AF803457

Divorce Therapy

THE *JOURNAL OF PSYCHOTHERAPY & THE FAMILY* SERIES:

- *Computers and Family Therapy*
- *Divorce Therapy*
- *Family Therapy Education and Supervision*
- *Family Enrichment*
- *Intrafamilial Abuse*
- *Severe and Chronic Disorders: New Perspectives on the Family*
- *Minority Family Therapy*
- *Feminist Family Therapy*

Divorce Therapy

Douglas H. Sprenkle
Editor

Routledge
Taylor & Francis Group
LONDON AND NEW YORK

First published 1985 by The Haworth Press, Inc.

Published 2014 by Routledge
711 Third Avenue, New York, NY 10017, USA
2 Park Square, Milton Park, Abingdon, Oxon OX14 4RN

Routledge is an imprint of the Taylor & Francis Group, an informa business

ISBN: 978-1-315-79145-6 (eISBN)

Divorce Therapy has also been published as *Journal of Psychotherapy & the Family*, Volume 1, Number 3, Fall 1985.

© 1985 by Taylor & Francis. All rights reserved. No part of this work may be reproduced or utilized in any form or by any means, electronic or mechanical including photocopying, microfilm and recording, or by any information storage and retrieval system without permission in writing from the publisher.

Library of Congress Cataloging in Publication Data
Main entry under title:

Divorce therapy.

"Has also been published as Journal of psychotherapy & the family, volume 1, number 3, fall 1985"—T.p. verso.
Includes bibliographies.
1. Divorce therapy—Addresses, essays, lectures. I. Sprenkle, Douglas H.
RC488.6.D58 1985 646.7'8 85-8657
ISBN 0-86656-467-5
ISBN 0-86656-472-1 (pbk.)

Divorce Therapy

Journal of Psychotherapy & the Family
Volume 1, Number 3

CONTENTS

FOCUS THREE: POST-DIVORCE RECOVERY AND REMARRIAGE

COMPREHENSIVE VIEWS OF THE FIELD

EDITOR

CHARLES R. FIGLEY, PhD

EDITORIAL COUNCIL

G. WALLACE DENTON, EdD
FRED PIERCY, PhD
DOUGLAS H. SPRENKLE, PhD

EDITORIAL BOARD

CONSTANCE AHRONS, PhD
JAMES F. ALEXANDER, PhD
CAROL M. ANDERSON, PhD
CAROLYN L. ATTNEAVE, PhD
DENNIS A. BAGAROZZI, PhD
MORTON BARD, PhD
DONALD R. BARDILL, PhD
AARON T. BECK, MD
MILO F. BENNINGFIELD, PhD
JESSIE BERNARD, PhD
PAULINE BOSS, PhD
ANN W. BURGESS, DNSc
THOMAS E. CLARK, PhD
STANLEY COHEN, PhD
WILLIAM DOHERTY, PhD
SPENCER ETH, MD
CRAIG A. EVERETT, PhD
CELIA J. FALICOV, PhD
C. RAYMOND FOWLER, PhD
IRA D. GLICK, MD
RICHARD GREEN, MD
BERNARD GUERNEY, JR., PhD
ALAN S. GURMAN, PhD
JAY HALEY
KENNETH V. HARDY, PhD
KENNETH HELLER, PhD
JUDITH HERMAN, MD
WILLIAM J. HIEBERT, STM
ALAN J. HOVESTADT, EdD
FREDERICK G. HUMPHREY, EdD
HARVEY JOANNING, PhD
VIRGINIA JOHNSON-MASTERS, DSc
FLORENCE W. KASLOW, PhD
BRADFORD P. KEENEY, PhD
DAVID KNISKERN, PsyD
CHARLES KRAMER, MD
JUDITH LANDAU-STANTON, MD
KITTY F. LAPERRIERE, PhD
MARCIA LASSWELL, MA
ARNOLD A. LAZARUS, PhD
RON LEVY, PsyD
JERRY M. LEWIS, MD
HOWARD A. LIDDLE, EdD
JACOB D. LINDY, MD
GAYLA MARGOLIN, PhD
WILLIAM H. MASTERS, PhD
SALVADOR MINUCHIN, MD
WILLIAM C. NICHOLS, EdD
WAYNE E. OATES, ThD
FRANK OCHBERG, MD
DAVID H. OLSON, PhD
PEGGY PAPP, MSW
NORMAN PAUL, MD
WILLIAM M. PINSOF, PhD
ROBERT S. PYNOOS, MD
CLIFFORD SAGER, MD
LEE SALK, PhD
VIRGINIA SATIR, DSS
WALTER SCHUMM, PhD
RICHARD C. SCHWARTZ, PhD
MILTON F. SHORE, PhD
CARLOS E. SLUZKI, MD
ROSS V. SPECK, MD
JOHN P. SPIEGEL, MD
FRED L. STRODTBECK, PhD
CHERYL L. STORM, PhD
CLIFFORD H. SWENSEN, PhD
HAROLD M. VISOTSKY, MD
JUDITH WALLERSTEIN, PhD
FROMA WALSH, PhD
KAREN S. WAMPLER, PhD
ROBERT S. WEISS, PhD
CARL A. WHITAKER, MD
LYMAN C. WYNNE, MD

Divorce Therapy

EDITORIAL NOTE

The *Journal of Psychotherapy & the Family* is very pleased to present this special issue that focuses on a critically important topic to the practice of psychotherapy: divorce therapy. As the divorce rate continues to be extremely high for the second straight decade, psychotherapists are called upon more and more to help their clients touched in some way by the trauma of divorce or its wake. The emotional distress of experiencing a divorce is both profound and long-lasting. It is clear from the emerging literature cited in this volume that divorce is both complex and impacts not only the divorcing couple and children, but other family members, friends and colleagues as well. Divorce is frequently the social context within which psychopathology and less impairing problems emerge. It has become a frequent topic in psychotherapy practice. This surge of attention is due to the profound societal impact of divorce. This collection is the first attempt to present a comprehensive approach to divorce therapy. It is especially oriented to subscribers of the *Journal:* psychotherapy practitioners. These include psychiatrists, psychologists, family therapists, social workers, educators, physicians, nurses, clergy, attorneys and social science researchers.

Dr. Douglas Sprenkle, editor of this special topic, *Divorce Therapy*, is a highly acclaimed scholar who, along with David Olson, developed the Circumplex Model of marital and family systems. He has been honored by national societies for his distinctive contributions to the field of marriage and family therapy and the author of over forty scholarly publications related to family intervention. Along with his colleague, Wallace Denton, one of Professor Sprenkle's most significant achievements has been the development of the Purdue Marriage and Family Therapy Program. It has an international reputation for one of the finest graduate training programs in family studies and therapy. His most current schol-

© 1985 by The Haworth Press, Inc. All rights reserved.

arly interest is the divorcing process and the most effective therapeutic methods for helping clients cope with divorce. One recent article on divorce research and therapy, for example, has received wide recognition as a seminal contribution to this area. Indeed, it serves as a foundation of this collection of papers to follow.

Dr. Sprenkle has assembled a collection of papers which focus on various aspects of divorce therapy, written by a highly knowledgeable group of scholar clinicians. The central theme of the collection, according to Dr. Sprenkle, is that clinical intervention related to the divorcing process—either by a family therapist or family physician—requires considerable knowledge and precision. As Dr. Sprenkle points out, this collection of papers is more than a "compendium of techniques but almost all are based on a foundation of theory and/or research about divorce" (p. 5). Moreover, this collection should serve for many years as the state of the art in divorce therapy, since it includes a concise summary of the research and clinical literature of the area while adding numerous insights, concepts, and methods as yet unpublished.

The *Journal* is dedicated to improving the arts and sciences of psychotherapy practice by focusing on the role of the family. We see the role of the family as being among the most important social support system to the well-being of its members. When the system begins to break apart, what transpires is in part chaos, relief, emotional pain, and a natural evolution of a dynamic system. This special issue, with its focus on the divorcing process, provides us with a rare view of the metamorphosis of the family system. We become aware of the variety of types, phases, events, and facets of the divorcing process. We learn of effective methods for facilitating emotional recovery from the divorcing process. This process is certainly a challenge to psychotherapy practice which, we believe, is illuminated by Dr. Sprenkle's collection.

C. R. Figley, PhD
Editor

INTRODUCING THIS VOLUME
AND DIVORCE STAGES
AS A FRAMEWORK FOR THERAPY

Introduction: Divorce Therapy

Douglas H. Sprenkle

This is one of the first collections devoted to a broad-spectrum coverage of divorce therapy. Books have been written about certain special topics like mediation (Coogler, 1978; Haynes, 1981; Irving, 1980), and treating postdivorce families (Hansen, 1982; Sager et al., 1983; Visher & Visher, 1979). In addition, there are several overview pieces about divorce therapy (Brown, 1976; Kaslow, 1981; Storm, Sprenkle & Williamson, 1985), but these are limited by the constraints of article or book chapter format. The current collection, then, offers the reader an opportunity to examine a wider variety of divorce therapy approaches than the more specialized volumes and also to explore them in more depth than the articles just cited. The collection also contains some approaches which have not been described in the literature.

As several of the collection's authors note, the interventions they describe have gained public as well as professional respectability only recently. This may help to explain why, although there is an enormous literature on divorce in general, attention to intervention has been late or underdeveloped. Have we now moved past the association of divorce with pathology and the sense that divorce therapy is somehow "anti-family" or "anti-marriage?" I hope so.

The collection also reflects a broad definition of the term, divorce therapy. Definitions found in the literature, even only several years ago, would be considered too narrow by the writers of the current volume. For example, Gurman and Kniskern (1978) defined the goals of divorce therapy as limited to "aiding the divorced or separated partner to deal with his/her loss, resolving ambivalence, fostering autonomy and self-esteem as a separate person" (p. 881). A broadened understanding is made explicit in the lead paper by Connie Salts, "Divorce Stage Theory and Therapy: Therapeutic Implications Throughout the Divorcing Process." Building on the work of Kaslow (1984) and Storm and Sprenkle (1982) Salts conceptualizes divorce therapy as helping couples and

Douglas H. Sprenkle, Ph.D., is Director of the Marriage and Family Therapy Program and Associate Professor in the Department of Child Development and Family Studies, 525 Russell Street, Purdue University, W. Lafayette, IN 47906.

© 1985 by The Haworth Press, Inc. All rights reserved.

families through the stages of: (1) predivorce decision making, (2) divorce restructuring, (3) postdivorce recovery. In the first, therapists focus on divorce as one alternative to relationship difficulties, help clients appraise the consequences of such a decision, and facilitate non-destructive communication about the decision so that family members are better prepared for the ensuing stages. In the second, the therapist facilitates the family members making the legal, emotional, financial, social and parental arrangements necessary for the transition from marriage to singlehood. During the final stage, the therapist facilitates the growth of the divorced spouses as autonomous individuals with stable lifestyles and helps them rebuild social relationships independent of the former lover relationship (goals similar to those enunciated by Gurman and Kniskern earlier in this paragraph). Continuing difficulties related to parent-child relationships, sibling relationships or custody/visitation issues are also often the focus of the therapist's attention at this post divorce stage. Finally, preparation for remarriage and facilitating the remarriage process can also be included here. Alternatively, remarriage might be considered a fourth stage (since a majority of divorcing families experience the remarriage of one or both spouses).

All divorce stage theories are more heuristic than literally descriptive since divorces vary widely and issues cycle and recycle among the stages. Nonetheless, Salts' time sequence stages are probably more accurate than divorce typologies based on the unfolding of certain emotions, as her review of the literature demonstrates.

Her typology also provides the organizational structure for the rest of the volume. The next paper specifically focuses on divorce decision making therapy. The second grouping of papers center on therapeutic interventions which help to restructure family life around the time of divorce. The third set focuses on interventions with the post-divorce family. As with the stages themselves, there is some overlap in the foci of the articles. The final two contributions are not stage-focused but deal more comprehensively with divorce therapy services and literature.

Nathan Turner ("Divorce: Dynamics of Decision Therapy") is one of the first scholars to direct therapists' attention to the intricacies of divorce decision making. Therapists are often puzzled by the decisional behavior of their clients—frequently marked by extraordinary ambivalence, seeming irrationality, decisional reversals, regressive behaviors, impulsive behaviors, and so forth. Turner makes sense of this puzzle by pointing to the social-psychological theories of decision making by Janis and Mann. Turner applies their work to divorce and delineates stages of decision making as well as the coping patterns of persons undergoing decisional stress. The common problems encountered by clients (and therapists) during this first of Salts' stages should be "normalized" for the reader by Turner's explication. This editor agrees with him ". . . that the specialized topic of the psychology of decision making during separation and divorce has been ignored or avoided for too long."

The contribution by Sutton and Sprenkle, "Criteria for a Constructive Divorce: Theory and Research to Guide the Practitioner," relates to all stages of the divorce experience. It is placed early in the collection because the paper is concerned with therapist goal setting. The authors assume that divorce therapy should be a goal-directed activity, informed, in part, by what research has shown to be constructive responses to divorce. Sutton and Sprenkle reject the notion that divorce adjustment is simply the absence of negative consequences and posit ten major criteria for constructive adjustment. These criteria are based not only on previous literature but on one of the first, and perhaps the largest, empirical investigations of the topic to date. The paper offers data not only on the relative salience of these dimensions for long term divorce adjustment but also therapists' assessment of their priority in therapy.

One of the major therapeutic issues in the second of Salts' stages—restructuring—is the reworking of parental roles and dealing with the stresses experienced by the children of divorce. William Nichol's contribution, "Family Therapy with Children of Divorce," begins with the assertion that children's "reactions" (which he prefers to "symptoms") are systemic attempts to restore harmony in the marital subsystem. As do other authors in this collection, Nichols takes a transgenerational perspective and notes that the therapeutic approach of choice for children entails attention to the divorcing parents, their children, and their grandparents. Although therapeutic help is normally not sought for children in the decision making stage, Nichols gives some attention to the important issue of informing the children. In the restructuring stage, the physical separation of the parents is typically the crucial stress point for children and Nichols offers a variety of ways in which transgenerational family therapy can be utilized to maintain a psychological "sense of family" for children in dire need of some continuity. He also gives considerable attention to the post-divorce recovery stage which he subdivides into the single parent household phase and the remarriage phase. Nichols also offers indications and contraindications for such therapeutic strategies as bringing former married persons together, and including grandparents, when there are difficulties pertaining to children.

Stanley Cohen, the Executive Director of the Association of Family and Conciliation Courts, offers an introduction to that form of intervention most intentionally related to restructuring—divorce mediation. He describes the rich history of mediation and speculates why the method, widely accepted in other aspects of life, has been only lately applied to divorce. Then he discusses differences between mediation and family psychotherapy and the manner in which divorce mediation services are offered. Although presenting a positive evaluation of the movement, supported by research, Cohen is quick to note its limitations. For example, almost all of the research is centered on the mediation of custody and visitation disputes. There are also certain types of couples for whom mediation will not work, and it will never completely replace the adversary legal process. Because of its positive potential, it is hoped that readers will consider expanding their repertoire to include mediation or referral to mediators.

One dimension of divorce restructuring which has gained considerable attention in recent years is joint custody. As with mediation, joint custody is an approach grounded in theory and research and has positive potential for diminishing the negative ramifications of the adversary legal system. However, as with mediation, ideological proponents of this method are too quick to view it as a panacea and too blind to its contraindications. The contribution by Sandra Volgy and Craig Everett, "Systemic Assessment Criteria for Joint Custody," will be useful to family psychotherapists helping either couples or courts determine the appropriateness of this option. The chapter is based upon the authors' work with over 300 families for whom joint custody was a possible alternative. The guiding concept of the chapter is that custody issues are embedded in prior patterns of family dysfunction and in the intergenerational system of which the nuclear family is a part. Utilizing principles from structural, intergenerational, and the authors' own systemic analysis they have delineated five criteria which may be used to determine if couples are adaptive enough to make joint custody work. The readers should note the similarities between these criteria and those advocated later in this collection by Crosbie-Burnett and Ahrons for successful transition to remarriage.

The third section of the collection focuses on post-divorce recovery. Here again, however, the authors give some attention to the other stages. Marcia Brown's contribution ("Creating New Realities for the Newly Divorced: A Structural Strategic Approach for Divorce Therapy with an Individual") is among the most creative but may also be the most controversial. The intent of her paper is to help the therapist contruct new psychological realities for the newly divorced or separated individual. All therapists working with this population are aware of the devastating impact of divorce and separation upon self-esteem, self-confidence, and life outlook. Strongly influenced by the work of Erickson, Watzlawick, Minuchin, and Fishman, Brown describes ways in which the therapist can build upon the client's language and current perspective to engender hope. The techniques are delicate and require consummate skill. "The strategy is analogous to disrupting the playback of a broken record by ever so slightly adjusting the needle. Since the client's unique reality is adjusted only slightly, there are no sure-fire reality creations which would be effective or even palatable to every newly divorced individual. The therapist has to adapt to the raw materials of each client's experience."

Brown's contribution is also unique in that it focuses on the individual. She notes the clinical reality that, while family and couple work is often desirable in divorce therapy, it is often not feasible. She also seeks to demonstrate that structural-strategic concepts are not limited by the unit of treatment.

The post-divorce experience most typically leads to remarriage of one or both partners. Margaret Crosbie-Burnett and Constance Ahrons offer therapists a detailed guide for the issues and problems families face at this time (''From Divorce to Remarriage: Implications for Therapy with Families in Transition''). Believing that the ''single parent family'' is a misnomer, and that the non-custodial parent is too often ignored, they develop their concept of the ''bi-nuclear'' family both to describe the post-divorce family and to indicate the context in which remarriage occurs. First, they discuss courtship expectations for remarriage and the common myths that therapists must help clients temper, such as, ''I must love my stepchildren.'' The major theoretical tenet of the paper is the boundary ambiguity inherent in remarried families and the greater need for boundary permeability than is true for nuclear families. Such issues as the movement between households, exchange of money, and shared decision making between co-parents (ex-spouses) reflect this need for permeability and underscores the potential for difficulties. Role-ambiguity in remarriage families is the twin of boundary ambiguity. Means whereby the therapist can help clients define roles, while at the same time encourage them to be flexible, are offered. The authors greatly respect the complexity of the bi-nuclear family and stress that solutions have to be individualized for each client/family.

Next, Mary Eno addresses the clinical implications of a topic heretofore ignored in the divorce literature, ''Sibling Relationships in Families of Divorce.'' Her contribution is based on clinical research completed as part of the Children of Divorce Project of the Philadelphia Child Guidance Clinic. While the material is clearly oriented towards the post-divorce period, the sibling dynamics described might well be operative in other stages. After making a case for the primacy of sibling relations in post separation families, Eno describes the ways in which siblings create a world for themselves which is separate from and sometimes unknown to other family relationships through such mechanisms as sibling rituals, sibling play, and sibling conflict. Through case illustrations, she also demonstrates how siblings are drawn into coalitions with divorced parents and how these liaisons affect adjustment. Clinical suggestions for both sibling sessions and family therapy sessions are offered which address these dynamics. The author's timely conclusion is that ''. . . it is clear that the sibling relationship can threaten a child's recovery or temporarily sustain a stable and lively micro-culture during an unstable time.''

The final section of this collection begins with Emily Brown's description of "The Comprehensive Divorce Treatment Center." As founder and director of the Divorce and Marital Stress Clinic in the Washington, D.C. area, Emily Brown has been a pioneer in providing comprehensive services for the divorcing family. It is, perhaps, a sign of the times that her work is being featured in this collection since ". . . historically, the marriage centers wanted no part of divorce . . . Those who saw a need for divorce counseling and tried to interest the established marriage and family agencies received a chilly response until very recently." In her paper, Brown delineates the goals and philosophy of her organization, its clientele, typical presenting problems, and describes the range of services offered. These include education programs and divorce mediation along with counseling and therapy. Clients can choose to use a single service or any combination of services in any particular order. Education programs and divorce adjustment groups heretofore not described in this collection, are discussed here. Brown closes with a discussion of issues related to funding, staffing, and community relationships.

A fitting close to the collection is Roslyn Cantrell's "Divorce and Divorce Therapy: An Annotated Bibliography." This paper will be useful for several reasons: (1) Because of the number of services and forms of intervention available for divorcing families, it has been impossible to cover all of them in this volume, and (2) resources for the lay person are also included and these may be used by the therapist for bibliotherapy.

Eleven categories are covered: adjustment for the divorcee; children's books; custody; extended family; mediation; parenting and children; post-divorce families; schools; theory, therapy and research; woman's issues; and workshops.

Hopefully, this collection indicates that, although divorce therapy is a late bloomer among the family of interventions, it is beginning to come of age. Let me conclude by noting three generalizations about the papers which support this assessment.

1. The papers are not simply a compendium of techniques but almost all are based on a foundation of theory and/or research about divorce. They support David Olson's (1976) argument that therapy will advance only through the synergistic interplay among theory, research, and practice. Kaslow (1981) has also written that what is needed is not simply new techniques for doing divorce therapy (as a variety of existing methods may be applied), but a deeper understanding of the phenomenon of divorce. The papers reflect a quest for this understanding.

2. Divorce is depicted as a highly complex series of processes (certainly not as an event!) which begin with decisional struggles and, for couples with children, end (if at all) with multifaceted post-divorce decisions, negotiations, and re-negotiations. The authors respect this complexity and emphasize that interventions must be tailor-made for each

situation. It is clearly not the case that "a divorce is a divorce is a divorce."

3. Divorce is also seen as having a ripple effect that impacts far more than the couple. Interventions must attend to components of a larger system including siblings, grandparents, friends, employers, and so forth.

The collection, however, represents only a beginning. The third theme is addressed but not well developed. Certain approaches, such as divorce recovery groups, are given minimal attention. The research base of divorce therapy must be strengthened as Sprenkle and Storm (1983) have outlined elsewhere. It is hoped, nonetheless, that these gaps will motivate the reader to contribute to this exciting and evolving field.

REFERENCES

Brown, E. M. (1976). Divorce counseling. In D.H. Olson (Ed.), *Treating relationships* (pp. 399-429). Lake Mills, Iowa: Graphic Publishing Co.

Coogler, O. J. (1978). *Structural mediation in divorce settlement.* Lexington, MA: Lexington Books.

Gurman, A. S. & Kniskern, D. P. Research on marital and family therapy: Progress, perspective and prospect. In S. Garfield & A. Bergin (Eds.), *Handbook of psychotherapy and behavior change.* (Second Edition). New York: Wiley, 1978.

Hansen, J. C. (Ed.). (1982). *Therapy with remarriage families.* Rockville, MD: Aspen Systems Corporation.

Haynes, J. M. (1981). *Divorce mediation: A practical guide for therapists and counselors.* New York: Springer Publications.

Irving, H. H. (1980). *Divorce mediation: A rational alternative to the adversary system.* New York: Universe Books.

Kaslow, F. W. (1981). Divorce and divorce therapy. In A. S. Gurman & D. P. Kniskern (Eds.), *Handbook of family therapy.* New York: Brunner/Mazel.

Kaslow, F. W. (1984). Divorce: An evolutionary process of change in the family system. *Journal of Divorce, 7*(3), 21-39.

Olson, D. H. (1976). Bridging research, theory, and applications: The triple threat in science. In D. H. Olson (Ed.), *Treating relationships* (pp. 565-579). Lake Mills, Iowa: Graphic Publishing Co.

Sager, C. J., Brown, H. S., Crohn, H., Engel, T., Rodstein, E., & Walker, L. (1983). *Treating the remarried family.* New York: Brunner/Mazel.

Sprenkle, D. H., & Storm, C. L. (1983). Divorce therapy outcome research: A substantive and methodological review. *Journal of Marital and Family Therapy, 9,* 239-258.

Storm, C. L., & Sprenkle, D.H. (1982). Individual treatment in divorce therapy: A critique of an assumption. *Journal of Divorce, 6,* 87-97.

Storm, C. L., Sprenkle, D. H., & Williamson, W. (In press, 1985). Innovative divorce approaches developed by counselors, conciliators, mediators, and educators. In R. Levant (Ed.), *Psycho-educational approaches to family therapy.* New York: Springer Publishing.

Visher, E. B., & Visher, J. S. (1979). *Stepfamilies: A guide to working with stepparents and step-children.* New York: Brunner/Mazel.

Divorce Stage Theory and Therapy: Therapeutic Implications Throughout the Divorcing Process

Connie J. Salts

ABSTRACT. This article provides a brief description of the research on the emotional process of divorce as it relates to therapy. Therapeutic implications during the predivorce decision making stage, the divorce restructuring stage and the postdivorce recovery stage are then discussed. Clinical suggestions are provided for the unit of treatment during each stage and for the use of specific techniques.

The purpose of this article is to address the implications of divorce stage theory for therapy. Divorce is a process involving decisions, changes, and adjustments resulting from increased dissatisfaction with the marital relationship (Salts, 1979). Divorce therapy is essentially a process which assists individuals, couples, and families experiencing divorce to make the changes necessary to establish relatively satisfactory lifestyles (Brown, 1976; Kaslow, 1984).

The divorce process has been further defined as consisting of stages which individuals and couples experience (Bohannan, 1970; Brown, 1976; Froiland & Hozeman, 1977; Herrman, 1974; Kessler, 1975; Kraus, 1979; Levy & Joffe, 1977; Smart, 1977; Weiss, 1975; Wiseman, 1975). Efforts to integrate the divorce stage theories have used emotions of individuals, actions and tasks of individuals and couples, time sequencing, and therapeutic implications to illustrate the similarities and compatibility of the theories (Kaslow, 1984; Price-Bonham & Balswick, 1980; Salts, 1979). This article will first provide a brief description of the research on the emotional process of divorce. Therapeutic implications throughout the divorce process will then be discussed using a three stage time sequencing of the major tasks involved in the divorce process.

EMOTIONAL PROCESS OF DIVORCE

The divorce stage theories focusing on emotions stipulate that each person experiences divorce differently and may skip stages or change the se-

Connie J. Salts, Ph.D., is Assistant Professor, Specialization in Marital and Family Therapy, Department of Human and Family Resources, Northern Illinois University, DeKalb, IL 60115.

© 1985 by The Haworth Press, Inc. All rights reserved.

quence of their occurrence (Froiland & Hozeman, 1977; Wiseman, 1975). Kolevzon and Gottlieb (1983:93) note that while dimensions of emotional "adjustment to divorce, such as feelings of hostility and anger, of depression, of lowered self-esteem and self concept, and of social isolation and abandonment, have been identified, there is little evidence to suggest the intensity or duration of these feelings, or to predict which divorce period will evidence challenges of coping with which dimensions of emotional adjustment." Their research findings provide no evidence to suggest that particular dimensions of emotional adjustment represent challenges that are unique to particular stages of divorce. The study's findings suggest that the first year of postdivorce adjustment appears to be the time when the emotional impact of divorce is most intense, and that during this time, the individual is faced with the challenge of adjusting to a range of co-existing intense emotions which appear to subside concurrently.

Although Kolevzon and Gottlieb's (1983) study was conducted with individuals who were already divorced, a plausible hypothesis, based on clinical experience, is that individuals experience a range of co-existing emotions which vary in intensity during the entire divorce process. Kolevzon and Gottlieb (1983) also suggest that a number of intervening variables serve to effect the intensity and the progressive decrease of the emotional challenges of divorcing individuals.

Crosby, Gage, and Raymond (1983:16) hypothesized that "persons who have experienced divorce will display a sequence of feelings and behavior which progresses in general sequence from denial to anger to bargaining to depression to acceptance." Results from the study suggest that there is great variance between the way any two people come to decision, acceptance, and resolution of divorce and that the grief-resolution process is most often marked by circularity rather than linearity. They also suggest that the grief resolution process associated with divorce cannot be separated from the following correlates of recovery: "economic stability, physical health, emotional health, experience with previous divorce or other crises, familial pressure, scripts and expectations, definitions of the meaning of the marriage and/or divorce, personal psychic factors, defense mechanisms, values, and religious beliefs" (p. 17).

The list of emotions that can be experienced throughout the divorce process is extensive (Kaslow, 1984). The intensity and timing of these emotions are affected by an equally long list of variables (Kolevzon & Gottlieb, 1983; Crosby, Gage, & Raymond, 1983). Therefore, it is important for a therapist to continually assess the emotional state of clients involved in divorce and to deal appropriately with these emotions throughout the divorce therapy process. In some cases the treatment plan will focus on helping the client deal directly with emotional adjustment, such as during the postdivorce stage, and the therapy goal may be to increase the self-confidence of the individual. In another case, the therapist may need to recognize and deal with the emotional status of the clients in order to achieve the larger therapy goal. For example, the therapy goal may be to help a couple to restructure their family following the decision to obtain a divorce. When the progress of therapy and restructuring become stalemated due to increasing feelings of anger, the therapist must recognize the role anger is playing in therapy and address the emotional adjustment of the couple.

How a therapist chooses to deal with a specific emotional challenge of an individual will depend upon the context within which the emotion occurs; whether the therapist is seeing the individual, the couple, or the family; the therapy goals; and the therapeutic style of the therapist. It is not within the scope of this article to address specific therapeutic techniques used to deal with the various emotions experienced throughout the divorce process. However, therapists working with clients experiencing any stage of divorce should familiarize themselves with several of the divorce stage theories referenced in this article.

THERAPY AND THE DIVORCE STAGES

A three stage time sequencing of the major tasks involved in the divorce process lends itself readily to discussing therapeutic implications throughout the divorce process: (1) predivorce decision making stage, (2) divorce restructuring stage, and (3) postdivorce recovery stage (Kaslow, 1984; Storm & Sprenkle, 1982).

Predivorce Decision Making

During this stage, the couple begins to consider divorce as an alternative to their relationship difficulties and to appraise the possible consequences of such a decision (Storm & Sprenkle, 1982). As the feelings of disappointment and disillusionment with the marriage or one's partner become more pervasive, one or both of the spouses are likely to decide to seek professional help.

Conjoint therapy is regarded as the appropriate treatment during the predivorce decision making stage (Storm & Sprenkle, 1982). Whitaker and Miller (1971) state that excluding one spouse from therapy may be making "an intervention in favor of divorce" (p. 254). The decision to divorce must be the client's and the therapist should remain as neutral as possible toward the decision regarding the maintenance or dissolution of the marital relationship.

If the therapist works from a family systems perspective, the children or parents of one or both spouses may be included in this predivorce decision making stage. Although the degree to which the family is included during therapy in the first stage of divorce is dependent to some extent on the type of relationship problems the couple is experiencing and the theoretical orientation of the therapist, it is recommended, since the final decision regarding divorce is a couple issue rather than a family issue, that a high emphasis be placed on conjoint therapy and a low emphasis on both individual and family therapy (Storm & Sprenkle, 1982).

When a couple seeks therapy for relationship problems, the amount of erosion the relationship has experienced will determine to some extent whether the therapy will become marital therapy or divorce therapy. The value orientation of the therapist toward "saving marriages" or conversely, "rescuing victims of bad marriages," will also affect the direction of therapy.

If the couple is oriented to making the marriage work, is seeking alternative ways of relating within the relationship, is motivated to make changes, and has not begun to consider divorce as the preferred alternative to the marital problems, the therapy is easily identified as marital therapy. The therapist continues to assess the spousal interactional patterns and develops a treatment plan consistent with his or her theoretical orientation of marriage and marital therapy.

Often, however, a couple will decide to seek marital therapy with one or both having the verbalized or nonverbalized stipulation: "If this doesn't work, then we'll get a divorce." If the therapist is not informed of an "if-then" stipulation, it becomes necessary to assess if one or both spouses are deliberating the decision to remain married.

Perhaps the most direct method to assess the couple's position is to ask each spouse about divorce using a circular questioning technique (Penn, 1982). An example of some possible beginning questions include: How often do you think/talk about divorce? What keeps you from thinking/talking about it? When do you think/talk about divorce the most? What comes to mind when you think/talk about divorce?

With this intervention, the therapist is not suggesting divorce as an alternative to the couple's marital problem, but is assessing commitment to the relationship and, ultimately, commitment to the marital therapy process. If early in the intervention it becomes apparent that the couple is committed to the relationship, the questions can easily be directed toward positive aspects of the marriage and the couple complimented on their motivation to work on improving their relationship. If the therapist determines that the couple has entered a phase in their marriage when one or both partners are considering whether or not to divorce, the therapist then places therapy in the context of the decision making stage.

The pre-divorce decision making stage can be viewed as having an early phase and a late phase. If couples are in the early phase, divorce has been considered as an option, but other alternatives are being heavily considered. When couples are in the late phase, events and decisions tend to occur rapidly, with divorce seen as the most likely alternative.

Early phase. When a couple is assessed to be on the early side of the divorce decision, the therapist can acknowledge this position, then establish that the reason the couple is seeking therapy is to work to improve the marital relationship. If both spouses readily agree with the position of the marital relationship and the purpose for seeking therapy, the therapist continues to assess the marital relationship and develops a treatment plan for marital therapy. Since therapy at this stage is in the context of decision making, the therapist needs to be aware that "stuckness" in the therapy process could indicate that divorce is being given greater consideration as an option by one partner.

Late phase. If the couple has moved to the late side of the decision making process, in addition to divorce being a prominent issue, there will be a reluctance or lack of energy available to commit oneself to work on changes in the marital relationship by at least one spouse. This reluctance and lack of energy are due in part to the extended period of marital difficulties most couples will have experienced and the attempts that have failed to improve the situation. At this point, the therapist may confront the couple regarding the assessment of each spouse's commitment to the relationship. The therapist can then suggest that perhaps the goal of therapy should first be to help the couple explore their needs as individuals and as a couple "to determine whether these needs can be met within the marriage (not necessarily by the marriage,) and to assess their alternatives" (Brown, 1976:412). Basically, the therapist is saying "Let's not start any marital therapy until we have decided if that is what you as a couple are ready for." The therapist then proposes a decision making contract to the couple by explaining the steps involved in effective decision making and how this will be implemented during the therapy sessions.

Effective decision making during the predivorce stage involves several steps: (1) identification and definition of needs and problems of the individuals and couple; (2) development of alternative solutions to meet these needs and to solve the problems; (3) consideration of the potential outcome of each alternative solution; (4) choice of the best and most fair solutions; (5) implementation of the choices; (6) evaluation of the outcome; and (7) further identification of needs and problems if the evaluation is not satisfactory.

The first task in predivorce decision making therapy is to identify and define the needs and problems of the spouses and the couple. The decision to be made at this point is not whether or not to get a divorce, as divorce is not a part of the problem. Divorce is one alternative solution to an unsatisfactory marriage. Therefore, the problem must be defined in terms of the relationship and individual needs. The therapist assesses the spousal interactional patterns and assists the couple to clarify what problems and needs exist within their relationship that make it unsatisfactory.

This process for the therapist involves the same assessment skills and techniques used with couples who are more committed to maintaining their relationship. Emotions, however, will be extremely intense during this phase, especially when one partner is more committed to maintaining the relationship.

Once the problems and needs have been defined, the next step in decision making is to develop a list of alternative solutions. The basic list for any couple includes maintaining the relationship as it is, making changes in the relationship, and obtaining a divorce. Clinical experience has shown that several alternatives can be generated for each couple by expanding on the various possible changes within their relationship during a brainstorming session. The number of possibilities is limited only by the therapist's and couple's creativity and freedom from criticism during this session. When brainstorming for alternative solutions, it is useful for all ideas, including the obviously irrational ones, to be written down for all to see. This procedure has been found to be helpful in creating a climate conducive for movement from the "heels dug in" stance many spouses assume during this phase of the divorce process.

After the list of solutions has been created, each of the various alternatives is explored. The ultimate satisfaction of the final decision will be greatly affected by the ability of the therapist to assist the couple to see the tasks involved in accomplishing each solution, the pros and cons involved in the tasks, the reasons why a solution might or might not work, and the potential realistic outcomes.

During this phase, pacing of therapy is important, although it is also difficult, since the partners are usually not at the same place in the process. The divorce process needs to be slowed down to provide the couple time to deal effectively with the decision, yet, at the same time, not so slow as to frustrate one partner into giving up the effort and making a panic decision.

While potential outcomes of alternatives are being discussed, new alternatives may become apparent and some alternatives eliminated by mutual agreement. The therapist assists the couple to express and deal with their feelings regarding each alternative, helps the partners to understand each other's position, and mediates a choice that is accepted as fair by both spouses. This is not an easy task, and the therapist may have to enforce effective communication rules (Stuart, 1980) during the session and use a wide range of therapeutic techniques in order for the couple to choose the best and most fair solutions.

Once agreement has been reached as to the best and most fair solution, the next step is the implementation. For some couples, the solution of choice will be to enter into a contract with the therapist to change the relationship in a further attempt to make the marriage work. Following the contracted therapy, the outcome needs to be evaluated in terms of whether the couple's needs are being met within the marriage. Lazrus (1981) provides a case example in which a couple, during marital therapy, had learned to replace feuds, quarrels, upheavals, and combative dealings with discussion, arbitration, debate, and fairplay. However, evaluation of the outcome and further identification of the problem revealed that this couple did not have the companionship or mutual happiness they desired. With the help of their therapist, they were able to move back to developing a new alternative which worked; an amicable divorce.

Divorce Restructuring

When divorce is the choice as the solution to marital dissatisfaction by one or both of the spouses, the couple moves into the second stage of the divorce process, divorce restructuring. If the couple has made the decision to divorce under the assistance of a therapist who effectively created a mutually acceptable decision making relationship in which the intense feelings surrounding divorce have been toned down, then the couple is ready to explore alternative ways of carrying out their decision to divorce. These new decisions will involve the necessary legal, emotional, financial, social and parental arrangements necessary to make the transition from marriage to singlehood (Storm & Sprenkle, 1982).

With the advent of divorce mediation (Coogler, 1978; Haynes, 1981), couples who have accepted the decision regarding divorce and who dislike the prospect of litigation are turning to this alternative to make decisions about custody, visitation, and distribution of assets (Kaslow, 1984). Although therapists not trained in divorce mediation may be able to help couples make decisions regarding these issues, financial and tax professionals should be consulted regarding the financial implications of custody and the distribution of assets. The therapist may also want to have contact with the spouses lawyers in order to encourage the maintenance of the mutually acceptable decision making relationship.

The role of the therapist during the restructuring stage is to help facilitate the timing of separation, to help the partners gain an understanding of the problems in the marriage relationship, and to provide an opportunity for the couple to deal with unresolved feelings. Conjoint or family therapy is recommended during this phase of the divorce process.

In the past, the meeting of divorcing partners was discouraged by the adversarial system for obtaining a divorce. With the increased development of no-fault dissolution of marital relationships and divorce mediation, the trend has been to encourage couples to resolve feelings of anger, disappointment and hurt to prevent these feelings from creating ongoing custody and visitation disputes (Storm & Sprenkle, 1982).

Research findings indicate that children's post divorce adjustment bear a direct correlation to the parent's adjustment (Wallerstein & Kelly, 1980). Partners may be more willing to continue to work through their emotional issues with each other when they are informed of the benefits for the children (Kaslow, 1984).

This period is a time of great stress (Brown, 1976) due to the multiple events that are often associated with the decision to divorce. Often, children are neglected emotionally during this period because parents are so overwhelmed by their own personal needs that they are not able to realize how much stress and emotional upheaval their children are experiencing. When the family can meet together with the therapist, a clearer understanding of what is happening and why can be provided to the children. As the separation and divorce decisions are implemented, new rules and roles evolve for parents and children in both households. Having the opportunity for each parent to openly discuss expectations with the children can often reduce future problems.

The amount of difficulty involved in working through the details of restructuring will depend to some extent on the process used to arrive at the decision to divorce. If one spouse has decided to leave the relationship and the other is desperately holding on, the restructuring will be much more difficult than when both spouses have decided that divorce is the best alternative. If the therapist was not involved with the couple during the decision making phase, reviewing this process with them can provide the setting to discuss and share the feelings each one has toward the decision. The intent of this intervention is not to change the decision to divorce, but to provide the opportunity for the couple to affirm that the decision is the best for them or to move an unwilling spouse to the point of acceptance. The therapist can reframe some behaviors of the partners in order to reduce feelings of hostility and a restructuring can be accomplished that is accepted as fair by both parties.

Although the recommendations for unit of treatment during the restructuring stage suggest a high emphasis on conjoint treatment, a moderate emphasis on family treatment, and a low emphasis on individual treatment (Storm & Sprenkle, 1982), the ideal situation does not always present itself at the therapist's door. Often the spouse who has not chosen to leave the marital relationship will seek help when the initial crisis period of physical separation occurs. Even the most engaging therapist will have difficulty convening the other spouse in many of these situations.

The individual may be so overwhelmed with feelings of rejection, frustration, and grief that he or she is unable to deal with the physical disorganization and the initial legal problems. Huber (1983) offers a therapeutic model based on Rational-Emotive Therapy which assists individuals to better understand and effectively cope with feelings of loss experienced in reaction to divorce. Even when the individual has the intense emotional reactions under reasonable control, the number of changes, problems and worries concerning money, jobs, children, family and friends, sex, and household maintenance often produce an overload for the individual's normal coping behavior. During this crisis period of restructuring, the therapist can provide the individual with directive assistance and information to help develop new skills for managing the practical problems (Fisher, 1974; Kessler, 1975) and at the same time be supportive and sensitive of the client's attempts to cope with the intense emotional reactions (Weiss, 1976; Levy & Joffe, 1977). Providing clients with reading materials about the divorce process (Kessler, 1977) can provide hope that the pain they are experiencing is normal for their situation and will decrease with time and support from professionals, friends, and family.

Post Divorce Recovery

As the changes continue and the individuals begin to complete the initial restructuring of their life styles, the focus of individual needs and therapy move to the recovery stage when "individual issues such as coping with loneliness, regaining self-confidence, and rebuilding social relationships are dealt with" (Storm & Sprenkle, 1982).

Unless there are continuing problems with parent-child relationships or custody/visitation issues, the individual is the unit of treatment during this stage (Storm & Sprenkle, 1982). It is during this phase that the divorce process can become a source of personal growth as the individuals battle within themselves to discover who they are. One's priorities must be assessed, values clarified, and personal goals and ambitions evaluated. When working with the individual during this time period, one effective technique is the two-chair dialogue to provide the client the opportunity to verbalize the conflicting desires within themselves. Providing guidance in decision making, and nonjudgmental support are the roles of the therapist for the individual client who is developing a sense of self satisfaction and autonomy. Some individuals, however, will be dealing with other serious problems (e.g., alcoholism, depression) and might require other appropriate therapy.

Participation in divorce adjustment groups (Kessler, 1977; Morris & Prescott, 1975) has been shown to be influential in improving the post-divorce adjustment for some individuals (Salts & Zongker, 1983). As in other forms of therapy, assessment of the individual's needs must be made before placement into a therapy group. Individuals who have not made sufficient progress in the restructuring stage of divorce are not ready for the personal growth task of the recovery stage (Salts, 1983). The focus of many divorce adjustment groups is on recovery, and premature placement in such a group could result in increased feelings of rejection, isolation and failure.

SUMMARY

The divorce process, starting with the first consideration of divorce by one partner and ending with the individual attaining a fairly stable and autonomous lifestyle, is a long term process, lasting approximately three years (Brown, 1976). It is also a difficult process which involves a variety of intense emotions, major decisions, and life changes as the couple moves through the predivorce decision making stage and the divorce restructuring stage, and the individuals accomplish postdivorce recovery.

There are no simple divorce therapy techniques. The therapist must assess the couple's relationship and the individuals' emotional reactions within the context of the divorce stage theory, assist individuals to effectively and appropriately deal with their emotional reactions throughout the process, and provide direction and support for the couple and the individuals in accomplishing the tasks of decision making and change. Recommended approaches to accomplish these therapy goals include the use of marital therapy, family therapy, individual therapy, and group therapy.

Marital and family therapy students often ask whether therapy during the predivorce decision making stage is marital therapy or divorce therapy. Just labeling the therapy could be an intervention in favor of one decision. Perhaps if the therapy is called couple therapy, then the therapist can move on to the business of assisting the couple to make decisions and changes regarding their relationship. During the restructuring stage, the therapist can continue to effectively provide couple therapy if the couple's decision to divorce is not viewed as failure of the previous therapy process by the couple or the therapist.

Just as the emotional divorce process is marked by circularity rather than linearity, so must the divorce therapy process. The effective therapist will be knowledgeable of divorce stage theory, skilled at assessment of couple relationships, perceptive of client emotional states, and aware and in control of their own personal value orientation toward "saving marriages."

REFERENCES

Bohannan, P. (1970). The six stations of divorce. In P. Bohannan (Ed.), *Divorce and after.* Garden City, NY: Doubleday.

Brown, E. M. (1976). Divorce counseling. In D. H. L. Olson (Ed.), *Treating relationships.* Lake Mills, IA: Grahic Publishing Company.

Coogler, O. J. (1978). *Structured mediation in divorce settlement.* Lexington, MA: Lexington Books.

Crosby, J. F., Gage, B. A., & Raymond, M. C. (1983). The grief resolution process in divorce. *Journal of Divorce*, 7, 3-18.

Fisher, E. O. (1974). *Divorce—The new freedom: A guide to divorcing and divorce counseling.* New York: Harper & Row.

Froiland, D. J. & Hozeman, T. L. (1977). Counseling for constructive divorce. *Personnel and Guidance Journal*, 55, 525-529.

Haynes, J. (1981). *Divorce mediation*. New York: Springer.

Herrman, S. J. (1974). Divorce: A grief process. *Perspectives in Psychiatric Care*, 12, 108-112.

Huber, C. H. (1983). Feelings of loss in response to divorce: Assessment and intervention. *The Personnel and Guidance Journal*, February, 357-361.

Kaslow, F. W. (1984). Divorce: An evolutionary process of change in the family system. *Journal of Divorce*, 7, 21-39.

Kessler, S. (1975). *The American way of divorce: Prescriptions for change*. Chicago: Nelson-Hall.

Kessler, S. (1977). *Beyond divorce: Participant's guide*. Fountain Valley, CA: National Institute for Professional Training.

Kolevzon, M. S. & Gottlieb, S. J. (1983). The impact of divorce: A multivariate study. *Journal of Divorce*, 7, 89-98.

Kraus, S. (1979). The crisis of divorce: Growth promoting or pathogenic. *Journal of Divorce*, 3, 107-119.

Lazrus, A. A. (1981). Divorce counseling or marriage therapy? A therapeutic option. *Journal of Marital and Family Therapy*, 7, 15-22.

Levy, T. M. & Joffe, W. (1977). *Counseling couples through separation: A developmental approach*. Paper presented at the annual meeting of the National Council on Family Relations, San Diego, October.

Morris, J. D. & Prescott, M. R. (1975). Transition groups: An approach to dealing with post partnership anguish. *The Family Coordinator*, 24, 325-330.

Penn, P. (1982). Circular questioning. *Family Process*, 21, 267-280.

Price-Bonham, S. & Balswick, J. O. (1980). The noninstitutions: Divorce, desertion, and remarriage. *Journal of Marriage and the Family*, 42, 959-972.

Salts, C. J. (1979). Divorce process: Integration of theory. *Journal of Divorce*, 2, 233-240.

Salts, C. J. (1983). Divorce adjustment groups are not for all divorcees. *The Personnel and Guidance Journal*, September, 37-39.

Salts, C. J. & Zongker, C. E. (1983). Effects of divorce counseling groups on adjustment and self concept. *Journal of Divorce*, 6, 55-67.

Smart, L. S. (1977). An application of Erikson's theory to the recovery-from-divorce process. *Journal of Divorce*, 1, 67-79.

Storm, C. L. & Sprenkle, D. H. (1982). Individual treatment in divorce therapy: A critique of an assumption. *Journal of Divorce*, 5, 87-97.

Stuart, R. B. (1980). *Helping couples change: A social learning approach to marital therapy*. New York: Guilford.

Wallerstein, J. S. & Kelly, J. B. (1980). *Surviving the breakup: How children and parents cope with divorce*. New York: Basic Books.

Weiss, R. (1976). *Marital separation*. New York: Basic Books.

Whitaker, C. A. & Miller, M. S. (1971). Evaluation of "psychiatric" help when divorce impends. In J. Haley (Ed.), *Changing families: A family therapy reader*. New York: Grune and Stratton.

Wiseman, R. S. (1975). Crisis theory and the process of divorce. *Social Casework*, 56, 233-240.

FOCUS ONE: DIVORCE DECISION-MAKING AND CRITERIA FOR A CONSTRUCTIVE DIVORCE

Divorce: Dynamics of Decision Therapy

Nathan W. Turner

ABSTRACT. This chapter applies social-psychological theory and research about decision making to separation and divorce. The chapter describes the stages in obtaining a stable decision and the typical coping patterns, most of which are dysfunctional, persons experience who are involved in decisional conflict. The article seeks to normalize the typical problems encountered at this time of stress and suggests clinical interventions related to the psychodynamics of decision making.

Divorce is among the most stressful experiences likely to be encountered in adult life. The stress involved is second in severity to the death of one's spouse (Holmes and Rahe, 1967, 1979).

When a person decides for divorce the individual often is under a very high level of stress and can unknowingly seek *premature closure* by making the decision in order to escape the anxiety, worry, and anger. When the level of stress is very high, the decisionmaker is likely to display *premature closure*—terminating the decisional dilemma without generating all the alternatives and without seeking or appraising the available information about the outcomes to be expected for the limited set of alternatives under consideration (Janis, 1982). Often the divorce oriented person is involved in a conflict of values. The person bounces between the value of remaining married versus the value of obtaining freedom from an oppressive situation. Despite the momentary feeling of elation over having made a decision to get a divorce, the decision can result in guilt, anxiety, and shame which adds to the pre-existing level of stress with which the individual is burdened (Janis, 1982). In a unique integration of decision making research with divorce decision making, Turner (1980) noted the following:

> One source of stress in decisional conflict is the feeling that one is risking major loss in whatever decision is considered. The intensity of the resulting stress symptoms depends upon the perceived magni-

Nathan W. Turner, Ed.D., is Assistant Professor of Psychiatry and Human Behavior at the Thomas Jefferson University Medical College, Philadelphia, Pennsylvania; and a psychotherapist in independent practice at 14 Elliott Avenue, #5, Bryn Mawr, PA 19010.

© 1985 by The Haworth Press, Inc. All rights reserved.

> tude of the losses the person anticipates from any of the decisions she/he may make. Common symptoms of stress in making such difficult decisions include a desire to escape, self-blame, and feelings of apprehensiveness (Janis and Mann, 1977). These symptoms of stress are common among clients in separation and divorce counseling. (p. 156)

Under high levels of stress, Janis (1982) concluded that the divorce oriented person begins to narrow the number of options seen, overlooks long-term implications, ignores information and data normally considered, becomes error prone in assessing expected results, and oversimplifies the decision making procedures one would normally utilize.

One reason for the level of stress is the accumulation of Life Change Units (LCU's), namely the total number of life changes which occurred during the period of time prior to the appearance of an illness or major emotional upset (Holmes and Rahe, 1967, 1979). Clusters of such events normally occur during marital separation and divorce. "Thus a person who separates, then reconciles, and then divorces within a six-month period accumulates a score of 185 for these events alone" (Jacobson, 1983, p. 10). Separation and divorce trigger changes in living arrangements, finances, personal living habits, sleeping and eating patterns, times together as a family, social life, and sexual partners. Added together such life changes (LCU's) present a potential for either physical or mental illness during and after separation and divorce. "Rahe believes that a dividing line of 150 LCU's occurring within six months exists between persons who tend to become ill and those who do not" (Holmes and Rahe, 1967, 1979; Jacobson, 1983, p. 10).

CONTEXT

It is interesting to observe that few authors have addressed theory, research or clinical interventions related to the massive amount of decision making required by those who go through separation and divorce. Broadhurst (1976), Janis and Mann (1977), Turner (1980) and Janis (1982) are the main published sources in this area. Jacobson (1983) has noted that the avoidance of painful topics like separation and divorce is a common phenomenon in the professional literature. It is the position of this author that the specialized topic of the psychology of decision making during separation and divorce has been ignored or avoided for too long. Few life scenarios require more decisions, and complicated decisions with long term consequences, than does divorce.

When the psychology of divorce decision making is considered, it is important to consider antecedent variables (those decisions which occurred prior to the marriage) as well as those which have occurred during the marriage (Turner, 1980; Jacobson, 1983). Antecedent behaviors, events, and decisions can become precipitating factors for future relationship disenchantment.

With this context in mind, let us now turn to the dynamics of decision therapy as originally developed by Janis (1983).

DECISION THERAPY

The prior research of Janis and Mann (1977, 1982) is the basic foundation for divorce decision therapy. If a client asks a counselor/therapist a question like, "What would be the best decision for me regarding my marriage?," the clinician can guide the client through a series of decision-making stages (Janis, 1983) to achieve a balanced decision.

FIVE MAJOR STAGES

The five major stages in making a stable decision are summarized in Table 1. In *stage one*, the immediate challenge to the person trying to decide for or against a separation or divorce is to decide to decide. In *stage two* it is crucial to survey all the alternatives in light of one's personal goals (to separate from one's spouse) and values (marriage is supposed to be a lifelong commitment). Most people search for all possible leads which have some potential for fulfilling their goals. A lead might be an offer of free housing in a close friend's home or the suggestion that one go for counseling.

In *stage three* the plusses and minuses of each alternative are deliberately weighed and considered. During this stage the individual must separate dependable information and suggestions from those which are undependable or merely based on others' limited personal experience with separation and divorce. By the end of this stage a person normally has begun to formulate a preliminary or tentative decision and course of action.

In *stage four* the person begins to seriously think about carrying out the decision made in stage three. Concomitantly, the individual begins to make plans for telling others about one's decision. After all, the "word" will get around town quickly. At this juncture, certain relatives and friends will probably disapprove of the decision and fear of social disapproval often serves as a deterrent to immediate action. Attention quickly turns to discovering new ways to avoid disapproval. It is normative for clinicians to see clients plateau at this stage and take large amounts of time to discover (a) new ways of informing people and (b) additional ways to deal with anticipated resistance.

In *stage five*, the recently announced decision to separate or divorce is

Table 1. Stages in arriving at a stable decision (based on Janis and Mann, 1977)

Stage	Key Questions
1. Appraising the challenge	Are the risks serious if I don't change?
2. Surveying alternatives	Is this (salient) alternative an acceptable means of dealing with the challenge?
	Have I sufficiently surveyed the available alternatives?
3. Weighing alternatives	Which alternative is best?
	Could the best alternative meet all essential requirements?
	If the best alternative is unsatisfactory, could one of the existing alternatives be modified to meet all essential requirement?
4. Deliberating about commitment	Shall I implement the best alternative and allow others to know?
	If the best alternative is satisfactory, what are the drawbacks or obstacles to implementing it and allowing others to know my choice?
5. Adhering despite negative feedback	Are the risks serious if I <u>don't</u> change?
	Are the risks serious if I <u>do</u> change?

Note. From Decision Making: A Psychological Analysis of Conflict, Choice, and Commitment (p. 172) by Janis, I.L. & Mann, L. 1977, New York: Free Press. Copyright 1977 by the Free Press. Reprinted by permission.

experienced with relief and even temporary euphoria. In many instances, the benignly calm scenario is all too quickly punctuated with unexpected resistance or setbacks. An individual can remain in stage five for an indefinite period of time; then either proceed with the original decision or receive such a powerful challenge that the process cycles back to stage one or two. A key dynamic at this juncture is the client's ability to handle *negative feedback* about the decision. Regression from stage five is normative yet very painful for most persons. It is important for the clinician to assist the client in viewing a regression to stage one or two as (a) normative and, perhaps, (b) necessary in light of unusually strong resistance from others. Above all, it is crucial that it *not* be viewed as a defeat (even though it feels that way) but as a developmental way to build up to a major life decision. In sum, making a major decision and then reverting to stage one or two can be framed as a necessary experience to test the authenticity of their decision.

Case Study - #1

Mrs. "A", age 34 (married 10 years with a daughter, age 9, and son, age 6), came in for counseling regarding her disenchantment with her husband. Presenting problems included his lack of affection, poor communication, and his late hours at work. She was an attractive woman who had taught school for two years prior to marriage. Her husband refused to come to therapy.

Early sessions covered issues regarding remaining in an unsatisfactory marriage or leaving it. Questions she raised included "should I leave him?" or, "should I stay and if I do what are the risks?" (Stage One).

As therapy progressed she began to survey her alternatives (Stage Two). She began to ask "if I could secure another teaching position would I survive economically with two children?" "Are there other forms of work for which I might be qualified?" "Should I go to an employment agency and check further job opportunities?" "Have I explored all the alternatives related to staying in this marriage?"

Next (Stage Three) the therapist guided her to consider which alternative was best. "Would X alternative meet your essential requirements?" After several months of weighing alternatives, she abruptly decided to separate from her husband for a few months to see if a separation would clarify her feelings. Her sudden decision appeared to be an avoidance of (Stage Four) seriously deliberating about her commitment to separate. Despite the therapist urging her to move more slowly, she persisted and had her husband move out.

After two months of separation, she decided (Stage Five) to continue the separation indefinitely despite negative feedback from her husband, her parents, and several close friends who thought she should reconcile.

After four months Mrs. "A" found herself ruminating about the same alternatives in Stage Two, but with more emotional depth. She was now asking "Could I *really* survive on a teacher's salary?" "Would my husband *really* pay child support?"

Again, it is important for the therapist to recognize that regression is *normative* due to the extreme stress of separation and divorce. Major reasons for cycling back are the failure to resolve the questions of the earlier stages or challenges to premature resolutions to these questions. Hence, decisional vacillation, ambiguity, ambivalence, and regression must be interpreted clearly and supportively to the client.

DECISIONAL CONFLICT AND COPING PATTERNS

The case just described is one example of decisional conflict which led to a less than quality decision. "Decisional conflict refers to opposing tendencies within the individual to accept and at the same time reject a given course of action" (Janis, 1983, p. 145). Common symptoms include vacillation, feelings of uncertainty and hesitation, and acute levels of guilt, shame, and anxiety whenever the individual focuses on the actual decision. The level of stress is typically proportional to the anticipated loss. Divorcees are frequently very concerned about social and emotional (e.g., threats to one's self-esteem and personal reputation) as well as material losses.

Janis and Mann (1983) have described how decisional conflict leads to five coping patterns, only the last of which is constructive.

Pattern one is unconflicted adherence. Here the individual incorrectly does not anticipate any significant loss or negatives in separation or divorce. A feeling of complacency and inertia is typical in this pattern. Information about risks and losses is ignored. "The danger in the inertia is that the actual problems and their . . . serious implications are mentally discounted or denied" (Turner, 1980, p. 157). *Pattern two is unconflicted change to a new course of action.* In this pattern the decision maker selects new courses of action uncritically. "Although serious risks may be involved, the person does not perceive the risks . . . [and] can make a series of incremental changes without ever canvassing or evaluating the full range of available alternatives" (Turner, 1980, p. 157). *Pattern three is defensive avoidance.* Common symptoms are procrastination, rationalizations to support weak or minimally viable alternatives and screening feedback which would expose deficiencies in one's choices. "Such defensive screening of information is necessary if the individual is to avoid major intrapsychic conflict" (Turner, 1980, p. 158). *Pattern four is hypervigilance.* During this pattern the decision maker is very anxious and subject to panic reactions. The individual tends to make impulsive decisions which are often error prone. The full range of consequences of one's decisions tend to be overlooked. Snap judgements, simplistic thinking, drastic actions, and perseveration are other common symptoms of this pattern. Finally, *pattern five is vigilance.* Here the individual is calmer and tends to search more thoroughly for all pertinent information bearing on the decisions related to separation or divorce. Careful search and appraisal require larger amounts of time. Regarding the process of vigilance, Turner (1980, p. 158) observed that:

> Self-confidence in one's ability to find better solutions and a realistic appraisal of the immediate results of deciding a course of action, balanced against a decision for a future course of action, are component parts of the process of vigilance. In brief, the alternative of making an immediate decision to separate or divorce (seen as a high risk) is balanced, during a state of vigilance, with a view that deciding later to separate or divorce may afford other advantages, as in financial or emotional aspects of the marriage.

People will evaluate the costs and benefits of a decision rationally "only when their coping pattern is vigilance" (Janis, 1983, p. 147). When any of the first four patterns are employed and things begin to go wrong, people will predictably overreact.

Janis (1983) makes clear that the primary coping patterns an individual selects are largely determined by the "presence or absence of three psychological conditions: (1) awareness of serious risks for whichever alternative is chosen (i.e., arousal of conflict), (2) hope of finding a better alternative, and (3) belief that there is adequate time in which to search and deliberate before a decision is required" (Janis, 1983, p. 149).

COMMON PROBLEMS

A series of common problems are embedded in the deficient decision-making patterns described above. The therapist must not only recognize that they are normative, but also normalize these problems for the client.

(1) *Excessive delay is very common.* The feelings of ambivalence and vacillation coupled with inertia can contribute to an excessive time delay. Therapists need to be aware that their own impatience can be projected onto the client and be cautious about urging them to move faster with their decisions and "get it done!" (2) *The clients need to make a decision* (gain closure) may bring temporary relief from anxiety and ambiguity but *often is premature.* (3) *Information overload* from considering too many variables and alternatives *can lead to distorted thinking and oversimplifying.* (4) *Emotional overload and* feelings of *high stress* lead to feelings of being pulled in opposite directions. (5) *Misinformation is a common problem.* It is easy to receive only half a story or description from one's children, spouse, or relatives and jump to conclusions. Misinformation can trigger needless misunderstandings and arguments. Indeed, it is

"missed information." (6) *Stereotyping others* and reinforcing one's innate prejudices with selected information and listening *is another common problem* which blocks effective communication and relating. (7) *Fear of the unknown can lead to excessive worry and preoccupation.* "What will happen if I . . ." is a common irrational thought that mainly serves to enhance worry.

INTERVENTIONS

Let us turn to some interventions which a clinician may use to facilitate a client/patient through a divorce or separation decisional crisis: (1) stress inoculation; (2) role-playing; and (3) balance sheet.

Stress Inoculation

"Stress inoculation involves giving people preparatory communications that contain realistic information about anticipated dangers and losses, self-help recommendations, and reassurances to prepare them to cope with an impending ordeal" (Janis, 1983, pp. 182-183). The concept undergirding stress inoculation is that prior to a major crisis related decision, people benefit from advance (a) information about it, (b) discussion of ways to cope, (c) development of contingency plans, (d) enhancement of self-confidence to deal with the situation and (e) extra time to appraise all possible alternatives.

There are three main steps in stress inoculation for persons making a decision to divorce or separate. *Step one* is to provide realistic information (for example, to challenge a person's perceived immunity to vulnerability) in order to motivate him to make realistic plans for the decisional crisis. *Step two* is to bolster the client's awareness of personal coping resources in order to nullify feelings of defeat, hopelessness or helplessness. *Step three* is to teach the person how to reassure and protect himself (Janis, 1983, p. 191). The third step is crucial in that a feeling of self-reliance is necessary to break the tendency to become overdependent on friends, relatives or other professional help. In recent years stress inoculation has been used by cognitive-behavioral therapists (Meichenbaum, 1977). One caution is that the clinician needs to make an early evaluation of the client's need for and tolerance of negative information. Janis and (1983) also found stress inoculation to have mixed results. In examining the various parts of the process, he concluded that one component that seems quite useful is assisting patients to reframe their future stresses as challenges which demonstrate their ability to deal with stress.

Additional components which have been helpful are (a) trying to build up a client's *expectations of being in control* of a stressful situation; (b) *increasing* the client's *sense of commitment* to his/her decision; and (c) building up the *client's sense of personal responsibility* for the decision (Janis, 1983, pp. 197-200).

The last two components are key ones in that sense of commitment and sense of personal responsibility ensure that the client take a proactive approach to his/her problem and not rely on the therapist to do most of the work.

To repeat, the therapist must allow for individual differences when employing stress inoculation and recognize that not all clients are going to react favorably to this approach.

Role Playing

Janis (1983) suggests a method of clinical intervention which is termed *emotional role playing*. It is a lengthy procedure with five successive stages. It appears to be a combination of role playing, psychodrama, and fantasy induction which can create very powerful clinical effects. Basically the therapist is expected to create a true to life situation to which the client may respond "as if" the experience were happening. The emotional impact of this technique once again calls for sage clinical judgment about the type of patient/client who should use it. The five stages include, for example, (1) a scenario in a waiting room for a doctor/therapist during which time the client is to share his/her feelings, worries and reservations aloud; (2) a scenario in the office during which time the therapist gives a realistic diagnosis of what will actually happen to the individual; (3) a scenario wherein the therapist calls for a consultation with another specialist about what should be done next for the client; (4) a scenario with the therapist about impending hospitalization or next steps with a consultation; and (5) a final conversation with the therapist about the cause(s) of one's current problem(s). Through this inductive process the clinician can provoke emotional insights about future coping abilities the client will have with anticipated problems. By anticipating the responses "before the fact" the client/patient has an opportunity to search for other alternatives and to discover better coping strategies.

An alternative procedure is an outcome psychodrama in which the person with decisional conflict concerning divorce is asked to assume one side of the polarity, e.g., "let us say you have decided to get a divorce." Then the therapist leads the person through all of the consequences of that decision. "You are now telling your husband/children. What are you saying? How does that feel?" The client is led further on. "You are now in court. What are you feeling as you look over at your partner across the room/as you leave the courtroom as a newly single person?" The sequence progresses. "It is now six months after the divorce. What are you doing? How do you feel? How much support are you receiving?"

The process is then repeated taking the other polarity: "You have decided to stay in your marriage. You are telling your husband of that decision. What are you saying? How does that feel?" By giving the client the freedom to fantasize about the consequences of both outcomes, there is the opportunity to clarify thoughts and feelings and to assess the emotional readiness for a given decision.

Balance Sheet

The decisional balance-sheet intervention was developed by Janis and Mann (1977) to enable clients to survey and evaluate various alternatives when making a major decision like separation and/or divorce. The balance sheet procedure calls for a decision maker to carefully investigate all alternatives and to systematically consider all major gains and risks which could be otherwise overlooked. The balance sheet process is an organized way to attempt to overcome the first four primary coping patterns and their defects discussed earlier.

Initially, the clinician asks the client to share all possible alternatives which he/she is considering and to detail the positives and negatives about each one. If necessary, the clinician may ask the client to develop additional alternatives if the client has too small a list of alternatives. Seven rules-of-thumb have been developed by Janis (1983) for generating additional alternatives: "(1) don't evaluate at the beginning; (2) generate as many alternatives as possible; (3) try to be original; (4) modify flawed alternatives; (5) ask other people (for ideas); (6) use contemplation as a source of ideas; and (7) avoid dichotomies (like 'either/or' ideas, questions or statements)."

Secondly, the clinician shows the client a sample balance sheet form as illustrated in Table 2. The importance of filling in positive and negative anticipated consequences for each alternative is explained by the therapist. The four categories listed in the lefthand column are carefully elucidated by the clinician. *Thirdly*, the client is requested to complete a separate balance-sheet page for *each* alternative considered. *Fourthly*, the client is then asked to check back over each cell on the balance sheet for gaps. Cells with the fewest items are usually the ones in which the client is feeling some form of self-disapproval and concern. The balance sheet method facilitates a detailed evaluation of the major alternatives clients consider when thinking of separation and divorce. It also assists them in clarifying their need for additional information and some kind of contingency plans. Although the balance sheet procedure may not be of value to all clients, for some it can enable them to stabilize their decisions and decrease postdecisional regrets (Janis, 1983, pp. 172-175).

Table 2. Decisional balance-sheet procedure. (Janis, 1983, p. 171, adapted)

Expected consequences	Positive anticipations	Negative anticipations
Tangible gains and losses for self	1.	1.
	2.	2.
	3.	3.
Tangible gains and losses for others	1.	1.
	2.	2.
	3.	3.
Self-approval or self-disapproval	1.	1.
	2.	2.
	3.	3.
Social approval or disapproval	1.	1.
	2.	2.
	3.	3.

CONCLUSION

This article has described many of the major dynamics of decision making during separation and/or divorce. Drawing on seminal research in the field of decision making psychology the various stages that one encounters in making a major decision have been described. The way that emotional stress impacts decision making was also discussed.

The nature and role of decision counseling, as developed by Janis and Mann (1977, 1982), was related. *Five stages* in obtaining a stable decision were interfaced with the *five primary coping patterns* persons experience in decisional conflict. Related to the coping patterns were *seven common psychological problems* that people encounter when making a major decision such as to separate or divorce.

Finally, *three forms of* major *clinical intervention* were described specifically related to the psychodynamics of decision making during separation and divorce. Although much research needs to be accomplished in this vital area, it is equally important to begin to interrelate existing decision making theory and research with one of the most volatile and complex life decisions a person ever makes. To decide to marry, separate, divorce or remarry is a decision of a magnitude that only happens a few times for most people. Therapists need to begin to interface current knowledge about decision making with clinical practice with the separating and divorcing population.

REFERENCES

Goldberger, L. & Breznitz, S. (Eds.). *Handbook of Stress, Theoretical and Clinical Aspects.* New York: The Free Press, 1982.

Holmes, T. H. Development and application of a quantitative measure of life change magnitude. In J. E. Barrett (Ed.), *Stress and Mental Disorder.* New York: Raven, 1979.

Holmes, T. H. & Rahe, R. H. The social readjustment rating scale. *Journal of Psychosomatic Research,* 1967, *11,* 213-218.

Jacobson, G. F. *The Multiple Crises of Marital Separation and Divorce.* New York: Grune & Stratton, 1983.

Janis, I. L. Decisionmaking under stress. In L. Goldberger & S. Breznitz (Eds.), *Handbook of Stress, Theoretical and Clinical Aspects.* New York: The Free Press, 1982.

Janis, I. L. *Short-term Counseling, Guidelines Based on Recent Research.* New Haven: Yale University Press, 1983.

Janis, I. L. & Mann, L. *Decision Making: A Psychological Analysis of Conflict, Choice, and Commitment.* New York: The Free Press, 1977.

Meichenbaum, D. H. *Cognitive-behavior Modification: An Integrative Approach.* New York: Plenum, 1977.

Turner, N. W. Divorce in mid-life: Clinical implications and applications. In W. Norman & Scaramella (Eds.), *Mid-life: Developmental and Clinical Issues.* New York: Brunner/Mazel, 1980.

Veninga, R. L. & Spradley, J. P. *The Work Stress Connection, How to Cope with Job Burnout.* New York: Ballantine Books, 1982.

Criteria for a Constructive Divorce: Theory and Research to Guide the Practitioner

Philip M. Sutton
Douglas H. Sprenkle

ABSTRACT. Ten criteria for a constructive divorce are described which are grounded in theory and research. They relate to acceptance of the end of the marriage, functional post-divorce relationship with the ex-spouse, emotional adjustment, cognitive understanding of the divorce, social support, parental adjustment, children's adjustment, use of opportunities for learning and personal growth, and general life adjustment and physical well-being. A study validating the criteria is described. The paper suggests that some divorces are clearly more constructive than others and therapists can utilize these criteria both to establish goals for therapy and to clarify values and therapeutic priorities.

This paper describes ten criteria for a constructive divorce that are based on theory and research. The purpose of the paper is to provide practitioners an opportunity to clarify their own understanding and values concerning divorce adjustment and the goals and outcomes of therapy with divorced or divorcing clients. The paper is based on two principles: (1) some divorces are clearly more constructive than others, and (2) divorce therapy should be a goal-directed activity.

The first principle is based on an even more basic assumption, namely, that divorce adjustment is a complex and multi-faceted process which may yield a variety of both positive and negative outcomes. Although marriage and family scholars have long recognized the complexity and variety of marriage and family forms and dynamics, researchers have only recently begun to distinguish different kinds of divorce (Sprenkle & Cyrus, 1983). It is a myth that "a divorce is a divorce is a divorce" (Baker, 1981).

The relative constructiveness of a divorce is a fairly recent focus of the

---

Philip M. Sutton, Ph.D., is a psychologist and family therapist at the Family Learning Center, 1513 Miami Street, South Bend, IN 46613.

Douglas H. Sprenkle, Ph.D., is the Director of the Family Therapy Doctoral Program, Department of Child Development and Family Studies, Purdue University, West Lafayette, IN 47907.

© 1985 by The Haworth Press, Inc. All rights reserved.

literature on divorce. Raschke (1982) has written extensively about the deviance perspective surrounding divorce and the tendency to define divorce adjustment as merely the absence of negative consequences. Sprenkle and Storm (1983) have noted that in much of the existing outcome research on divorce therapy, divorce is depicted as an unintended outcome of marriage counseling or a negative consequence of conciliation counseling. Divorce has been regarded as an inherently pathological outcome of marital distress, rather than as a legitimate, if indeed painful, solution to some marital and family distress. We believe that this bias toward seeing divorce as pathological should not prevent scholars from discovering constructive aspects of divorce or therapists from seeking to facilitate constructive outcomes.

The intent of this paper is *not* to suggest that divorce is easily growthful, creative, or freedom-producing, or that divorcees will readily or necessarily achieve constructive adjustment to divorce. We recognize that divorce adjustment is a long-term process which typically requires two to four years of effort in order to achieve a constructive resolution of divorce-related changes and distress (Weiss, 1975). But time alone is insufficient for achieving positive outcomes after divorce, and some divorcees never adjust constructively to their divorce. Our intent is to stress that divorce can have a range of long-term outcomes, positive as well as negative, and to present the mediating and ultimate criteria which research and theory suggest are most salutary for constructive adjustment.

The second basic principle of this paper reflects our agreement with Feldman ". . . that in many ways the most important initial task of family therapy is goal setting" (1976, p. 111). We believe that without a clear delineation of goals, therapy can become a "seat of the pants" activity (Nichols, 1973), and meaningful assessment of therapeutic outcomes is made very difficult. Appropriate goal-setting is important especially for therapeutic work with divorced and divorcing clients, because divorce therapy requires an understanding of the divorce adjustment process, rather than unique therapeutic skills (Kaslow, 1981). We hope that the criteria for constructive, long-term divorce adjustment will be useful to therapists both as guidelines for the process of divorce therapy and as benchmarks for evaluating its effectiveness.

CRITERIA FOR CONSTRUCTIVE, LONG-TERM ADJUSTMENT TO DIVORCE

The term "constructive divorce" was first introduced into the literature by Kenneth Kressel and his colleagues. They based their work on in-depth interviews with twenty psychotherapists (Kressel & Deutsch,

1977), twenty-one clergymen (Weinglass, Kressel & Dutch, 1978) and seventeen lawyers (Lopez-Morillas, 1977), who had expertise in working with divorcing individuals. Using this work as a foundation, Sprenkle (1981) delineated eight criteria or goals of constructive or adaptive divorce adjustment and these were expanded to ten criteria by Sutton (1983). The ten criteria are not only described here in narrative form, but were used to develop an instrument called the Divorce Adjustment Values Inventory (DAVI) (Sutton, Sprenkle & Hackney, 1983). Sample items from this inventory are listed later in this paper.

Before reading the criteria themselves, readers should note the following caveats:

(1) It is much easier to delineate these criteria than to actually help divorcees to achieve them. It is almost impossible for any one person to achieve all of these goals either quickly or completely. Since the criteria are for long-term adjustment, it is assumed that progress is typically slow, if not plodding. In addition, the "graph" of divorce recovery is typically jagged rather than straight, and divorcees' forward steps are often matched by retreats. We are describing goals to guide the therapist's work rather than delineating the typical process of adjustment (Sprenkle and Cyrus, 1983).

(2) The criteria are not comprehensive nor exhaustive. It is not possible to cover all contingencies. For example, second or third divorces following complex step family forms may require unique criteria. Most of the criteria, however, are applicable to all divorce situations.

Dimension One: Acceptance of the End of the Marriage

The cornerstone of the process of divorce adjustment is accepting that one is not, and will no longer be, married to one's ex-spouse (Fisher, 1981). This entails developing an identity that is tied neither to one's former marital status or one's ex-spouse (Kitson & Raschke, 1981).

This process is made difficult by the bonding that frequently develops between spouses. Weiss (1975) has written perceptively about the "persistence of attachment" between spouses that persists even after the "erosion of love." Kitson (1982) offers some empirical evidence that lingering attachment is associated with "higher divorce distress."

Not all contact or even positive feelings between former spouses, however, should necessarily be considered destructive. Ahrons (1980a) stressed the difference between "normal" attachment to the ex-spouse and "pathological" attachment. She questions the tendency of many therapists to pathologize what may be harmless or constructive caring or friendship between former intimates. Nonetheless, it is important for many clients to be convinced that it is no use investing in a relationship for which there is no return. It is helpful if clients realize that even though divorcing is painful, a worse fate is being married to someone who does not wish to be married to them.

Dimension Two: Functional Post-Divorce Relationship with the Ex-Spouse

This process entails making "peace" with the ex-spouse, hopefully both within oneself and between oneself and one's former mate. Sprenkle and Cyrus (1983) write:

> Eventually the divorcee must learn that nastiness only begets nastiness and that acting in aggressive (active or passive) and hostile ways only hurts oneself. Part of 'becoming free' of the other person is the capacity not to engage in tit-for-tat retribution. The ultimate expression of this freedom is the capacity to forgive the other for his contribution for the demise of the marriage. (page 68)

One method whereby spouses can have a cooperative relationship is by compartmentalizing their relationships. Past areas of conflict can be either resolved or avoided, and past roles and other aspects of their relationship can be limited to what is mutually acceptable. In a study of post-divorce relationships between divorcing parents, Ahrons (1980b) found that the most successful divorcing parents were those who were able to separate parental and spousal roles, while the least successful parents were those who continued to act out their marital conflicts and were unable to negotiate new boundaries for their post-divorce relationship. Part of developing a functional relationship with the ex-spouse is the ability to develop a balanced view of the ex-spouse and come to appreciate what is good about the ex-spouse as well as his/her foibles and weaknesses.

Dimension Three: Emotional Adjustment

Divorce almost always entails negative emotional consequences (Goode, 1956; Raschke, 1974; Weiss, 1975; Kitson, 1982). Raschke (1974) found that almost 40% of the variance in response to her Post-Divorce Adjustment Stress Scale was accounted for by respondents' unpleasant emotional states. What we are stressing here is that the divorcee not get stuck in *long-term* self blame, guilt, or anger. The divorce literature, for example, is replete with illustrations of persons who "feed" on a relationship of anger and remain hostility "junkies", engaging in such non-constructive responses as vandalism, withholding visitation, verbal abuse, beating, and even murder.

The authors recognize, however, that in the short-term, certain negative emotions may have constructive value. Anger may, for example, galvanize energy and help a person to get through the crisis of separation. Certainly the expression of grief and sadness is also appropriate and valuable. Adequately mourning the death of the marriage and the loss of one's spouse, lifestyle, identity, children, etc., has been described as a necessary stage in the process of adjusting to divorce (Fisher, 1981).

Dimension Four: Cognitive Adjustment (Development of Realistic Understanding)

It is important that divorcees understand their own contribution to the dysfunctional behavior patterns which led to the failure of the marriage. To the degree that one accepts responsibility for failure, one is also empowered to be able to do something about it. This is not possible when one is locked into a blaming stance.

We believe it is useful when each partner is aware of the ways in which marital failure is related to struggles in his or her family of origin (Napier & Whitaker, 1978). It is also useful for each partner to learn about his or her reasons for choice of mate so that one does not or is at least less likely to repeat the same mistake (Kressel & Deutsch, 1977).

Sutton (1983) has noted: ". . . eventually, the divorcee should be able to acknowledge that not all marriages are doomed to failure; not all women are 'turkeys'; that good relationships and marriages are possible; that marriage can be a good way to live (even if I choose not to marry); that one's self worth does not depend upon living up to either one's own or another's expectations . . ." (pp. 42-43).

Dimension Five: Social Support and Adjustment

We believe it is very important that divorcees find sources of support other than their ex-partner. By social support we accept Kitson and Raschke's (1982) definition of formal and informal contacts with individuals and groups that provide emotional or material resources. In general, research demonstrates that social support and participation are highly related to low stress and better adjustment (Goode, 1956; Weiss, 1975; Kitson & Raschke, 1982; Hynes, 1979). In most studies, higher dating activity is related to higher adjustment (Hetherington, Cox & Cox, 1976; Raschke, 1974). There is also at least suggestive evidence that participation in therapy and divorce adjustment groups facilitates constructive outcomes (Sprenkle & Storm, 1983). But a paradox of adjusting to divorce through social participation is that many divorcees must learn to live as single persons and to deny the temptation to escape from divorce-related distress through another intimate relationship (Fisher, 1981). Divorcees must learn to relate out of ''strength'' and not simply out of ''need''.

Dimension Six: Parental Adjustment

As previously noted, it is best for divorcees to compartmentalize negative feelings about the ex-partner and work together cooperatively as parents. A number of studies have demonstrated that a co-parenting relationship free of conflict and hostility is positively related to children's adjustment (Ahrons, 1980a; Jacobson, 1978b; Wallerstein & Kelly, 1980; Goetting, 1981; Hetherington, Cox & Cox, 1981). It is therefore important that ex-spouses communicate directly and not through their children. Parents should not be competing for their children's affections and should not be overly emotionally dependent on their children. When remarriage occurs, biological and stepparents should support each others' interactions and stepparents should develop respect, if not necessarily affection, for their stepchildren. And, parents should come to feel more competent and comfortable in post-divorce parenting roles.

Dimension Seven: Children's Adjustment

Jacobson (1978a,b,c) has stressed the significance of parents' discussing the reasons for the separation and divorce with their children in age appropriate ways. Parents should help dispel any beliefs by their children that the children may have caused the divorce. It is essential that children believe both parents still love them even if the parents no longer love each other. Furthermore, it is essential that children do not feel that loving either parent will jeopardize their place in the affections of the other. Children should be encouraged to express their painful emotions so that they can feel listened to and cared for; although therapists should realize that children of different ages have different capacities for understanding and articulating their situation (Longfellow, 1979; Wallerstein & Kelly, 1980). Children should also not nourish fantasies or beliefs about their parents' reconciling.

It is constructive for children to have regular contact with the noncustodial parent, provided this is not a dysfunctional relationship (Wallerstein & Kelly, 1970; Weiss, 1975). Contact with both sets of grandparents and relatives (again barring unusual circumstances) is also constructive (Ahrons, 1983).

Children who are adjusting well to divorce should be doing satisfactory work in school, be reasonably active in social and recreational activities, and have satisfactory peer relationships. Finally, it is constructive if children *believe* that their divorced parents are adjusting well, and it is crucial for children's adjustment that their parents *are* adjusting well, so that the children receive the consistent care and stable environment which fosters their adjustment (Herzog & Sudia, 1973; Wallerstein & Kelly, 1980).

Dimension Eight: Use of Opportunities for Learning and Personal Growth

Although divorce is typically painful and traumatic, it can be an opportunity for personal growth. Sometimes, it reflects a wise and mature decision to end a relationship rather than continuing in a destructive situation (Fisher, 1978, 1981; Framo, 1981). Divorced persons can emerge emotionally, socially, and spiritually stronger than when they began the divorcing process. This may be due to the fact that divorce frequently forces people to clarify their values and revise their priorities (Sutton, 1983). Hence, it "shakes up the system" in ways that might not have happened otherwise. An important therapeutic goal is to help the individual develop feelings of competency and mastery as a single person. We like to remind clients that "in divorce, you always get custody of yourself."

An important part of this growth process is finding sources of meaning in one's life other than the ex-partner. This frequently entails establishing a new identity and setting new goals for oneself. It may also involve developing a new set of roles, such as learning to cook, becoming a professional person, or caring for children alone (Sprenkle & Cyrus, 1983). The desirable result is that the divorcee becomes more "self-caring and self-esteeming" and that s/he is in a better position to make use of the "new beginning" that can be created out of the end of a marriage.

Dimension Nine: Process and Outcome of a Legal Settlement

The legal process itself frequently exacerbates the pain of divorce (Spanier & Casto, 1979; Irving, 1980; Coogler, 1978). Divorces are most constructive if they are not contested, or at least neither partner feels embittered by the adversary process. Divorcees must learn to walk a fine line between taking care of themselves through being assertive about their own rights, and not using the legal process as a punitive measure (Irving, 1980; Sprenkle & Cyrus, 1983). The literature also suggests that individuals who are active participants in the settlement process and who are not overly influenced by guilt and resentment become better adjusted. Naturally, it is more constructive for divorcees to believe that they neither gave nor took too much and to be satisfied with the terms of custody and visitation. It is also more constructive of divorcees to pay child support regularly and to not withhold support or visitation because of conflicts with the ex-spouse. Finally, the literature suggests that pre- and post-settlement behaviors may be a "barometer" to indicate how well the psychological divorce has proceeded (Kressel et al., 1977, 1978).

Dimension Ten: General Life Adjustment and Physical Well-Being

Many definitions or measures of divorce adjustment have equated adjustment to divorce with the absence of negative consequences (Goode, 1956; Raschke, 1982). Separated and divorced persons have been shown to have more physical and mental health problems than married persons (Bloom, Asher & White, 1978). Factors such as physical health, abuse of alcohol and drugs, sleep patterns, eating habits, hygiene and grooming, job performance, the ability to make appropriate decisions, the absence of memory difficulties, and the avoidance of major financial difficulties may indicate more or less adjustment to divorce-related difficulties. The presence or absence of these difficulties may not necessarily indicate the quality of post-divorce adjustment since such difficulties may have preceded the divorce and have been its cause. At least, experiencing difficulties with life adjustment and physical well-being would make achieving a constructive divorce more difficult (Kitson, 1982; Sutton, 1983). But, resolving such difficulties could also be an appropriate goal in therapy for helping clients adjust constructively to divorce.

EMPIRICAL VERIFICATION

The following is a brief summary of the study by Sutton (1983) which sought to verify the saliency of the dimensions discussed above. Those interested in more detail, such as matters related to reliability and validity, should consult Sutton (1983) and note that several other publications are planned which will report the results in more detail.

Each of the ten dimensions was operationalized with from ten to fifteen items to comprise the Divorce Adjustment Values Inventory (Sutton, Sprenkle & Hackney, 1983). Sample items for each of the ten dimensions follow:

(1) *Acceptance of the end of the marriage*
"Divorcees no longer hope for reconciliation after the divorce"
"Divorcees 'let go of,' disengage emotionally from, the ex-spouse"

(2) *Functional post-divorce relationship with the ex-spouse*
"Divorcees express appreciation to the ex-spouse for the good parts of their past life together"
"Divorcees express both the strong and weak points of the ex-spouse"

(3) *Emotional adjustment*
"Divorcees do not have excessive self-blame or guilt about the divorce"
"Divorcees have finished mourning the death of the marriage"
(4) *Cognitive adjustment*
"Divorcees understand their part in the marital breakdown"
"Divorcees realize how they could be a better partner in the marriage"
(5) *Social adjustment*
"Divorcees develop a support group"
"Divorcees avoid committed, intimate relationships until after they have adjusted to the divorce"
(6) *Parental adjustment*
"Divorcees can cooperate with the ex-spouse about parenting issues"
"Parents are not competing for their children's affections"
(7) *Children's adjustment*
"Children do not blame themselves for their parent's divorce"
"Children are reasonably active in social or recreational activities"
(8) *Opportunities for learning or personal growth*
"Divorcees learn how to relate as single persons"
"Divorcees use time alone to increase self-understanding"
(9) *Satisfactory process and outcome of settlement*
"Divorcees actively participated in the settlement process"
"Divorcees do not withhold child support or visitation because of conflicts with the ex-spouse"
(10) *General life adjustment and physical well-being*
"Neither too much nor too little sleep"
"Eating neither too much or too little"

A random sample of 400 clinical members of the American Association for Marriage and Family Therapy rated each item, in terms of its importance for long-term adjustment, on a five point scale from "low" (1) to "medium" (3) to "extremely high" (5). Respondents were also asked to rank order the ten dimensions in terms of the relative priority the respondents assigned to each dimension in therapy both when divorce involves children and when it does not.

Results showed that the mean rating of the items, by dimension, is high. All dimensions except #2 (functional post-divorce relationship with ex-spouse) had a mean rating of over 3.5 (range 3.58 to 4.21). The mean ratings for dimension two was 2.68. These results suggest that these therapists believed the dimensions are, indeed, important to long term adjustment. As the reader examines the *relative* importance of the dimensions in the first column of Table 1, s/he should realize that these comparisons are among ratings that were high to begin with.

Examining both importance ratings and priority in therapy rankings (see Table 1) we see that dimensions one (acceptance of the end of the marriage) and dimensions six (parental adjustment) and seven (children's adjustment) were both rated and ranked highly. The high marks for dimension one corroborates the research noted earlier that lingering attachment is a major cause of post-divorce stress. Interestingly, and perhaps because of this belief, dimension two (functional relationship with the ex-spouse) was given the lowest importance rating and priority in therapy unless children are involved (when the ranking moves up two places). This suggests that the respondents may not accept the recent research trend (Ahrons, 1980a) which suggests that a continuing relationship between ex-spouses can be functional and important even when children are not involved.

The high importance given to dimensions six (parental adjustment) and seven (children's adjustment) suggests the great concern that therapists

Table 1

Summary of Comparisons Between Dimension Ratings and Rankings

	Importance Ratings	Priority Rankings for Therapy	
Dimensions of Adjustment	Item Mean	With Children	Without Children
1 Acceptance of Divorce	2	1	1
2 Relationship with Ex	10	6	8
3 Emotional Adjustment	5	1	1
4 Cognitive Adjustment	5	5	3
5 Social Adjustment	8	6	3
6 Parental Adjustment	1	3	--
7 Children's Adjustment	2	3	--
8 Personal Growth	8	10	5
9 Settlement	2	8	7
10 General/Physical Well-being	5	8	5

have about the effects of divorce on children and also the close linkage between children's adjustment and parents' adjustment which is indicated in the literature.

It is interesting that respondents rated dimension nine (process and outcome of the settlement) as one of the most important concerns for long term adjustment, but gave it a relatively low priority in therapy. Perhaps this suggests that it is still the case, as Kressel and Deutsch (1977) noted, that most therapists do not believe it is their role to work out the details of a settlement. The burgeoning growth of divorce mediation, and its apparent effectiveness, may lead therapists to modify this value.

Conversely, dimension three (emotional adjustment) is given the highest priority for therapy (along with dimension one) but was considered less important for long term adjustment. Perhaps the higher priority rating reflects the immediacy of the therapeutic challenge to deal with people's emotional distress.

Dimension eight (opportunities for learning and personal growth) was considered among the least important for long term adjustment and was also given the lowest priority in therapy when divorce involved children. When children were not involved, however, this dimension was ranked relatively higher.

In summary, these data suggest that, although therapists consider all ten dimensions important, they give greatest value to and prioritize their work around helping former marital partners disengage and attending to parental and child issues. Responding to emotional issues is also a dominant therapeutic priority.

CONCLUDING REMARKS

In this paper, we have presented ten criteria for constructive, long-term adjustment to divorce along with a brief summary of the theory and research which support these criteria. We have also discussed the results of a study of a national sample of marriage and family therapists' views of the importance of these criteria for long-term adjustment and the priority of these criteria in therapy. In general, the therapists who participated in the study appear to have endorsed the importance of the ten criteria for divorce adjustment and to have prioritized these criteria with respect to therapy.

We hope that readers of this paper will use our ideas to clarify their own understanding, values, and therapeutic priorities regarding constructive adjustment to divorce. As we noted at the beginning of the paper, some divorces are clearly more constructive than others. We believe that having one's goals of divorce therapy more clearly in focus should enable therapists to help their divorced and divorcing clients achieve more constructive, long-term adjustment.

REFERENCES

Ahrons, C. R. (1980a). The continuing coparental relationship between divorced spouses. Paper presented at the 1980 annual meeting of the American Orthopsychiatric Association in Toronto, Canada.

Ahrons, C. R. (1980b). Joint custody arrangements in the postdivorce family. *Journal of Divorce, 3*(3), 189-206.

Ahrons, C. (1983). Predictors of paternal involvement postdivorce: Mothers' and fathers' perceptions. *Journal of Divorce, 6*(3), 55-69.

Baker, L. (1981). The transition to divorce: Discrepancies between husbands and wives. Unpublished doctoral dissertation. Purdue University.

Bloom, B. L., Asher, S. J. & White, S. W. (1978). Marital disruption as a stressor: A review and analysis. *Psychological Bulletin, 85*, 867-894.

Coogler, O. (1978). *Structured mediation in divorce settlement.* Lexington, Mass.: Lexington Books.

Feldman, L. (1976). Goals of family therapy. *Journal of Marriage and Family Counseling, 2*, 103-113.

Fisher, B. (1978). *When your relationship ends: The divorce process rebuilding blocks.* Boulder, CO: Family Relations Learning Center.

Fisher, B. (1981). *Rebuilding: When your relationship ends.* San Luis Obispo, CA: Impact Publishers.

Framo, J. (1981). The integration of marital therapy with sessions with family of origin. In A. Gurman and D. Kniskern (Eds.), *Handbook of Family Therapy*, New York: Brunner/Mazel.

Goetting, A. (1981). Divorce outcome research: Issues and perspectives. *Journal of Family Issues, 2*(3), 350-378.

Goode, W. (1956). *After divorce.* Glencoe, IL: Free Press.

Herzog, E. & Sudia, C. (1973). Children in fatherless families. In B. Caldwell and H. Ricciuti (Eds.), *Review of child development research* (Vol. 3), Chicago: University of Chicago Press.

Hetherington, E., Cox, M. & Cox, R. (1976). Divorced fathers. *Family Coordinator, 25*, 417-428.

Hetherington, E., Cox, M. & Cox, R. (1981). The aftermath of divorce. In E. Hetherington and R. Parke (Eds.), *Contemporary readings in child psychology* (2nd edition). New York: McGraw-Hill.

Hynes, W. (1979). *Single parent mothers and distress: Relationships between selected social and psychological factors and distress in low-income single parent mothers.* Unpublished doctoral dissertation, The Catholic University of America, Washington, D.C. (DAI, 40/3A, p. 1686).

Irving, H. (1980). *Divorce mediation: The rational alternative.* Toronto: Personal Liberty Publishers.

Jacobson, D. (1978a). The impact of marital separation/divorce on children: I. Parent-child separation and child adjustment. *Journal of Divorce, 1*, 341-360.

Jacobson, D. (1978b). The impact of marital separation/divorce on children: II. Interparent hostility and child adjustment. *Journal of Divorce, 2*, 3-19.

Jacobson, D. (1978c). The impact of marital separation/divorce on children: III. Parent-child communication and child adjustment, and regression analysis of findings from overall study. *Journal of Divorce, 2*, 175-194.

Kaslow, F. (1981). Divorce and divorce therapy. In A. Gurman and D. Kniskern (Eds.), *Handbook of family therapy*, New York: Brunner/Mazel.

Kitson, G. (1982). Attachment to the spouse in divorce: A scale and its application. *Journal of Marriage and the Family, 44*(2), 379-393.

Kitson, G. and Raschke, H. (1981). Divorce research: What we know; what we need to know. *Journal of Divorce, 4*(3), 1-38.

Longfellow, C. (1979). Divorce in context: Its impact on children. In G. Levinger and O. Moles (Eds.), *Divorce and separation: Context, causes, and consequences.* New York: Basic Books.

Lopez-Morillas, M. (1977). *The role of the divorce lawyer: An in-depth survey of matrimonial lawyers.* Unpublished manuscript, Social Psychology Laboratory, Teacher's College, Columbia University.

Napier, A. & Whitaker, C. (1978). *The family crucible.* New York: Harper and Row.

Nichols, W. (1973). The field of marriage counseling: A brief overview. *The Family Coordinator, 22*, 3-13.

Raschke, H. (1974). *Social and psychological factors in voluntary postmarital dissolution and adjustment.* Unpublished doctoral dissertation, University of Minnesota at Minneapolis (DAI, 35/08a, p. 5549).
Raschke, H. (1982). *Divorce and marital separation.* Unpublished manuscript, Austin College.
Spanier, G. & Casto, R. (1979). Adjustment to separation and divorce: A qualitative analysis. In G. Levinger and O. Moles (Eds.), *Divorce and separation: Context, causes and consequences.* New York: Basic Books.
Sprenkle, D. (1981). *Is there life after divorce?* Paper presented at the Department of Child Development and Family Studies Symposium on Divorce, Purdue University, West Lafayette, IN.
Sprenkle, D. & Cyrus, C. (1983). Abandonment: The sudden stress of divorce. In C. R. Figley and H. I. McCubbin (Eds.), *Stress and the family* (Vol. 2). New York: Brunner/Mazel.
Sprenkle, D. & Storm, C. (1983). Divorce therapy outcome research: A substantive and methodological review. *Journal of Marital and Family Therapy, 9*(3), 239-258.
Sutton, P. M. (1983). *Defining divorce adjustment: A study of marriage and family therapists' criteria for constructive long-term adjustment to divorce.* Unpublished doctoral dissertation. Purdue University.
Sutton, P., Sprenkle, D. & Hackney, H. (1983). *The Divorce Adjustment Inventory (DAI).* Unpublished manuscript, Purdue University.
Wallerstein, J. & Kelly, J. (1980). *Surviving the breakup: How children and parents cope with divorce.* New York: Basic Books.
Weinglass, J., Kressel, K. & Deutsch, M. (1978). The role of the clergy in divorce: An exploratory survey. *Journal of Divorce, 2,* 57-82.
Weiss, R. (1975). *Marital separation.* New York: Basic Books.
Weiss, R. (1976). The emotional impact of marital separation. *Journal of Social Issues, 32,* 135-145.

FOCUS TWO: RESTRUCTURING—THERAPY FOR CHILDREN, MEDIATION, AND CUSTODY

Family Therapy with Children of Divorce

William C. Nichols

ABSTRACT. This paper describes a transgenerational family therapy perspective as the approach of choice to providing therapeutic assistance to children of divorce. Major stress points for such children—the separation/divorce (breakup of the nuclear family household) and the remarriage of the parent/s—are placed within the broad framework of pre-divorce, divorcing, and post-divorce stages. Primary attention clinically is given to the major issues for children of divorce: loss and reactions to continuing marital discord.

There is little question that divorce is a stressful experience for children. Only the most highly partisan advocate of divorce as a doorway to freedom and new vistas of creative living for adults would maintain that children do not suffer from marital breakup and family reorganization. The needs of children in marital disruption and divorce have been well-documented. As summarized from available empirical research and clinical studies and observations, two major clusters of difficulties generally plague children during marital separation/divorce and afterwards: (1) the losses that they suffer as a result of the breakup and (2) the effects of continuing parental discord (Nichols, 1984). The purpose here is not to document the incidence and severity of the impact of marital breakup and family reorganization on children. Rather, it is to deal with the question of appropriate therapeutic assistance for those children requiring help when their parents divorce. What kind of help is needed and when is it needed?

THERAPEUTIC INTERVENTION: SYMPTOMS AND SYSTEMS

Various kinds of therapeutic intervention for children have been recommended: child therapy, children of divorce group therapy during the actual time of divorce, parent-child therapy, children's activity group therapy, and family therapy during the post-divorce stage (Kaslow,

William C. Nichols, Ed.D., is a Diplomate in Clinical Psychology (ABPP) and a Family Therapist in independent practice at 30200 Telegraph Road, Suite 455, Birmingham, MI 48010.

© 1985 by The Haworth Press, Inc. All rights reserved.

1984). The concern in this paper is with therapeutic intervention within the context of the changing family, particularly the continuing parental relationship and needs of the children as change is occurring. The specific focus here is on the ways in which family systems perspectives and family therapy approaches are helpful and useful. The time frame includes divorce and the early years of family reorganization through remarriage of the parents. Family therapy, as used here, refers to an orientation, a perspective in which issues are seen in the context of family structure and process, and not to a particular set of techniques or the number of individuals seen in an interview.

Until very recently the major focus of therapeutic work during separation/divorce and afterward has been on individuals. The best-known and the more creative approaches to working with children of divorce in the past have followed an individual, intrapsychic orientation (e.g., Gardner, 1976). Individual psychodynamic therapies assume that internal dynamics are the major forces determining behavior and that external events serve primarily as a source of stress to activate internal problems. These theories employ techniques which focus on intrapsychic mechanisms of the individual (Robinson, 1979). Consequently, the needs of the divorcing adults and their children have been considered separately and, when psychotherapy was employed, traditional individual modalities were used for both groups. Children were treated in child therapy with an individual orientation and adolescents in individual psychotherapy. Adults might receive therapy for themselves separately. If adults were brought into the child's treatment, the focus was still on the child as an individual. Typically, the custodial parent—who is still the mother 90 percent of the time—would be the parent brought into the child's treatment. Recently, for example, an individually oriented therapist described the use of conjoint mother-daughter treatment with adolescent daughters of divorce. The purpose of the conjoint therapy was to facilitate the youngsters' movement into individual psychotherapy and to begin dealing with the girls' psychological separation from mother (Kalter, 1984). There are some suggestions that the traditional child guidance model may not be the most appropriate way to work with children of divorce, given some of the high attrition rates and other nonproductive outcomes of such work (Rembar, Novick, & Kalter, 1983).

Individual psychotherapy for children of divorce is likely to be sought when they are displaying psychological/psychiatric symptoms or engaging in problematic behaviors. The interpretation of symptoms and problematic behaviors is different in individual treatment and family therapy approaches. Both view symptoms as connected with conflict, but family therapy locates the conflict in the transactions between the needs of the developing individual and the family system. A dysfunctional family that does not have an emotionally secure and stable marriage impairs or arrests the movement of children toward differentiation from their family of origin and into a life of their own where they can form appropriate new attachments.

Perhaps, it is more accurate to talk about pathological *reactions* rather than symptoms. As Framo (1972) has pointed out, the term symptom is derived from an individual, medical framework and in some ways does not apply to pathological reactions coming out of a system such as the family. Psychopathology may not have to be regarded as an intrapsychic conflict, but as a particular kind of relationship between intimately related people, according to Framo. Psychodynamic apparatuses certainly do operate within individuals, but form comparatively weak systems when faced with the multigenerational organization of a troubled family. The symptoms or reactions of anxiety, depression, and even psychosis often occur when the developmental strivings of the individual encounter opposing pressures from a dysfunctional family (Robinson, 1979). Viewing symptoms or pathological reactions as stemming from family transactions makes particular sense when one is dealing with children of marital breakup and family reorganization. The disruption of the child's development and the need to get him/her back on track should be one of the major concerns of the therapist.

What is actually happening to the child of divorce from a systemic point of view is that the youngster is reacting to family changes stemming from a rupture of the marital relationship. This results in greater or lesser alterations to the parent-child subsystem and, sometimes, in the sibling subsystem of the nuclear family. The child's reactions can be regarded as a systemic attempt to restore harmony to the marital subsystem and, often, to return the family system to the condition prevailing before the marital breakup. The marital breakup and subsequent family systems alteration can be viewed as a kind of "second order change" and as such a "sidewise leap" to another kind of systemic structure and functioning. In a sense the child's symptoms can be regarded as a systemic attempt to avoid second order change and/or as a byproduct of radical change in the family system.

There are several transition points in the life of a changing family where reactions (symptoms) may be expected to appear among children, whether or not there is marital breakup and family reorganization. The question, always, is whether the behaviors about which the family is concerned are, indeed, symptoms reflective of significant difficulty or whether the behaviors are essentially an age-appropriate set of actions that are normal. The criteria to be used in assessing the child's "needs, difficulties, and strengths within the context of the family setting" have been described elsewhere as including specific attention to separation/divorce, symptomatic/problematic behavior, and network of support (Nichols, 1984, pp. 32-34).

The effects of divorce and remarriage on youngsters certainly are related to their age and developmental stage, which reflect differences in the child's adolescent's ability to reason and take social perspectives (Longfellow, 1979). The broad age ranges used in this paper are the young child or pre-school period (ages 0-5 years), the middle years or elementary period (6-12 years), the adolescent period (13-18 years), and the young adult period (19 years and upward). Chronicity of the reactions or symptoms is an important guide (Gardner, 1976). The presence or absence of a support system for the child, including a supportive sibling subsystem; or for the custodial parent in the single parent household may be significant factors in the child's adaptation, along with other factors in the environment. Both factors in the social environment and the child's perspective play important roles in dealing with the effects of divorce.

A transgenerational perspective in which careful attention is given to the divorcing parents, their children, and their grandparents appears to be the therapeutic approach of choice for divorce situations. Therapy and various kinds of interventions are aimed at dealing with the continuing relationships of the three generations during and after the ending of the marital relationship (Beal, 1980). Originally, of course, the marital pair link two families, as well as three (and more) generations. Not only the emotional unhooking of husband and wife but also the alteration of their relationships with their children and with their own parents are proper concerns for the therapist who would help children of divorce. Considerable attention has been given to age and stage of the children at the time of the divorce, but little attention has been paid to the age and marital cycle stage (Berman & Lief, 1975) of the parents at the time of divorce. These factors may have implications for both the impact of the divorce on the children directly and indirectly through their effect on the parents' differentiation from and relationship to their own parents and family of origin.

DIVORCE STAGES AND STRESS POINTS

The various frameworks of the divorce and divorce adjustment process that have been devised over the years (e.g., Bohannon, 1970; Kessler, 1975; Kaslow, 1984) essentially reflect what happens with the husband and wife. That is, most of the reactions and needs described for the various stages in such frameworks pertain to the adults in the family. The needs of the children basically are dependent on what happens with their parents. Rather than using the frameworks as they are, therefore, it is necessary to make some adaptations in order to use them in working with children. Here, we shall use a broad framework of pre-divorce, divorcing, and post-divorce stages, giving attention to the major stress points appearing for children within those stages.

Two major stress points for children emerge from the actions of the parents: the breakup of the nuclear household (separation and divorce) and the remarriage of the parent/s (Sager et al., 1983). This is not to imply that children of divorce may not experience stress or need help at other points, but that these are the most predictable and major times of difficulty. Therapy with stepfamilies not only at the point of formation, which will be a concern of this paper, but also at subsequent stages is an important new therapeutic concern, for example (Nichols, 1980). Marital discord without divorce also may be a major source of stress for children, but that topic lies outside the parameters of this paper. The concern here is with the period from the marital breakup through remarriage.

Divorcing parents have two overlapping but distinct adjustments to make: adjustment to the dissolution of the marriage and establishment of a new life style, according to Spanier and Casto (1979). Their research indicates that forming a new life style is more essential to the overall adjustment of the adults than coping successfully with the marital dissolution. The time from the point of divorce until recuperation and reestablishment of a functional equilibrium seems to take about two years for adults (Kaslow & Hyatt, 1981; Kessler, 1975; Bohannon, 1970). Acquiring the position of adjustment helps to prepare most adults for eventual remarriage. The situation is both similar and different for children. Those who were functioning well prior to the separation/divorce often appear to be recuperating adequately one to two years following the divorce (Wallerstein & Kelly, 1980). For some children, completion of the period of recuperation and readjustment by the adult brings some relief from their own pain during the early adjustment period. For many children, the subsequent decision of a parent to remarry brings another disruption. While some children view the remarriage positively, others experience it as "a second divorce" (Sager et al., 1983).

Pre-Divorce Stage

Most therapists evidently have little experience with children of divorcing parents prior to the separation stage, particularly as compared with the numbers that show up a few months to a year following the separation/divorce. Parents or other family members such as grandparents are not very likely to seek a therapist for preventive work or to find assistance for the child in coping with the effects of marital discord and/or a dissolving marriage. Instead, they are likely to contact a therapist only when the child has displayed symptomatic behavior that solidly grips their attention.

Several factors deter parents from seeking help for their children during the pre-divorce stage. Some parents are too wrapped up in their own concerns—pain, misery, pursuit of freedom, for example—to give adequate attention to the needs of their children. If the marriage is disintegrating, their energies are likely to be bound up in dealing with their own reactions or, in some cases, turning toward a relationship with a new lover. Denying that parental actions are affecting the children negatively is common. Some couples do argue over their children's adjustments during marital discord, and cannot cooperate sufficiently to get help or to permit the other spouse to do so because any request for help is viewed as reflecting negatively on their parenting. Two ideas often expressed are "He/she is too young to understand what's going on" (for younger children) and "They are too involved in their own world, with their own friends and activities to be bothered" (for older children and adolescents). These forms of denial and stigmatization contribute to slowness in securing help for children prior to separation.

Most therapeutic work during the pre-divorcing stage, therefore, is with the parents. The first task of the therapist involves helping them to decide what they are going to do with their marriage and, if and when they do decide to end it, helping them to make the break in the least painful and most productive manner possible. Divorce therapy, a subject in its own right, also involves helping the partners to detach themselves and to work through in many cases the processes of withdrawing lingering vestiges of dependency and inappropriate expectations. One aspect of the process has been referred to as "decourting" by Napier (1977). They also need help in advancing their efforts to continue differentiating themselves from their respective families of origin. The second major task of the therapist is to assist them to begin addressing their children's needs during the breakup and afterwards.

As separation approaches parents sometimes begin to ask such questions as "What should the children be told?", "Who should tell them," and "When should they be told?" Gardner's book entitled *The Boys and Girls Book About Divorce* (1970) provides examples of the kinds of questions that children ask as divorce impends or occurs and illustrates appropriate parental responses. The book is useful with school-age children and older offspring, as well as being a helpful guide for parents.

Several courses are open to the therapist in helping the parents to deal with such questions. Careful exploration with some couples may establish that the children are not manifesting major dysfunction and that the parents have the ability to talk with the children adequately and appropriately. Here, the sharing may be done at home. In other instances, the clinical decision may be to recommend that all members of the nuclear family meet with the therapist and that the children be told in that setting of any parental decisions and the reasons for them. Whatever the location, home or the therapist's office, the children need to find out in the context of the total family as much as they can about what is happening and what it means for them. Children do not need to be left with an informational vacuum into which they can pour their anxieties and fears and create unnecessary pain for themselves. Also, they certainly need the opportunity to express their own concerns and reactions within the total family context.

Divorcing Stage

Regardless of whether difficulties have been recognized or acknowledged previously, the physical separation of the spouses makes it evident that marital discord and disruption are occurring. Whatever may have been denied from the children, it is evident with separation that change is underway and that estrangement exists between the partners. The marital breakup, which sets into motion a rather lengthy divorce readjustment process of some months and years for both parents and children, disrupts not only the family life cycle but also the individual life cycles of the members. The evidence seems to point to the physical separation as probably the most critical time in the divorcing process for children of all ages in the family (Bloom, White, & Asher, 1979; Sager et al., 1983).

Young children appear to be the group most severely affected by the marital breakup at the time it occurs (Wallerstein, 1984). They may find separation and divorce more difficult to comprehend and handle because of a lack of intellectual development and cognitive skills (Longfellow, 1979) and because of greater dependence on parents than is the case with school-age children and adolescents. Helping them to deal with feelings of confusion and self-blame, often stemming from illogical reasoning, is very important (Wallerstein & Kelly, 1975), as is the provision of a consistent caretaker (Beal, 1980; Goldstein, Freud, & Solnit, 1973) and physical contact with adults.

For children of divorce at all ages, the therapeutic challenge is to help them deal with their feelings of loss as the separation/divorce occurs, while simultaneously working with the parents whenever possible to minimize continuing parental conflict and to encourage cooperation in parenting. An exceedingly important part of working for the adjustment of children is the effort of helping them to construct and maintain an image of a "psychological family" (Sonne, 1980). Involvement of the grandparents and other extended family members in non-partisan roles both in the therapeutic sessions and in the general life of the children can help in this task. Extended family members can assist in offsetting feelings of loss on the part of the children (as well as on the part of the adults, for that matter), can provide buffers against continuing parental discord, and can encourage a sense of security regarding "family" through their own behaviors as family members. Provision of models of marriage by grandparents and other members of the extended family may prove to be most significant in the construction and maintenance of a construct of a psychological family.

Consistent with a family systems perspective is the recent suggestion that "children who are disturbed by parental separation may in turn be a source of stress for their parents" (Bloom, White, & Asher, 1979, p. 195). Examination of the emotional triangle that frequently develops when a child (or various children alternately or in serial fashion) line up with one parent against the other can lead to amelioration of stress. Similarly, exploration of what is happening, with the parents and the children present, can elucidate patterns of "emotional blackmail." Often a child or children exploit the parents' sense of uncertainty and feelings of guilt in order to gain what they want or punish the parents because of the marital discord and breakup. Conjoint sessions also can make clear to the parents their children's needs for continuing access to both parents and for continuing love.

Wallerstein and Kelly (1977) have described an intervention process of six weekly sessions for divorcing families held between one and six months following the divorce. Such time-limited and sharply focused sessions, in which it is made clear to all participants that family adjustment and problem-solving and not marital therapy form the agenda, can be very helpful. Inclusion of extended family members on a tailored and prescriptive basic—e.g., bringing in all members residing in the nuclear family's household or participating in the family's living on a regular basis, regardless of residence—can be helpful as well by reducing tensions between the divorcing spouses and providing reassurance for the children that not all important figures in their world are leaving them. The major focus in any case is the continuation of vital parenting functions while the marital relationship is dissolving (Beal, 1980).

A divorcing stage in which both parents continue to reside in the same household is different from one in which a parent departs and a physical separation occurs. The continuing residence pattern provides the family and the therapist with the opportunity to work on adaptation to the fact that a divorce is going to happen. However, it also provides a setting in which the children sometimes feel that they are receiving two messages. It may encourage the children to hold fantasies that the divorce is not going to happen and that the parents are going to remain together. Helping the parents to give their children consistent and supportive messages during this time, including realistic and valid reassurances about their relationship with and feelings for the children and behavioral demonstrations of parental cooperation for the sake of the children, generally proves helpful for all family members. There seems to be no simple or easy way for family members to live through this time of limbo.

Post-Divorce Stage

The post-divorce stage, as conceptualized for purposes of this paper, has two phases for children. The first, of course, is the phase of single parent living in which most children reside with one parent and spend some time with the other. Living in a household in which the two biological parents are not living together may bring relief for the children in some cases. Freedom or relief from the tensions between the parents in the family's former daily living pattern or from the tension of waiting for separation/divorce to occur often is experienced along with the pain of losing one parent.

Children may need to be assisted to recognize that it is all right for them to be relieved. They can be helped to recognize and acknowledge that they are ambivalent about the physical separation of the parents and breakup of the household, that it is all right to miss father while being glad that the omnipresent strain of family living is gone. This recognition and acceptance can take place far more readily when both parents are present in a therapy session than it possibly could with only the therapist and the child present. Being able to recognize and deal with such feelings with both parents can move the youngsters forward in the direction of resuming their normal growth and development which has been disrupted by the separation and divorce.

Dealing with the losses experienced by the children and helping them with their grief reactions has several important facets. For example, the losses may include not only the absence of a parent from the home and the child's daily life but also a change in residence, altered relations with extended family members, loss of friends, and reduced material circumstances. Once again, the age of the children has relevance for how losses are perceived and handled. Another significant factor in helping children deal with loss is the manner in which their parents, particularly the custodial parent, respond to the losses and changed circumstances.

The most direct way to help children deal with their losses in some instances is through the indirect route of helping the parents to cope with their own losses and grief reactions. Helping the parents to "resolve their personal loss and grief without projections of responsibility to others is of utmost importance," according to Beal (1980, p. 261). Working thus with parents helps them to avoid extruding their difficulties from their own disordered relationship onto the children and pulling the youngsters into the familiar scapegoated or parentified roles. Not only does a successful outcome from such efforts with parents help free children from being inducted into such roles but it also releases children to express their own reactions and to mourn their own losses.

Helping the parents to resolve their conflicts to the extent possible is, of course, another part of contributing to the adaptation and adjustment of the children. As the issue has been succinctly stated, "Resolution of conflicts and completion of mourning for the marriage are essential in order to minimize the continued fights through the children" (Sholevar, 1981, p. 470).

Play therapy for younger children and for many school-age children as well can be helpful for the expressing and acting out of reactions of loss, bewilderment, fear, and, with the older children, anger (particularly if as noted earlier the actions are taken in sessions with the youngsters and their formerly married parents present). Direct expressions of feelings by older children, adolescents, and youth are more effective when they can be done with the parent/s present, rather than alone with a therapist. The ability of the therapist to structure the session, to serve as a buffer, and to interpret meanings and needs is crucial to productive handling of such reactions in family sessions.

Evidence is accumulating that the kind of network of support that the custodial parent has helps to determine the availability of that parent to provide for the needs of the children (Wallerstein & Kelly, 1980). The emotional stability and mental health of the custodial mother, which is related to having such supports for herself, is in turn very important to the adaptation of the child (Longfellow, 1979).

There are not enough data on the needs of children who live in joint custody situations to provide strong guidance as to therapeutic requirements for such youngsters during the early post-divorce period. It may be that smaller proportions of individuals involved in joint custody circumstances, as compared to single parent custody arrangements, require professional assistance. Such a finding would not be unexpected, since the successful construction of a joint custody agreement requires at least a modicum of cooperation between the parents. Unfortunately, much of the writing on joint custody has either been based on very small and non-representative samples or has been done by advocates of that approach. The major issue for many parents and children is not necessarily physical custody but access of child and parent to one another.

The second phase of post-divorce living for most children involves the remarriage of one or both parents. This is, as noted above, the second major stress point for children of divorce. Researchers and clinicians have viewed the chief issues facing children at remarriage as complex. Visher and Visher (1979) named the major issues as dealing with loss, questions about where he/she belongs, membership in two households, divided loyalties, unreasonable expectations, fantasies over the natural parents reuniting, guilt over thinking he/she caused the divorce, and, in the case of adolescents, problems of identity and sexuality. Sager and associates (1983) found the experience of remarriage from the child's perspective as involving positive potential, multiplicity of relationships, divided loyalties, pseudo-independence, and incest fears. The tendency to regard the remarriage as a second divorce is especially likely to prevail if the youngster has been exceptionally close to the marrying parent during the post-divorce stage, according to their findings. For all children the fact of remarriage tends to challenge the common fantasy of having their parents remarry.

Again, there are important age differences in the reactions of the youngsters to this major stress point, as there were differences to the marital breakup according to the age of the children. Adolescents, for example, may have much more difficulty entering a new household than do younger children, unless the parent and his/her new spouse as well as the non-custodial parent exercise a considerable amount of understanding and flexibility (Sager et al., 1983). Important therapeutic issues for parents and stepparents during the period leading up to and immediately following remarriage are their concerns about separating what is normal, expectable behavior on the part of children and teenagers from their reactions to the remarriage.

Bringing together the biological parents, the intended or new spouse, and the children for the purpose of working on the practical and emotional problems of the remarriage can be productive. The focus is kept always on the continuing needs of the adults to provide parenting for their children and on the needs of the children and the stepparents to work out effective ways of relating and dealing with one another. Various combinations of post-divorce, pre-remarriage, or early remarriage sessions may be arranged, from those involving all participants as just described to those including only the former spouses. Different members of the family may need to be seen individually in order to make it possible for them to work productively in therapeutic sessions with other members and subsystems of the total family. Again, as has been emphasized throughout this paper, devoting such sessions to working on specific issues and keeping the structure firm, the focus steady, and the time short makes it possible to gain the participation and cooperation of more families than myth and common belief would indicate is possible. Ahrons (1981), Brown (1981), Nichols (1984), and Sager and associates (1983) provide clinical and/or research evidence supporting the idea that such cooperation around the best interests of children can be secured.

Certainly, there are some contraindications to bringing formerly married persons together for the purpose of resolving difficulties pertaining to their children. Among the major reasons for not attempting to work conjointly with divorced parents is the persistence of hostility on the part of one or both of them that makes such work nonproductive. This means that a therapist should think things through very carefully before expending time and effort on working with individuals who do not demonstrate some slight degree of cooperativeness with the former spouse with regard to the children. Similarly, the tendency of a parent to be punitive against children specifically as a result of or in reaction to the therapeutic sessions is a strong contraindication to seeing the children and their formerly married parents together. Another contraindication is the tendency of one or both parents to use the children in a struggle against the other. As noted earlier, it may be possible in some instances to work separately with one or both of the adults in such a way as to prepare them to work cooperatively and productively in conjoint sessions for the good of the children. Similarly, it may be possible in some cases for the therapist to work separately with the adults, engaging in a kind of shuttle diplomacy that secures their cooperation even though they will not meet together. Borderline personality characteristics in one or both of the parents also makes it unwise to attempt to assemble children and their formerly married parents for therapeutic intervention and assistance.

Extending the therapeutic focus to include a three-generational perspective and members of the grandparental generation in the post-divorce period may have significant outcomes for the children. Some of this may be indirect, such as the reduction of stress between the divorced parents which enables them to give attention and commitment to parental responsibilities. Strong support by the older, third generation can enable the parents to be aware that there is no disapproval by their own parents and imputation of family disloyalty because they are cooperating, even though they are divorced. Bitterness by the older generation sometimes works the other way, of course, to prevent cooperation between their child and his/her former spouse. Some of the impact on children may be more direct, as in the case of grandparents who step appropriately into the picture to give direct support to the child as a result of therapeutic intervention. Aunts and uncles also can be used as surrogate authority figures and as significant other adults in the lives of the children.

With regard to the grandparents, the extent and manner in which members of the third generation may be productively brought into the therapeutic process depends in large measure on how they are handling the divorce itself. We have very little research evidence bearing on the impact of the divorce of an adult son or daughter on their parents. What evidence there is seems to suggest that the divorce of an adult son or daughter may be problematic for the parents (Johnson & Vinich, 1981). Some research shows that third generation respondents felt that their offspring's divorce had a negative impact on their lives. There were differences between paternal and maternal grandparents in terms of contacts and relationships with their grandchildren. Paternal grandparents were more likely to report negative effects (Ahrons & Bowman, 1981). Spanier and Hanson (1981) concluded from their research findings that the potential advantages of support and interaction offered through participation of extended family members in the lives of separated persons may be moderated by several familial sanctions, including disapproval and criticism. The picture seems to be somewhat different once the divorce has occurred and the members of the older generation have had time to adjust to it as fact. For conjoint sessions with extended family, as with other parts of the reorganizing family, the therapist generally needs to structure the session—i.e., laying out the purposes and establishing the boundaries in terms of the purpose, length of time for the interventions, and limits of permissible behavior. The therapist needs to maintain control. This involves not only the structuring of the variables named but also lessening suspicions so that the sessions are made as safe as possible for parents, children, grandparents, and other participants.

CONCLUSION

This paper has been concerned with the use of family systems perspectives and family therapy approaches in dealing with the needs of children of divorce through the stage of early remarriage by their parent/s. The two major sets of problems—losses suffered in the marital breakup and family reorganization and reactions to continuing parental discord—need continuing attention and assistance in order to help children and adolescents resume their normal growth and development toward maturity. The children encounter major stress points at the time of the separation/divorce and at the time of remarriage.

This paper did not deal with the techniques of family therapy intervention to any significant degree, because of space limitations. Family therapists will use the techniques and specific approaches and interventions they ordinarily use. This paper has provided a broad framework and map of the territory.

REFERENCES

Ahrons, C. (1981). The continuing coparental relationship between divorced persons. *American Journal of Orthopsychiatry, 51*, 415-428.

Ahrons, C. & Bowman, M. E. (1981). Changes in family relationships following divorce of adult child: grandmother's perceptions. *Journal of Divorce, 5*(1/2), 49-68.

Beal, E. W. (1980). Separation, divorce, and single-parent families. In E. A. Carter & M. McGoldrick (Eds.), *The family life cycle: a framework for family therapy* (pp. 241-264). New York: Gardner Press.

Berman, E. M. & Lief, H. I. (1975). Marital therapy from a psychiatric perspective: an overview. *American Journal of Psychiatry, 132*, 583-592.

Bloom, B. L., White, S. W., & Asher, S. J. (1979). Marital disruption as a stressful life event. In G. Levinger & O. C. Moles (Eds.), *Divorce and separation* (pp. 184-200). New York: Basic Books.

Bohannon, P. (1970). The six stations of divorce. In P. Bohannon (Ed.), *Divorce and after* (pp. 33-62). New York: Doubleday.

Brown, E. M. (1981). Divorce and the extended family: a consideration of services. *Journal of Divorce, 5*, 159-171.

Framo, J. L. (1972). Symptoms from a family transactional viewpoint. In C. J. Sager & H. S. Kaplan (Eds.), *Progress in group and family therapy* (pp. 271-308). New York: Brunner/Mazel.

Gardner, R. A. (1970). *The boys and girls book about divorce.* New York: Bantam Books.

Gardner, R. A. (1976). *Psychotherapy with children of divorce.* New York: Jason Aronson.

Goldstein, J., Freud, A., & Solnit, A. J. (1973). *Beyond the best interests of the child.* New York: The Free Press.

Johnson, E. S. & Vinich, B. H. (1981). Support of the parent when an adult son or daughter divorces. *Journal of Divorce, 5*, 69-77.

Kalter, N. (1984). Conjoint mother-daughter treatment: a beginning phase of psychotherapy with adolescent daughters of divorce. *American Journal of Orthopsychiatry, 54*, 490-497.

Kaslow, F. W. (1984). Divorce: an evolutionary process of change in the family system. *Journal of Divorce, 7,* 21-39.
Kaslow, F. W. & Hyatt, R. (1981). Divorce: a potential growth experience for the extended family. *Journal of Divorce, 5,* 115-126.
Kessler, S. (1975). *The American way of divorce: prescription for change.* Chicago: Nelson Hall.
Longfellow, C. (1979). Divorce in context: its impact on children. In G. Levinger & O. C. Moles (Eds.), *Divorce and separation* (pp. 287-306). New York: Basic Books.
Napier, A. Y. (1977). Followup to divorce labyrinth. In P. Papp (Ed.), *Family therapy: full length case studies* (pp. 133-142). New York: Gardner Press.
Nichols, W. C. (1980). Stepfamilies: a growing family therapy challenge. In L. Wolberg & M. Aronson (Eds.), *Group and family therapy 1980* (pp. 335-344). New York: Brunner/Mazel.
Nichols, W. C. (1984). Therapeutic needs of children in family system reorganization. *Journal of Divorce, 7*(4), 23-44.
Rembar, J., Novick, J., & Kalter, N. (1983). Attrition among families of divorce in an outpatient psychiatric population. *International Journal of Family Therapy, 5,* 227-236.
Robinson, L. R. (1979). Basic concepts in family therapy: a differential comparison with individual treatment. In J. G. Howells (Ed.), *Advances in family psychiatry, I.* (pp. 428-435). New York: International Universities Press.
Sager, C. J., Brown, H. S., Crohn, H., Engel, T., Rodstein, E., & Walker, L. (1983). *Treating the remarried family.* New York: Brunner/Mazel.
Sholevar, G. P. (1981). The emotional impact of family disruption on children. In G. P. Sholevar (Ed.), *The handbook of marriage and marital therapy* (pp. 461-474). New York: SP Medical and Scientific Books.
Sonne, J. C. (1980). The psychological family and family image construction in uprooted children. *Family Therapy, 7,* 255-284.
Spanier, G. B. & Casto, R. F. (1979). Adjustment to separation and divorce: a qualitative analysis. In G. Levinger & O. C. Moles (Eds.), *Divorce and separation* (pp. 211-227). New York: Basic Books.
Spanier, G. B. & Hanson, S. (1981). The role of extended kin in the adjustment to marital separation. *Journal of Divorce, 5,* 33-48.
Visher, E. & Visher, J. (1979). *Stepfamilies.* New York: Brunner/Mazel.
Wallerstein, J. S. (1984). Children of divorce: preliminary report of a ten-year follow-up of young children. *American Journal of Orthopsychiatry, 54,* 444-458.
Wallerstein, J. S. & Kelly, J. (1975). The effects of parental divorce: experiences of the preschool child. *Journal of the American Academy of Child Psychiatry, 14,* 600-616.
Wallerstein, J. S. & Kelly, J. (1977). Divorce counseling: a community service for families in the midst of divorce. *American Journal of Orthopsychiatry, 47,* 23-29.
Wallerstein, J. S. & Kelly, J. (1980). *Surviving the breakup: how children and parents cope with divorce.* New York: Basic Books.

Divorce Mediation: An Introduction

Stanley N. Cohen

ABSTRACT. This chapter is an introduction to a form of intervention designed to counter the detrimental effects of the adversary legal system—divorce mediation. Following a history of the movement, the author discusses differences between mediation and marital and family psychotherapy. The different types of mediation services currently being offered are described. Mediation is evaluated in terms of who uses the services and factors affecting utilization; the effectiveness of mediation; client, dispute, and mediator factors related to mediation success; and client satisfaction. The limitations of mediation, as well as its promise, are also delineated.

INTRODUCTION

The social reality of high divorce rates, along with the profound adjustments in marital and parental relationships that accompany divorce, have resulted in an expansion of the type of services offered by marriage and family therapists. Practitioners are now as apt to be asked to help couples deal with divorce related economic, personal, and social issues as they are to provide persons with assistance in solving their marriage and family problems.

Most recently, mediation has emerged as a specific type of intervention geared to help divorcing couples in conflict over custody, visitation, spousal and child support, and other economic issues. It provides an opportunity to minimize potential conflict for couples considering divorce, in that in examining options, they can make constructive decisions in a more informed manner. Mediation is, also, a means of addressing post-divorce, child-related and economic problems which carry over from the marriage and prevent its successful termination. Mediation is available, too, in post-divorce situations when new disputes related to remarriage, visitation, and child support defaults arise that need resolution.

The mediation process should be viewed as an alternative to self-help and litigation. It stresses and provides an opportunity for the participants

Stanley N. Cohen, Ph.D., is the Executive Director of the Association of Family and Conciliation Courts and Professor, the Department of Psychiatry, Oregon Health Sciences University, 8131 SW Sam Jackson Park Road, Portland, OR 97201.

© 1985 by The Haworth Press, Inc. All rights reserved.

to work cooperatively and to assume responsibility in making decisions that can have a profound impact on the well-being of themselves and their children during and after divorce. Mediation, then, is viewed as being a more constructive alternative to resolving divorce disputes than the adversarial arena of the courtroom.

Folberg (1983) has defined mediation as:

> . . . a process by which disputants attempt to reach a consensual settlement of issues in dispute with the assistance and facilitation of a neutral resource person or persons. At the very least, the process consists of systematically isolating points of agreement and disagreement, developing options, and considering accommodations. (page 8)

Although it is a method used to resolve other forms of interpersonal and intergroup conflict, this paper is concerned only with divorce mediation. The following topics will be addressed:

1. The history of divorce mediation.
2. Differences with marriage and family therapy.
3. The manner in which divorce mediation services are offered.
4. Evaluation.
5. Potential, limitations, and future directions.

DIVORCE MEDIATION: A BRIEF HISTORY

The current enthusiasm and advocacy for mediation belies its long history as a means by which interpersonal disputes have been resolved. In their excellent historical reviews, both Brown (1982) and Folberg and Taylor (1984) point out that mediation has been used in a variety of societies for thousands of years. In ancient China, for example, mediation was the principal means by which conflict between disputing parties was resolved. It continues to be practiced in the People's Republic of China, and enjoys an important place in the present Chinese legal system.

A rich history of conciliation and mediation is found, also, in the customs of Japan. In older times, village leaders were expected to help their community members settle a range of interpersonal disagreements. Prior to World War II, the courts of Japan were structured formally to provide for the conciliation of personal disputes. Such a system continues to flourish today.

Similarly, in parts of Africa a respected community leader served as a mediator to assist disputing parties in resolving their grievances cooperatively. As elsewhere, the intent was to get the disputants to settle their differences without resorting to the use of an arbitrator or judge.

Turning to the United States, we find that the principal method used by early Quakers to resolve disputes was mediation and arbitration. Ethnic and religious groups who culturally were attuned to the use of mediation and conciliation established similar systems after immigrating to the United States. One illustrative example is the Chinese Benevolent Society which was created to resolve disputes between community members and disagreements within the family. Another example is the Jewish Conciliation Board which was formed in New York City in 1920. The community-based system, which continues to function, is a derivation of the Jewish Religious Court—a system used by ancient Hebrews for conciliation and mediation of interpersonal conflict between community and family disputants.

More recently, a number of developments have been instrumental in recognizing the value of mediation in the United States. For example, the Federal Mediation and Conciliation Service, which was established in 1947, provides assistance in resolving disputes to both industry and labor. The Dispute Resolution Act was passed by Congress in 1980. This piece of legislation provided support to establish and evaluate alternative approaches to the settlement of a variety of community disputes without the need for court intervention. In addition to these national trends, strides have been made by state and local governments to develop and implement localized centers for resolving conflict emanating from a wide range of issues such as domestic violence, consumer complaints, landlord-tenant disputes, and neighborhood disagreements.

The preceding brief historical overview has highlighted what is really an old and worldwide tradition. The increasing use of dispute-resolution techniques in labor/management, neighborhood, and local community settings was mentioned. While family disputes have been within the province of previous mediation efforts, it is interesting to note that the specific application of mediation in response to divorce disputes has a very short history. As pointed out by Brown (1982),

> practically none of the books on divorce, children of divorce, or child custody that were published prior to 1981 even mention the word "mediation." (page 3)

How does one account for the long delay and apparent resistance in applying mediation principles to the resolution of divorce disputes, particularly since there has been a demonstration of the effectiveness of such an approach in resolving conflict in other areas of human relations? The question is a complex one and cannot be answered fully in this paper. The answer, in part, may be due to two factors, one of which has been addressed by the author and a colleague in a recent article:

> A belief commonly held by most Americans is that the family requires unconditional and permanent bonds between its members for

> its survival. Historically, and up to the present time, marriage has been defined as a lifelong commitment between two adults that typically involves maintaining a household and raising children. In other words, marital and parental relationships are thought to be one and the same. Simply stated, if your marriage dissolves or ends, so does your family.
>
> The divorced parent not living in the household often believes he (and it usually is the father) has no role in the parenting of the children. This attitude apparently stems directly from a misconception that family life can occur only when the parents are living together. The fact is that parenting relationships are not intended to be terminated by divorce. Indeed the laws explicitly emphasize a reordering of parental and parent-child relations, the intent being to secure access to the child by the out-of-home parent. At the same time, the manner in which parenting responsibilities are to be shared during and after divorce have been clouded by the way family law has categorized the role of divorced parents in custodial and noncustodial terms. What is of particular concern to many noncustodial parents is that they have no legal basis to be involved in the lives of their children except on a limited basis. Recent changes in family law—for example, joint custody—have clarified and provided a legal basis by which both parents have the opportunity to participate in decisions related to the rearing of their children.
>
> In summary, the ideal American family is one that is intact, nuclear, and child-centered. This ideal is deeply embedded in the cultural fabric of our society going back to colonial days. Family life also has been romanticized as a life-long commitment between two adults with no distinction having been made regarding the functional differences between marital and parental relationships and the implications of disruption to family members when a divorce occurs. (Cohen and Jones, 1983, pp. 468-469)

Given these deeply rooted notions about the life-ending nature and importance of family life to the well-being of children, it is not too far-fetched to assume that any attempts to provide alternatives that promote access out of dissatisfying and dysfunctional marriages would be resisted strongly. Such a procedure, in fact, could be viewed as breaking up families—the antithesis of a constructive intervention.

The second reason for the delay of mediation relates to the history of attempts by human institutions to control divorce. In ancient times neither marriage nor divorce were treated in a legal context. Both were private matters and not subject to control by the state. The rise and influence of Christianity, however, altered the concept of marriage in that it was defined as a sacrament and, therefore, not subject to dissolution. Consequently, for centuries marriage as well as divorce was controlled exclusively by the church. Eventually, government assumed control over marriage and divorce, but access to dissolving one's marriage was as difficult as when the matter was under the jurisdiction of the church. Domestic relations law gradually developed grounds which had to be established before the court would grant a divorce. One had to "prove" that the other party was unfit to continue the marriage. The system was structured as an adversarial setting, which pitched party against party. It is no wonder that divorce was viewed as a contentious and competitive process that served to exacerbate and sustain bitterness even among couples who might only have held minimal animosity towards one another. The author believes it is no coincidence that social and legal resistance to mediation prevailed as long as adversarial legal procedures were so entrenched.

Conversely, as divorce has come to be accepted as a fact of contemporary life, through a confluence of social, economic, and legal changes, it is not surprising that the "door" for mediation was opened. Beginning with California's ground-breaking legislation in 1970, no-fault divorce has become widely accepted in this country and divorce mediation has achieved respectability as a constructive alternative to the traditional adversary system.

CONTRASTING MEDIATION WITH MARRIAGE AND FAMILY PSYCHOTHERAPY

It is not unusual for an emerging discipline to seek out and clarify its uniqueness from other allied professions. The discussion that follows is based on Kelly's (1983) attempt to delineate basic differences between divorce mediation and psychotherapy.

Kelly differentiates between the two by examining several aspects of mediation including:

> . . . the goal of mediation, the nature of the mediation process, the role of the mediator, the role of diagnosis, the place of emotional expression in the mediation process, and the mediator's techniques and interventions. (page 35)

Goal of Mediation

The principal goal in mediating a divorce is the negotiation of specific issues identified and agreed upon by the parties and mediator. The specificity of the goal (a settlement) stands in contrast to psychotherapy goals which generally are broad based, such as improving marital relationships, enhancing one's personal life, and so forth.

While there is general agreement about the primary goal of divorce or post-divorce mediation, there is less consensus regarding subgoals pertaining to issues like restructuring of parental and parent-child relationships, developing means for resolving subsequent disputes, and enhancing a constructive adjustment to the divorce. In these areas, the boundaries between mediation and counseling are not clear-cut.

Mediation Process

The process of mediation is viewed as being goal-focused, task-oriented, and time-limited. While crisis counseling, behavioral, and other forms of short-term, present-centered psychotherapy share these characteristics, there are marked differences from many forms of psychotherapy which emphasize the value of history and insight, and which focus on the long-term resolution of intrapsychic and interpersonal dynamics.

To reach a settlement, clients and mediator have to deal predominantly with tasks that are concrete and thus the focus is on problem-focused information and issues. Clients have to be specific in identifying and valuing assets, liabilities, and other property. Developing plans for custody, visitation, and child support are other examples of very concrete operations. Intrapersonal material and the quality of a person's relationship with his or her spouse are deemphasized. While the business of mediation may evoke emotional reactions, they need to be contained. In contrast, psychotherapy often seeks to expand rather than contain the exploration of psychological material. The mediation experience undoubtedly elicits this material but the mediator does not interpret or explore it.

The mediation format is also different from the way in which many practice psychotherapy. Early on, client and mediator expectations, an explanation of the structure of the process, and "rules of the game" are outlined explicitly so that the mediator and the clients can move as quickly as possible to the work of reaching an agreement on the issues in dispute. By contrast, psychotherapy often moves more slowly, placing an emphasis on what is troubling an individual or couple. The therapist may use several sessions establishing rapport and gathering personal and marital histories in order to develop a treatment plan for resolving a couple's problems.

Role of Mediator

A divorce mediator functions in an active manner. In many respects, the mediator serves as an educator to the couple, providing them with information that is needed for an equitable negotiated settlement. At the same time, he or she remains task-oriented, keeping the clients on target with regard to the aims, procedures, and scope of the mediation. The mediator, of course, does not make decisions, but facilitates the couple's decision-making abilities while remaining impartial and maintaining a balance between the parties.

While working with the clients, the mediator may function in a way similar to an active family therapist who is working on a specific family problem. But, there are some critical differences. The mediator must have skills above and beyond those offered by a therapist. The competent mediator must have a working knowledge of domestic relations law, common monetary practices, budgetary needs, the provisions of the divorce law regarding the division of assets and liabilities, and income tax considerations. This specialized knowledge, in addition to specific information about the impact of divorce on parents and their children, makes the mediator's role more specialized than the traditional therapist who deals with a dissatisfying marriage.

Diagnosis

Diagnostic activity is limited to the purposes of mediation, and primarily is used for strategy building. Generally speaking, a mediator assesses the client's reaction to the divorce, the power relationship between the couple, and present and future needs of the parties and their children. He or she, typically, is not interested in the past history of a couple unless it bears directly on the ability to reach a settlement.

The Place of Emotions in Mediation

The experienced mediator is aware of the strong emotions that may surface as a couple works toward reaching a divorce settlement. The extent to which emotional expression facilitates or impedes the mediation process dictates how much of these feelings will be allowed to surface in the sessions by the mediator. By contrast, in some psychotherapies emotional expression and a sharing of feelings are valued for their own sake.

Conflict Management

The mediator assumes an active role in managing conflict when it emerges. This is done to provide safeguards that allow for the process to move on in a rational task-oriented manner. Obviously, sustained interpersonal conflict impedes progress and may result in one or both parties abandoning their efforts at reaching a negotiated settlement.

Some psychotherapies, on the other hand, encourage the expression of conflict. The conflict management techniques used by mediators would be seen as counterproductive since understanding the dynamics of a couple's conflict is deemed necessary to work towards its resolution.

Negotiation Strategies

Clients who elect to mediate their divorce vary in their readiness to reach an agreement. The process is straightforward and relatively quick when the clients are open and flexible. However, when faced with rigid clients and little room to "trade," the mediator is in need of bargaining skills to avoid an impasse and termination. Since therapists generally have no training in bargaining techniques, their approach relies more heavily on exploration, interpretation, and emotional and behavioral techniques.

The preceding discussion has underscored key differences in the techniques mediators and therapists use in helping their clients resolve interpersonal problems and conflicts. The discussion clouds the fact that the majority of persons who currently practice mediation come from mental health backgrounds. The transition from therapist to mediator has been made without a great deal of difficulty for some professionals. The theoretical orientation of the therapist affects the ease of this transition. For example, it is much more difficult for a psychodynamically-oriented therapist, who works primarily with individuals in a long-term manner, to feel comfortable with mediation. On the other hand, those therapists whose orientation is behavioral, work conjointly with couples, use a crisis or short-term counseling model, and are familiar with conflict resolution techniques probably will make an effective transition to mediator. If the reader conceptualizes the two examples as opposite ends of a continuum, you may informally assess the extent to which your orientation lends itself to the practice of mediation. Beyond the transition issue, almost all therapists will need to enhance their skills and knowledge about divorce law and procedures, bargaining and dispute resolution strategies, state and federal tax considerations, the divorcing process and how it impacts on parents and children, and the economics of divorce.

MEDIATION AS IT IS PRACTICED IN COURT RELATED AND NON-COURT RELATED SETTINGS

There are two settings where divorce mediation services are offered—court related and non-court related. The focus of what is mediated varies both across and within these settings.

Court-Connected Services

Mediation services developed as an extension of ongoing service provided by professionally staffed counseling units that were attached administratively to a judicial jurisdiction. These units were called conciliation courts and originally provided marriage counseling focusing on the reconciliation of couples who had either filed for divorce or were considering such an action. The oldest conciliation court was established in Los Angeles in 1955, and served as a model system for such services in California and throughout the country. Parenthetically, while the focus of service was reconciliation, the counseling approach was similar to divorce mediation in that short-term counseling was offered to assist couples to negotiate a formal reconciliation agreement. As the divorce rate began to climb, conciliation courts expanded their services to include divorce counseling and custody evaluations. In response to a growing awareness of the value of mediation as an alternative to court litigation of divorce disputes, the State of California enacted legislation that mandated mediation services for any couple that was in dispute over custody or visitation issues. While mandated mediation services have not been totally accepted by judicial systems throughout the country, a proliferation of court-connected mediation programs has occurred.

Typically, court-connected mediation services are limited to the resolution of custody and visitation disputes. Response to this type of divorce mediation has been equivocal. As is pointed out by Milne (1983):

> Separating the mediation of parent-child issues from financial and property issues allows children to be treated as an issue in their own right, and it lessens the potential for using them as pawns in the negotiation process. However, separation of issues can segment a divorce agreement artificially when property, finances, and children are indeed related and when decisions made in one area affect decisions made in the other area. (page 19)

There has been criticism of court-connected mediation programs that allow for information obtained during the mediation process to be given to the judge and the parties' attorneys. Implicit in this criticism is the covert ability of the mediator to influence an agreement made by the parties. Those who support this practice point to the fact that court-connected mediators often work with highly conflicted couples who are not likely to reach an agreement through less aggressive means.

Non-Court Related

One type is the private practitioner whose practice is restricted to mediation. More typical is the mental health professional who provides divorce mediation in addition to other services (Pearson, Ring, and Milne, 1983). To a lesser degree, lawyers also provide divorce mediation. More often than not, they continue to practice law while offering mediation to selected clients.

Sometimes practitioners from different disciplines work together as co-mediators. The team is usually composed of an attorney and a counselor. These practitioners usually maintain their separate legal and counseling services and co-mediate on a part-time basis.

Private mediation operates on a fee-for-service basis and independently establishes policy and procedures. Services vary with regard to issues mediated, the model of mediation used, and the professional orientation of the mediator. These disparities occasion criticism and call for the development of mediation standards.

Agencies and clinics (both public and private) that offer divorce mediation typically also offer a wide range of services. Within these agencies, certain individuals are advocates of divorce mediation. They may have participated in mediation training and offer the service as part of their professional practice. Some agencies specifically advertise divorce mediation as one of the services provided; many of these agencies are advocates for children, and are therefore motivated to provide mediation dealing with custody and visitation.

EVALUATION OF DIVORCE MEDIATION PROGRAMS

In an article that reviews the development of family and divorce mediation, Brown (1982) notes that:

> Among those who have practiced mediation during the past few years, there has been near unanimous agreement that it is an effective means for resolving divorce and family disputes. Nevertheless, there is a paucity of empirical data that would confirm the validity and reliability of the divorce mediation model. Fortunately, however, in addition to the court-connected custody/visitation projects previously mentioned, there are several ongoing or recently completed studies that will help fill this research deficit. (page 31)

This section summarizes selected research findings that have been recently reported about divorce mediation. The discussion is framed around two projects. One project, the Denver Custody Mediation Project (Pearson and Thoennes, 1984), evaluated the effectiveness of private-based mediation in resolving custody and visitation disputes out of court. The second project focused on the effectiveness of court-connected mediation in Los Angeles, Minneapolis, and Connecticut (Pearson and Thoennes, 1984) in resolving custody and visitation issues. This project was called the Divorce Mediation Research Project. These projects, under the direction of Jessica Pearson, are viewed as offering a relatively reliable assessment of mediation because of their scale, design, and longitudinal design (Pearson and Thoennes, 1984, page 1). The findings reported in this paper include the following:

Who Used Mediation?

Mandated court-connected services, not unexpectedly, attract the highest participation rates. In the Los Angeles County Conciliation Court (where mediation is mandatory) there were close to 4500 mediations of custody and visitation in 1982. Typically, however, mediation services that are voluntary do not draw large numbers of participants. The Denver Project offered free mediation services, and half of the parties chose not to use the service (Pearson and Thoennes, 1982). A 1981 survey of public and private mediation programs found that over 93 percent of those services identified as private-based conducted less than 50 mediations annually, and slightly over half saw fewer than ten cases.

Why the reluctance to use mediation voluntarily? Pearson and Thoennes (1984) suggest that differences in those who mediate as opposed to those who do not may explain some of the resistance. The pro-mediation subjects score higher on traditional socioeconomic indicators, and seem to communicate better with their spouses. Women who try mediation find it less distant and impersonal than the court system. Men apparently opt for mediation because they see their chance of winning custody as being low in the courtroom. Further, men who are ambivalent about the divorce or who are reconciliation-prone seem eager to try mediation.

Attorneys play an important part in their clients' choices about using mediation. Among those who tried mediation, 72 percent of the women and 69 percent of the men indicated they were encouraged by their attorneys. Among those who reject mediation only 18 percent of the women and 32 percent of the men report their attorneys suggested that they try mediation (Pearson, Thoennes, Vanderkooi, 1982).

The preceding suggests low participation in mediation may be associated with low public awareness and attitudes of lawyers. As long as mediation maintains a low community profile, it may only be used by higher-income and better-educated couples, or by those who are required to mediate their disputes by court jurisdictions such as is the case in California.

While some criticize making mediation of divorce issues compulsory, the evidence seems to support compulsory service. Between 60 and 70 percent of those using court-connected mediation service in Los Angeles, Minneapolis, and Connecticut favor such programs. The pro-position (85 percent) is even higher, of course, among those parties who reached agreement. What is more interesting is that between 62 and 68 percent of those couples who *failed* in their mediation attempts also support a mandated approach to the resolution of divorce disputes.

EFFECTIVENESS OF MEDIATION

Mediation agreements vary and are difficult to compare primarily because there are different definitions as to what constitutes agreement. In addition, it is hard to ascertain the extent to which "unsuccessful" couples reached a settlement later. Some programs report high agreement rates of 70 percent (Irving, 1982) and 80 percent (Wixted, 1982). Included in these figures, however, are agreements to continue further mediation sessions as well as temporary agreements.

More frequently, however, mediation services report agreement rates ranging from 40 to 65 percent. In the three court-connected mediation services that were studied by Pearson and Thoennes (1984), the resolution of child custody or visitation disputes approximated 40 percent. An additional 20 to 30 percent of couples using mediation reported partial or temporary agreements.

It should be noted that most civil complaints terminate either by dismissal, default, or by negotiated settlement. To find out whether mediation is as effective as pending litigation, Pearson and Thoennes (1984) compared disputing parties who used mediation with another group who went to court to resolve the issues. These results are from the Denver Study of a private, voluntary service. Sixty percent of those who mediated their disputes reached agreement and a majority of those who tried but could not reach a mediated agreement were able to stipulate to an agreement prior to appearing in court. In contrast, only half of the non-mediation group stipulated before going to court, while the remaining disputants relied on a judicial resolution of their disagreements. Put another way, over 80 percent of the couples using mediation produced their own agreements during or after the experience. On the other hand, half of the parties not exposed to mediation relied on the court to resolve their divorce disputes.

CLIENT, DISPUTE, AND MEDIATOR FACTORS RELATED TO MEDIATION SUCCESS

Pearson and Thoennes (1984) found no set of variables highly predictive of success in mediation when client and case attributes were analyzed. However, there were patterns that were suggestive of success in mediation. As mentioned previously, higher income couples were able to mediate more often than lower income couples. Successful mediation couples appear also to be more willing to communicate or cooperate with each other. When pathology (alcoholism, drug and spousal abuse) is evident, there is a lower likelihood of success.

When the nature of disputes is reviewed, there appears to be a relationship between mediation success and the scope and duration of the disagreement(s). In other words, successful mediations are more likely to occur if cases are mediated early on in the divorcing process and there are no ongoing multiple disputes. This is particularly true if the cases do not involve serious disputes about child and spousal support and the division of property. This information points to the need to divert divorce disputants to mediation as soon as possible.

Pearson and Thoennes (1984) also found that successful mediation was related to mediator experience. For example, 30 percent of cases seen by new mediators resulted in resolution of the disputes; successful mediation increased to over 60 percent when the mediator was more experienced.

Agreements are also more likely to occur when mediating couples perceive the mediator to be neutral, thus underscoring the importance of impartiality in the sessions. Further, successful mediation is tied to a perception by clients that the mediator should be task-oriented and focus on solutions to the disputes. Clients who reached full agreement in mediation reported (Pearson and Thoennes, 1984):

> . . . the mediator understood the . . . problems . . ., gave the respondent a chance to express . . . views, reduced . . . tension . . ., focused . . . on the children, did not spend . . . time on the past, provided information about child development and adjustment, and helped to identify . . . custody and visitation alternatives. (page 18)

TYPES OF MEDIATED AND ADJUDICATED AGREEMENTS

One assumption underpinning the concept of mediation is that it fosters accommodation and compromise. This appears to be the case. Couples who reach agreement in mediation appear to choose joint custody. This type of arrangement rarely is selected by non-mediating couples. In addition, Pearson and Thoennes (1984) found that in those cases where sole custody was agreed upon in mediation, more visitation time was provided than in non-mediated sole-custody agreements. It appears that the mediation process allows for more give-and-take between couples than is the case when such disputes are adjudicated.

Client Satisfaction With Mediation

Individuals who have used mediation generally report high satisfaction with the process, regardless of the outcome. These persons also indicate satisfaction with mediation, would recommend it to a friend, and believe it should be mandatory for couples with custody disputes. By contrast, for those not using mediation, the majority report dissatisfaction with custody investigations and the workings of the legal system in general as it pertains to resolving divorce disputes.

Three factors have been cited by those clients supportive of mediation (Pearson and Thoennes, 1984). First, mediation is viewed as helping couples focus on their children's needs. Secondly, the mediation process is viewed as providing an opportunity to air grievances—a chance to express a point of view about the dispute. A third feature thought to be valuable by user advocates of mediation is that the process helps keep the discussion on target. Mediators prevented arguing, thus focusing on the issues to be resolved—namely custody and visitation. In addition, successful mediation clients were somewhat more satisfied with the outcomes than those using adversarial means to resolve custody and visitation issues.

Despite high levels of satisfaction with mediation, there were also dissatisfactions voiced by its users. Half of the clients in the Pearson study of the three court-connected mediation services reported tension and unpleasantness in the sessions. A slightly smaller percentage of clients reported feeling defensive. Considering the emotionality around issues of custody and visitation, these comments should not be totally unexpected. Other dissatisfactions revolved around misconceptions about mediation. For example, many parties thought that the process might save the marriage, and began the sessions angry and upset. Others thought the mediators would make the final custody decision.

Finally, mediation seems to have little impact on the relationship between the couple. About 20 percent of the parties reported that mediation helped them understand their ex-spouse's point of view, and only a third felt it had helped them understand themselves (Pearson and Thoennes, 1984). Mediation, then seems limited in affecting long-term relationship patterns; thus, mediation should not be viewed as a substitute for counseling and support services even though custody and visitation issues had been resolved through its use.

In general these results support an independent review of empirical mediation studies by Sprenkle and Storm (1983). They found that "ideal" candidates for mediation are couples mediating around a limited number of issues, whose level of conflict is moderate or less, and both parties feel able to represent themselves. Both have begun the process of letting go and accept the divorce. Mediation occurs early before the entanglements of the adversary process of court orders. There are no third parties directly involved, such as grandparents or lovers. Both parties sense some ability to communicate and cooperate. Money is not a major issue in the divorce and there are sufficient resources to carry on as single persons. Finally, the attorneys support the mediation.

THE PROMISE, LIMITATIONS, AND FUTURE DIRECTIONS

The thrust of this article has been to introduce the concept of mediation. Readers are urged to review the references in this paper, as well as the separate chapter on divorce literature in this collection for a more comprehensive understanding of the scope and practice of mediation.

While mediation currently enjoys an increasing acceptance among clients, mental health professionals, judges, and attorneys, perspective should be maintained about its "universal" appeal and effectiveness. For example, mediation should *not* be viewed as a mechanism by which all divorce related disputes can be settled, notwithstanding assertions to the contrary by some of its ardent advocates. There will continue to be the need for adjudication for some individuals and/or couples who either are not amenable to mediation or who want their "day in court." Indeed, this is their legal right.

As with any emerging discipline, it is important to examine the development and practice of mediation critically in order to enhance its professional growth. Issues that seem pertinent to making mediation an identifiable service that can be offered to the public include: (1) continuing to clarify and develop a generic framework under which all forms of public and private divorce mediation can be given shape without compromising the divergent ways in which it is currently practiced; (2) educating the public; (3) working with legal, judicial, and mental health professionals in providing an understanding of the interdisciplinary nature of mediation; (4) developing realistic standards and practices of mediation that reflect and distinguish its legitimacy as a discipline; (5) continuing to support the need for research related to the effectiveness of mediation, as well as information pertinent to those qualities important in the training of competent mediators; research also needs to be broadened to include studies of the mediation of child support and property settlement; and (6) promoting training programs that reflect the legal and behavioral science perspective that is a distinguishing characteristic of the practice of mediation.

In summary, the future of mediation appears promising. It has achieved a high degree of public support considering its recent arrival as an alternative means to resolve divorce related disputes. There has been a proliferation of both private and public services and further growth seems assured as mediation becomes more well-known. Training opportunities have become established so that persons interested in providing such services can enter the field. Within a short time there has been an active interest in research, and there are at least two professional journals (the *Mediation Quarterly* and the *Conciliation Courts Review*) that primarily publish articles related to divorce mediation. At the same time, the promising future may be jeopardized if the leaders and advocates of the movement do not come together to clarify and organize the gains that have been made. As one advocate stated in a recent article (Milne, 1983):

> To look to the future is visionary. Conscientiously to shape the future is vigilant. Let us work together to share the future of divorce mediation so that we can provide families in conflict with a cooperative means of resolving issues. (page 31)

REFERENCES

Bane, M. J. *Here to stay: American families in the twentieth century.* New York: Basic Books, 1976.

Brown, D. G. "Divorce and Family Mediation: History, Review, Future Directions." *Conciliation Courts Review*, 1982, 20 (2), 1-37.

Cohen, Stanley N. and Jones, F. Nolan. "Issues of Divorce in Family Therapy." *Handbook of Family and Marital Therapy.* New York and London: Plenum Press, 1983.

Folberg, J. "Mediation Overview: History and Practice." *Mediation Quarterly*, 1983, 1, 3-13.

Folberg, J. & Taylor, A. "Mediation: A Comprehensive Guide to Resolving Conflicts Without Litigation." San Francisco, Washington, London: Jossey-Bass, 1984.

Irving, Howard et al. "Final Research Report of the Conciliation Project: Provincial Court (Family Division)," Toronto: Ministry of Attorney General, 1982.

Kelly, Joan B. "Mediation and Psychotherapy: Distinguishing the Differences." *Mediation Quarterly*, 1982, 1, 33-44.

Milne, A. "Divorce Mediation: The State of the Art." *Mediation Quarterly*, 1983, 1, 15-31.

National Center for Health Statistics. Annual summary of births, deaths, marriages, and divorces. 1980. Monthly vital statistics report, 29:13, Washington, D.C.: U.S. Government Printing Office, 1981.

Pearson, J., Ring, M., and Milne, A. "A Portrait of Divorce Mediation Services in the Public and Private Sector." *Conciliation Courts Review*, 1983, 21 (1), 1-24.

Pearson, J. and Thoennes, N. "Research on Divorce Mediation: A Review of Major Findings," in 13th Quarterly Report. Department of Health and Human Services, Children's Bureau, 1984.

Pearson, J. and Thoennes, N. "Mediating and Litigating Custody Disputes: A Longitudinal Evaluation." Forthcoming in *Family Law Quarterly*, Winter, 1984.

Pearson, J. and Thoennes, N. "Mediation of Contested Child Custody Disputes." *The Colorado Lawyer*, 11:2, 1982.

Pearson, J., Thoennes, N., and VanderKooi, L. "The Decision to Mediate: Profiles of Individuals Who Accept and Reject the Opportunity to Mediate Contested Child Custody and Visitation Issues." *The Journal of Divorce*, VI:1, 1982.

Sprenkle, D. H., & Storm, C. L. (1983). Divorce theory outcome research: a substantive and methodological review. *Journal of Marital and Family Therapy, 9*, 239-258.

Wixted, Sandra. "The Children's Hearing Project: A Mediation Program for Children and Families," Alternative Means of Family Dispute Resolution, Washington, D.C.: ABA Special Committee on Alternative Means of Dispute Resolution. 1982.

Systemic Assessment Criteria for Joint Custody

Sandra S. Volgy
Craig A. Everett

ABSTRACT. This paper reports historical trends and recent literature regarding joint custody. Based on a systemic theoretical position and over 300 clinical divorce cases, the authors present five criteria reflecting family structure and process from which to evaluate the efficacy of joint custody arrangements.

The rate of litigated child custody and visitation disputes in this country has been rising rapidly. The factors which have accelerated this figure are numerous (see Everett & Volgy, 1983). However, one of the more prominent factors has been the increasing liberalization of the courts in considering creative and unique solutions to custody disputes. Historically in early judicial decisions, custody was awarded to the father who exercised absolute control over the children, considered "property" of the father. Later, tradition and judicial precedence shifted to a focus on the needs of the child for maternal contact. What became known as the "tender years doctrine" has dominated judicial decisions until quite recently and continues to exert a strong influence in many regions of the country (see Folberg and Graham, [1979] for a thorough review of the historical aspects of custody from a legal perspective). More recently the work by Goldstein, Freud, and Solnit (1973) argued that one parent should be given sole custody and have absolute control over visitation and all other aspects of child raising. This has been interpreted in light of the tender years doctrine as favoring the mother for sole custody. Present estimates report as high as ninety percent of all custody orders in this country award sole custody to the mother. However, there has been a significant liberalization of visitation guidelines for the non-custodial parent over the past

Sandra S. Volgy, Ph.D., formerly Coordinator of Child Advocacy Services, Pima County Conciliation Court, Tucson, Arizona, is a Clinical Psychologist, Family Therapist and Mediator in Private Practice, Tallahassee, FL 32306.

Craig A. Everett, Ph.D., is Associate Professor and Director of Family Therapy Training, Interdivisional Doctoral Program in Marriage and the Family, Florida State University, Tallahassee, FL 32306.

© 1985 by The Haworth Press, Inc. All rights reserved.

twenty years which has served to increase post-divorce contact between fathers and children.

Since the early 1960's, there has been a gradual shift towards the integration of male and female social roles in this country. Women have pursued employment and careers in steadily increasing numbers until, at present, they represent over fifty percent of the work force. Women have moved away from traditionally defined jobs into executive, managerial and professional positions where the demands on their time and energy have increased dramatically. Similarly, men have begun to redefine their roles away from that of "only" the breadwinner in the family and have begun to invest more of their time and energy into self-enhancement programs, creative hobbies and child care responsibility. The concept of the house-husband is no longer startling or associated with radical, counterculture lifestyles.

During this shifting of social roles toward greater androgyny and integration, parents in the midst of dissolving their marriages began to question the traditional adversarial process in deciding custody/visitation matters. The historical judicial precedents did not fit the reality of contemporary families in which both parents had provided substantial child care and had attained good parenting skills, as well as both parents having been employed outside the home. In searching for alternatives, divorcing parents became the primary promoters and supporters of joint custody legislation.

Joint or shared custody is a custodial choice which is rapidly gaining support among courts and mental health professionals who make recommendations to judges regarding custody and visitation. Many experts in family law believe it will be the mandated custody of choice in most states by 1990. By September, 1980, fifteen states had statutes affirming the right of both parents to be judged equally as potential custodians for their children. Another four states had laws which authorized joint custody and twelve more were considering bills which would require judges to begin with a presumption for joint custody (see Folberg & Graham, 1979; Axelrod & Everett, 1983). In January, 1980, California passed legislation which defined joint custody as a the presumptive choice in custody disputes and required judges to submit written justification for *not* awarding joint custody. However, a great deal of controversy surrounds the issue of the advisability of joint custody for both parents and children. To date there are limited data to either support or refute its effectiveness.

With the popular interest in joint custody and the recent legislative support, family therapists as well as other mental health professionals are confronted increasingly with divorcing couples who wish to explore joint custody options. As these requests proliferate, it is encumbent upon the mediator to be aware not only of the legal implications within his/her state but also to be able to discuss with the couple the implications of joint custody with respect to family patterns and issues of child development.

Joint custody has often received idealized reviews in the popular press and within various professional circles. However, clinicians should be aware that joint custody may be proposed as a legal ploy or bargaining tool to manipulate the other spouse or to enhance one's bargaining power in the dissolution. Similarly, at an emotional level, spouses still struggling with the painful aspects of separation may perceive of joint custody as a tool for clinging to the marriage or as a weapon for retaliation and control.

The patterns of joint custody arrangements present a complexity of legal issues which range from support and taxes, to school districts and legal residences. In addition, joint custody raises a number of family and emotional concerns which include the stability and the continuity of a child's environment, differing parenting patterns, and issues of values and lifestyles. Often the ambiguity inherent in some joint custody orders or agreements serves to further dramatize the emotional confusion of post-divorce parent-child relationships and to escalate post-divorce animosities.

The value of joint custody is that it most clearly approximates the normative family system and supports the continuation of parent-child roles which were present prior to the separation and divorce. This seems to mitigate many of the negative aspects of divorce for children. Unfortunately much of the literature with regard to joint custody, both pro and con, is written from an advocacy position often with emotional biases and little substantiation. Detractors of joint custody frequently raise concerns regarding a potential lack of stability for the child or confusion with regard to custodial and residential roles and environments. Others cite the difficulties for parents in maintaining close communication patterns and tolerating differences between them when often these were the very problems in the marriage which led to the divorce.

SYSTEMIC ISSUES IN FAMILY DISSOLUTION AND CUSTODY PATTERNS

As we have reported elsewhere, the "victim" of the divorce is never simply the children but the loss of the viability and organization of the family process (Everett & Volgy, 1983). Studies which focus solely on the impact of divorce on the marital partners or the children are at best naive because they fail to identify the circularity and power of the broader family system. The event of divorce is much like a pebble being tossed into a pond that produces increasingly larger ripples. The effects on the family system encompass not only the spousal, parent-child, and sibling subsystems but spread intergenerationally to grandparents and the broader social network.

Thus, custody disputes are generally embedded within the prior patterns of family dysfunction reflecting early marital disappointments, anger or guilt. Similarly, the mediated resolution of such custody disputes must look beyond the immediate needs of a child or parent to the broader resources and limits of the intergenerational family system. This is particularly true in cases moving toward joint custody where the former spouses must re-establish a new working alliance as co-parents. For example, it has been our observation that many of the most bitterly disputed and litigated custody cases have included a grandparent actively involved behind the scenes, either emotionally or financially. In addition, grandparents are often particularly concerned when they feel access to the grandchildren may be denied by a son-in-law or daughter-in-law.

Thus the ongoing success and effectiveness of any mediated custody arrangement, and particularly joint custody, is dependent upon the family's experience of the divorce process and subsequent reorganization of the post-dissolution parent-child subsystem. We have defined elsewhere the developmental sequence by which a family system moves through a period of *structural decoupling* and into a process of structural recoupling (Everett & Volgy, 1983). In the former period the system disengages from the prior roles and loyalties. Marital bonds are withdrawn and parental ties are altered. While the basic systemic organization of the nuclear family ceases here, the continuing parent-child subsystem evolves into a new post-dissolution organizational structure. This process will be shaped by patterns of custodial and/or non-custodial interaction, geographical residences, remarriage, the blending of step-siblings and step-parents, and the continuing roles of grandparents. It should be recognized that dysfunctional patterns which were present in the prior nuclear system will continue at differing levels of intensity through this structural decoupling and recoupling process. These patterns are critical in evaluating and predicting the potential outcome of any custodial arrangement. For example, where a child was parentified in the former nuclear system by being given excessive adult responsibilities for caretaking and nurturing, the decoupling process may be slowed and inhibited due to spousal ambivalence and reluctance to reassume parental control. Following disengagement the recoupling process may be characterized by competitive struggles between the parents for the parentified child's alliance through custody. This may result in patterns of withholding visitation, attempts to bias the child against the other parent, and an inability to re-establish a new parental alliance for the purposes of co-parenting.

The development of a joint custodial pattern must be considered in the context of the entire matrix of interlocking systems which impact on both parents and children. Systemically, joint custody represents a new family form, particularly where relatively equal residential sharing occurs, and operates with two or more co-existing parent-child subsystems with alternating residential environments each headed by one parent. Ahrons has termed this a binuclear system (Ahrons, 1979). It develops as if the original spousal subsystem undergoes a process of systemic mitosis (as in the division of cells). Here the subsystem subdivides with one parent in each new cell and the sibling subsystem is replicated in both cells. In this systemic reorganization the structure of joint custody most closely duplicates the original nuclear system as compared to other types of custody. Each new cell or parent-child subsystem carries its own intergenerational loyalties and social network ties. In sole custodial arrangements the reorganization occurs within one cell in which the children remain and which is headed by one parental decision-maker. The other cell contains only the non-custodial parent and does not form an equivalent functional subsystem. In other custodial arrangements such as split or divided custody the sibling subsystem is divided along with the spousal subsystem such that only fragments of the original system remain. Alternating custody operates similarly to joint custody except that decision-making is not shared and the two subsystems do not typically function in concert with one another nor do they often exist within the same social and community systems.

In recent years, research has been reported which strongly supports both the viability and superiority of joint custody over sole custody arrangements. The primary impetus from the mental health field came almost simultaneously from two groups of landmark studies on the effects of divorce on children (Wallerstein & Kelly, 1974, 1975, 1976, 1977, 1980; Hetherington, Cox & Cox, 1976, 1978; and Hetherington, 1979a, b, c, d). Both studies, completed independently in different parts of the country and with a fairly diverse group of sole custody parents, found that the quality of the relationship of the child to the non-custodial father was a critical factor in the child's post-divorce adjustment and that the more frequent access to *both* parents, the better the child's adjustment. In addition, it was found that the less hostility and bitterness the parents experienced toward each other, the better the child responded to the divorce.

Other researchers later found that parenting skills and competence of both parents was improved with frequent visitation or joint custody, that support payments were more timely and less litigated and that relitigation in all areas was significantly reduced with joint custody arrangements (Luepnitz, 1982; Grief, 1979; Folbey & Graham, 1979; Roman & Haddad, 1978).

The positive aspects of joint custody for children have also been examined and researchers have found that psychosocial adjustment is negatively affected by loss of time with a non-custodial father (Jacobson, 1978), that quantitative skills (Shinn, 1978) and inadequate development of appropriate sex-typed behavior (Biller & Bahm, 1971) are also negatively affected by father absence. Other studies have shown that lack of parental contact was related to delinquency and anti-social acting out (Anderson, 1968; Douglas, 1970), childhood depression (Caplan & Douglas, 1969), and dysfunctional heterosexual relationships for girls (Hetherington, 1972). Children in many of the studies cited reported that typical sole custody visitation relationship did not compensate for the loss of the non-custodial parent in their lives.

In studies specifically of joint custody and parent and child satisfaction with it, joint custody arrangements have been seen as having a great many more advantages for parents and for their children (Brown et al., 1976; Luepnitz, 1982; Nehls & Morgenbesser, 1980; Ahrons, 1980) and as being strongly preferred by parents and children as a custody option (Grief, 1979; Ahrons, 1980; Luepnitz, 1982; Morgenbesser & Nehls, 1980).

ASSESSMENT CRITERIA

The following criteria have been evolved from the authors' clinical work with over 300 cases in either custody evaluations or mediated custody agreements over the past five years. These criteria are intended to provide descriptive resources by which the clinician can evaluate the potential efficacy of proposed joint custody arrangements. They may be utilized also by the therapist in assisting parents in examining the pros and cons of joint custody options.

Before examining one specific systemic criteria, there are a variety of pragmatic issues which effect the potential outcome of joint custody arrangements. These are factors that are commonly considered in formal custody evaluations for other types of custody as well. It should be noted that these considerations are for assessing options for combined joint legal *and physical* custody. As physical residence of the children begins to more closely approximate a sole custody (every other weekend plus holidays) arrangement, these issues become somewhat less relevant with regard to the efficacy of joint custody. This definition should be assumed in the use of the words "joint custody" which follows.

Pragmatic Issues

It is useful to compare the parent's values and attitudes regarding parenting and to consider the degree to which they are similar which will facilitate comfortable shared parenting. If they are quite dissimilar, it is important to consider whether *both* parents have the ability to tolerate their differences in these areas. If this is problematic, a power struggle will quickly develop and control issues will begin to outweigh other more positive aspects of the arrangement.

It is also important to assess the personal and emotional stability of each parent in the context of both past and future relationships. Often, attorneys and others who may be strongly influenced by the parents erratic and hostile behavior during the divorce will assume that one or both are unstable and incapable of good parenting because of divorce adjustment struggles. If their pre-divorce behavior is considered along with a prediction of their behavior following the adversary divorce, then a better indication of their overall stability can be obtained. As a concomitant of the above, it is important that both parents be able to accept responsibility for their own actions and behavior in the present, even if it is at times erratic or embarrassing. If they are only able to blame the other spouse for their action, the advisability of shared parenting diminishes.

Another important assessment factor is the degree of trust they report in each other's parenting ability. It is not necessary that they trust the other person in any other area of functioning but it is imperative that they believe that the other parent will take care of the children adequately and make decisions which will safeguard the children's welfare. If such trust is not present, the clinician should explore the specific areas where trust is lacking and see if trust in that/those area(s) can be developed through exchange of information or improved communication skills. If it cannot be developed, at least to a minimum degree, it is unlikely that joint custody will be tolerated for very long by the untrusting parent.

Another consideration is how motivated both parents are to provide to the children continual access to the other parent regardless of whether it is convenient or comfortable. Essentially, they must believe in this as a value for the children and as essential for their healthy emotional development. Since joint physical custody is often less convenient for parents because of the increased transportation difficulties, the increased need for contact with the former spouse, higher financial requirements, and for some parents less emotional comfort, high motivation is often required for it to succeed. The clinician should assess motivation as a determinant.

The last pragmatic issue to be considered in assessing the efficacy of joint custody is each parent's current and future capacity for parenting skills and for comfortably sharing the children. Future capacity must be considered because at the time of the separation or divorce one of the spouses may have been the primary caretaker for the children and the other may have had limited experience in childcare. However, with time, experience, and perhaps special parent education courses, the less experienced parent may be easily capable of equal parenting skills and knowledge. The parents' individual feelings about sharing the children are important to assess since discomfort in this area can lead to continual resistance at the time of transferring the children or in issues of sharing necessary information regarding the children's needs and concerns. It is especially common in our society for mothers to have a great deal of difficulty sharing the children's caretaking with a former spouse. This becomes increasingly difficult for a mother as the age of the child decreases. Fathers are usually less accustomed to having dominant control of children's lives, especially at younger ages and therefore welcome the notion of sharing childcare. Often, the mother's severe resistance to sharing the younger child is related to her need to retaliate for marital differences rather than reality-based concern regarding the father's ability to care for the child appropriately. If the therapist can explore these concerns and examine their accuracy, sometimes the more correct issues will become clearer.

Systemic Criteria

The following systemic criteria (Volgy & Everett, 1985) are intended to reflect the broad intergenerational and structural influences both in the pre-existing family system and in the reorganized post-dissolution system. We have identified and defined five family structure and process variables: external family boundaries, intergenerational enmeshment, structural decoupling, structural recoupling, and internal subsystem boundaries.

1. External Family Boundaries

Family boundaries circumscribe the nuclear system and define how members of the family and information passes both in and out of the system. These boundaries range along a continuum typically from closed to open to diffuse. In evaluating systems for joint custody, clinicians should trace the boundary patterns from the pre-divorce nuclear system, including their relative flexibility or rigidity, into the post-divorce process of developing separate systems and thus new boundaries. In some cases these are continuous and in others they may change significantly. The specific concern regarding joint custody is the children's ability to move comfortably between the newly evolving systems.

In cases where the former nuclear system was characterized by closed boundaries family members experienced less contact with either external family of origin members or social network resources. Where the relative isolation carries over to the new post-divorce systems we found that both parents and children have difficulty tolerating and encouraging an open flow of information and time sharing between the systems. Similarly, both parents will have difficulty accepting the viability of the other system and may tend to sabotage authority in the other parent. Such parents are often uncomfortable sharing or receiving information outside of their immediate system and therefore such withholding can mitigate against successful joint custody.

Where the boundaries of the nuclear family have been highly diffuse, the system is often characterized by a lack of consistent internal structure and intrusive external influences which may result in somewhat chaotic functioning. Children in such systems are exposed to a lack of parental consistency in rule-making and expectations. Parents in such a system may have had difficulty maintaining authority and protecting the system from excessive intergenerational interference. When these boundary patterns are replicated in the new post-divorce systems, the children will be caught between two systems lacking consistent definition and structure. Parents may defer responsibility or control of the children to the other parent or external resources such as the school or grandparents. The actual patterns of the children moving between residences may be altered upon impulse without predictability or structure for the children's needs.

2. *Intergenerational Family Ties*

The relative closeness or distance that exists through family relationships is often described respectively as *enmeshed* or *disengaged* (see Minuchin, 1974). These patterns carry across intergenerational boundaries and are reflected, for example, by the relative involvement of grandparents (first generation) in their children's (second generation) marriage and with their grandchild (third generation). These ties may range from cut-off and distant (disengaged) to intrusive and manipulative (enmeshed).

It is important to evaluate these patterns both with the predivorce nuclear system and subsequently with the post-separation/divorced parents. We have identified excessive intergenerational enmeshment as a "red flag" issue for the clinician. Where close alignments and high loyalties continue between first and second generation family members, i.e., grandparents and parents, at least two patterns potentially disruptive to joint custody occur. First, grandparents have access to intrude into the parent-child subsystem which can sabotage the authority and quality of parent-child attachments. To the extent that this occurred in the pre-dissolution nuclear system, the probability of its continuation post-divorce is high. Secondly, where parents maintain continuing access to their families of origin for support or nurturance, there is a likelihood that under pressure or stress they may seek to develop coalitions and triangular alignments with their own parents against the spouse or former spouse. To the extent that either of these patterns occurred in the pre-dissolution nuclear system, there is high probability that they may occur even more dramatically post-divorce. In fact aspects of these patterns, i.e., the inability of the parents to contain and protect their spousal subsystem from external/intergenerational influences, probably represented the underlying clinical dysfunction in the nuclear system.

Where the intergenerational ties are emotionally cut-off (see Bowen, 1978) or excessively disengaged, we have observed that the post-divorce parents and their children tend to lack both emotional support and access to financial assistance from their families of origin. This tends to leave the single parent somewhat more isolated, having to rely on the development of a new social network or occasionally pulling a child into an awkward alliance for emotional support. These factors often contribute to an inability by these parents to establish stable post-dissolution co-parenting structure. This was evidenced dramatically by a case with delinquent adolescents referred for family therapy. The joint custody arrangement, agreed to one year previously by the parents, had been characterized by chaos and an inability of the parents either to work together or to set limits on the three children. Both parents were isolated from other family members and had invested heavily in career and social endeavors with little involvement in parenting. They acknowledged having agreed to joint custody with the covert intention of the other spouse taking the "burden" of parenting off their respective shoulders.

3. Structural Decoupling

In nearly fifty percent of the joint custody cases that were identified initially as failures, we attributed the etiological dysfunction to patterns of excessive intrusiveness or retaliation by one or both parents. The request for joint custody was seen as either a covert mechanism by one spouse to cling to the former marriage and reengage the spouse by defining a prominent role with the children or an effort to manipulate and control the other parent through presumed joint custodial control of the children. These situations are the result of incomplete structural decoupling where the spouse(s) have failed to withdraw their former emotional attachment from the marital relationship and continue either to cling to it or act out against it.

The systemic issue involves the structural termination of the former spousal subsystem while at the same time evolving a new relationship within a parent-child subsystem (recoupling). In other words, parents must learn to be parents without being spouses. Here triangular patterns which existed in the nuclear sytem, particularly within the former parent child subsystem, not only may continue post-divorce but may become dramatized (see Everett & Volgy, 1983). For example, a child that was scapegoated prior to the separation/divorce may tenaciously cling to that role and even act out in more delinquent ways. This reinforces circularly both the child's role of pulling the parents back together again and the inadequately decoupled parents needs to remain involved with one another, in this case with the focus on the child.

In situations where one parent has more successfully decoupled than the other, a dramatic imbalance may occur which can sabotage a joint custody arrangement. Here the children become caught in the middle with the least decoupled parent seeking to hold the children closer with the hope of pulling the other spouse back. When that fails both parents may retaliate in the form of covert coalitions with the children or in specific acts such as sabotaging the children's time with the other parent. Similarly, the children may resent the "healthy" decoupling of one parent, protect the parent who is still clinging to the former marriage, and attempt to force or negotiate a reconciliation. While such patterns may occur in sole custodial arrangements, the possibility of shared power in the joint custodial relationship may not only trigger these but exacerbate their potential destructiveness.

4. Structural Recoupling

The post-dissolution process of recoupling involves the establishment of a new parent-child subsystem structure without the former marital component. Developmentally, the relative ease with which this stage is accomplished is based in part on the degree of successful structural decoupling. However, the structural process of recoupling begins systemically at the moment former spouses begin to relate to one another and their children from separate households regardless of their relative emotional detachment or the form of custody.

In joint custody, where the degrees of power and control are intended to be relatively equalized, this recoupling process is particularly critical. Each parent's ability to tolerate such shared power must be evaluated in the context of two simultaneously evolving systems that must become both separate yet integrated (as in the former mitosis example). These new parent-child systems must be balanced in terms of their internal organization, i.e., the authority/control of each parent and their stability, e.g., not too enmeshed or disengaged from intergenerational loyalties.

The relative effectiveness of this recoupled parental structure is often tested both by the ability of each side to integrate comfortably new social contacts and potential partners and by the ability of the other parental system to tolerate this. The entry of a new partner into either or both parental systems creates a transitional imbalance that can escalate into retaliatory behavior destructive to a joint custodial arrangement. This is particularly true if one parent has not successfully decoupled from the prior marriage or if one's own potential for evolving a new social network is deficient. The entry of a new partner and potential remarriage triggers latent issues from the former marriage in terms of disappointment, rage or fantasies for reconciliation.

Clinicians must be careful to identify these post-dissolution issues, helping former spouses realize that they may not evolve new social networks at the same pace. It has been our observation clearly that the more effectively *both* parents are able to evolve new social contacts and thus maintain a relatively balanced degree of new system development, the greater will be their ability to tolerate a shared custodial system. If a significant imbalance in the structural recoupling occurs, a joint custodial system may not last over time.

5. Internal Subsystem Boundaries

This identifies the development of new boundaries within the simultaneously evolving parent-child systems. Boundaries defining subsystems are evaluated according to the range of closed, open or diffuse as in the external system boundaries (see #1). Here they will define the relative degree of separation or intrusion between each parent and the children within each respective system. Boundary patterns that existed within the former nuclear system may not always be replicated in the new post-dissolution systems. For example, formerly firm and open boundaries in the nuclear system may become ill-defined and diffuse post-divorce as one parent pulls a child closer for emotional support in a pseudo-spousal role or as another parent reactively moves closer to his/her family of origin and closes off contact with the children.

The reciprocal role of the children within both new subsystems will be highly influenced by these new internal boundaries. It has been our observation that the boundaries between the executive parental role and the children's subsystem must be fairly similar. This is critical due to the alternative residential patterns in joint custody and the simultaneous operation of each parent-child subsystem. If there is considerable disparity, it is likely that the children will begin to refuse to participate cooperatively in one or the other systems. For example, if in one system the children are allowed to join the executive subsystem (diffuse boundaries) and make co-decisions with the parent they may resist or react to involvement in the other system where the boundaries with the parent are often not firmly delineated. The older the children the more likely they will favor the system that allows them more power and less definition of role or structure.

CONCLUSIONS

We have summarized the historical issues involving custody in this country and reviewed the relative pros and cons of joint custody from the literature. Based on a systemic theoretical position regarding the family dissolution process, we have extracted from over 300 clinical divorce cases five central criteria regarding the efficacy of joint custody.

We support joint custody for families in every possible situation where it can be effective and productive. However, as clinicians and mediators, particularly having been associated with court programs, we have seen not only the failures of custody patterns but the toughest possible cases in which to evolve potential shared parenting arrangements. The descriptive clinical criteria are offered as guidelines and "red flags" for those working with similar cases. We have identified the need for more empirical research with regard to joint custody and hope these preliminary criteria will serve both as a stimulus and potential hypotheses for clinicians and researchers.

REFERENCES

Ahrons, C. (1979). The Binuclear Family: Two households, one family. *Alternative Lifestyles,* (2), 4, 499-515.

Ahrons, C. (1980). Joint custody arrangements in the post-divorce family. *Journal of Divorce,* 3 (3), 189-207.

Anderson, R.E. (1968). Where's dad? Parental deprivation and delinquency, *Arch. Gen. Psychiatry,* 18, 641-649.

Axelrod, P. & Everett, C.A. (1983). Joint Custody. In A.M. Haralambie (Ed.), *Handling Child Custody Cases.* Colorado Springs, Shepards/McGraw-Hill, p. 52-63.

Biller, H.B. & Bahm, R.M. (1971). Father absence perceived maternal behaviors and masculinity of self-concept among Jr. high school boys. *Develop. Psych.,* 41, 1978-181.

Brown, C.A., Feldberg, R., Fox, E.M., and Kohen, J. (1976). Divorce: Chance of a new lifetime, *J. Soc. Issues,* 32: 119-133.

Bowen, M. (1978). *Family Therapy in Clinical Practice.* New York: Jason Aronson.

Caplan, M.G. & Douglas, V.I. (1969). Incidence of parental loss in children with depressed mood. *J. of Child. Psychol. Psychiat.,* 10, 225-232.

Douglas, J.W.B. (1970). Broken families and child behavior. *J. Royal College Physicians,* 4, 203-210.

Everett, C.A. & Volgy, S.S. (1983). Family assessment in child custody disputes. *Journal of Marital and Family Therapy,* (9), 4, 343-353.

Folberg, H. Jay & Graham, M. (1979). Joint custody of children following divorce. *U.C. Davis Law Review,* 12 (2), 523-582.

Goldstein, J., Freud, A., & Solnit, A.J. (1973). *Beyond the Best Interests of the Child,* New York: The Free Press.

Grief, Judith B. (1979). Fathers, children and joint custody. *Am. J. of Orthopsychiatry,* 49, 311-319.

Hetherington, E.M. (1972). Effects of father absence on personality development in adolescent daughters. *Devel. Psychol.,* 1, 313-325.

Hetherington, E.M., Cox, M., & Cox, R. (1976). Divorced fathers. *Family Coordinator,* 25, 417-428.

Hetherington, E.M., Cox, M., & Cox, R. (1978). The aftermath of divorce. In J.H. Stevens, Jr. & M. Matthews (Eds.), *Mother-child, father-child relations.* Washington, D.C.: NAEYC.

Hetherington, E.M. (1979a). The development of children in mother-headed families. In H. Hoffman & D. Reiss (Eds.), *The American Family: Dying or developing.* New York: Plenum.

Hetherington, E.M. (1979b). Stress and coping in divorce: A focus on women. In J. Gullahorn (Ed.), *Psychology and women in transition.* B.H. Winston & Sons.

Hetherington, E.M. (1979c). Family interactions and the social, emotional and cognitive development of children following divorce. In V.C. Vaugh & T.B. Brazelton (Eds.), *The Family: Setting priorities.* New York: Science and Medicine Publishers.

Hetherington, E.M. (1979d). Play and social interaction in children following divorce. *J. of Social Issues*, 4, 26-50.

Jacobson, Doris S. (1978). The impact of marital separation/divorce on children: I. Parent-child separation and child adjustment. 1(4), 341-361.

Kelly, J.B. & Wallerstein, J.S. (1975). The effects of parental divorce: I. The experience of the child in early latency: II. The experience of the child in late latency. *Amer. J. of Orthopsychiatry*, 45, 253-254.

Kelly, J.B. & Wallerstein, J.S. (1976). The effects of parental divorce: Experiences of the child in early latency. *Amer. J. of Orthopsychiatry*, 46, 20-32.

Kelly, J.B. & Wallerstein, J.S. (1977). Brief interventions with children in divorcing families. *Amer. J. of Orthopsychiatry*, 47, (1), 23-39.

Luepnitz, D.A. (1982). *Child Custody: A Study of Families After Divorce*. Lexington, MA: D.C. Heath & Co.

Minuchin, S. (1974). *Families and Family Therapy*. Cambridge, MA: Harvard University Press.

Morgenbesser, M. & Nehls, N. (1980). *Joint Custody: An alternative for divorcing families*. Chicago: Nelson-Hall Press.

Nehls, N. & Morgenbesser, M. (1980). Joint Custody: An exploration of the issues, *Family Process*, 19 (2), 117-127.

Roman, M. & Haddad, W. (1978). *The Disposable Parent: The case for joint custody*. New York: Holt, Rinehart & Winston.

Shinn, M. (1978). Father absence and children's cognitive development. *Psych. Bulletin*, 85, 295-324.

Wallerstein, J.S. & Kelly, J.B. (1974). The effects of parental divorce: The adolescent experience. In J. Anthony and C. Koupernik (Eds.), *The Child in His Family: Children at psychiatric risk*. New York: John Wiley & Sons.

Wallerstein, J.S. & Kelly, J.B. (1975). The effects of parental divorce: Experiences of the preschool child. *Journal of the American Academy of Child Psychiatry*, 14, 600-616.

Wallerstein, J.S. & Kelly, J.B. (1976). The effects of parental divorce: Experiences of the child in later latency. *Amer. J. of Orthopsychiatry*, 46, 256-269.

Wallerstein, J.S. & Kelly, J.B. (1977). Divorce counseling: A community service for families in the midst of divorce. *Amer. J. of Orthopsychiatry*, 47, (1), 4-22.

Wallerstein, J.S. & Kelly, J.B. (1980). *Surviving the Breakup: How children and parents cope with divorce*. New York: Basic Books.

Volgy, S.S. & Everett, C.A. (1985). Joint Custody Reconsidered: Criteria for Mediation. *Journal of Divorce*, 8, 3/4, (in press).

FOCUS THREE: POST-DIVORCE RECOVERY AND REMARRIAGE

Creating New Realities for the Newly Divorced: A Structural-Strategic Approach for Divorce Therapy with an Individual

Marcia D. Brown

ABSTRACT. Not every divorcing client comes equipped with a family system that is willing to participate in divorce therapy. This paper emphasizes that a divorce therapist can still use a systemic approach with an individual who seeks help even without the luxury of the family's presence in-session. Case vignettes serve to illustrate how a clinician can create new and more productive realities for the newly divorced client during early therapy, mid-therapy, and late therapy. The structural-strategic orientation suggested culminates in a single case study which links theory and technique with actual practice.

The purpose of this paper is to help the therapist construct new realities for the newly divorced or separated individual. It is based on the assumption that the meaning the client attributes to divorce can become either a nodal point for accentuating pain or a motivation to seek alternative self-definitions. The client may focus on the former; the divorce therapist must capitalize on the latter. The theoretical framework presented will be structural-strategic family therapy although the focus will be on utilizing the tenets of this approach to work with an individual.

Key figures in strategic and structural family therapy have much to say concerning the interplay between the client's and the clinician's presentation of reality. Erickson (1962) notes that children try to discover what is strong, secure, and safe and will look for definitive boundaries from those around them. According to Erickson, the task of the therapist is to present "secure realities," setting the parameters to optimize security. Watzlawick (1978) suggests that children and most adults behave as if words "exactly represent reality." He takes the position that "language does not so much *reflect* reality as *create* it." This opens up new opportunities to shape the client's world-view by the therapist's very words and the ways those particular words are phrased. Minuchin and Fishman

Marcia D. Brown, A.C.S.W., is a family therapist at Lutheran Child and Family Services, Indianapolis, IN and a doctoral candidate in Marriage and Family Therapy in the Department of Child Development and Family Studies, CDFS Bldg., Purdue University, W. Lafayette, IN 47907.

© 1985 by The Haworth Press, Inc. All rights reserved.

(1981) advise that the art of family therapy is to experience reality as each client experiences it. They say that the therapist should contest the unworkable reality that has been formed by the client's vacillation between the dubious security of the known and the uncertain exploration of adaptive means to meeting changing conditions. Old patterns are undermined to make way for the new via therapeutic challenges which may be direct or indirect. The goal is to reframe the original view of the problem, making it imperative that an inner search occurs for alternative affective, cognitive, and behavioral responses.

This paper will guide the reader through several case vignettes in which new realities are created for persons who have experienced recent separation and/or divorce. It will examine this process in early therapy (where the focus is on reacting to the crisis), in mid-therapy (where the thrust is on acting as well as reacting), and in late therapy (where the emphasis is on personal growth and self-direction). A single case description at the end ties these processes together.

While not all divorces are the same and the processes described here can occur early or late depending on circumstances, the therapist should be able to adapt the concepts and techniques described here. The choice to focus on the individual was deliberate. It will hopefully demonstrate that structural-strategic concepts are not limited by the unit of treatment. It also recognizes the reality that while family and couple work is often desirable in divorce therapy (Sprenkle & Storm, 1983), it is often not feasible. The principles enunciated here, however, can be applied to couple and family sessions.

Creating new realities offers the therapist considerable leeway in building upon the client's language and perspective without leaving her/him stuck in the mire of destructive patterns and obsessions. The strategy is analogous to disrupting the playback of a broken record by ever so slightly adjusting the needle. Since the client's unique reality is adjusted only *slightly*, there are no sure-fire reality creations which would be effective or even palatable to every newly divorced individual. The therapist has to adapt to the raw materials of each client's experience. It should also be emphasized that reality creation represents only *one* avenue within a clinician's full repertoire for facilitating growth, *not* a panacea for all situations. Clients who need to feel like they are being heard, for example, are not likely to be receptive to new realities.

EARLY THERAPY

Joining and Identifying the Immediate Problem

The first example illustrates the interviewer's clarification of the immediate problem at the outset of therapy (Haley, 1976b).

Example (1)

Client: I don't know where to begin.
Therapist: I'm interested in what your situation was that prompted you to call for an appointment.
Client: Since my wife left me, I can't seem to concentrate. I'm a Ph.D. student in analytic chemistry and the outline to my dissertation proposal is due in two weeks. Nothing I read seems to register.
Therapist: How long has it been that you've had difficulty concentrating?
Client: Let's see . . . Cindy told me on Friday evening she just didn't want to work on the relationship anymore. I thought she'd be back. It's been over a week now. I guess it's been worse since I got served papers a couple days ago. I had no idea things would move this fast.

The client is not called upon to explain the demise of the marriage or any other unanswerable question at the beginning. The therapist conveys interest in the recent past and assists the client in identifying his current reality, namely, shock and bad timing for his dissertation proposal. The client describes the sequence of events as happening *to* him and he targets poor concentration as his most pressing problem. The therapist structures questions around the symptom and assesses the client's functioning versus his *perceived* level of functioning. The fact that the therapist is asking answerable questions set a precedent that therapist and client can communicate and forms a context that associates therapy with success, an important initial building block (Rosen, 1982).

Divorcing clients have probably already gotten the message that they are "wrong" in someone's eyes and may anticipate that the therapist will likewise sit in judgment. This is not the time to point out personality flaws or explore past mistakes even if asked, "What's wrong with me that she would leave me?" A choice point here would be to ask further historical questions but the next example shows how the interview can be kept present-oriented and still gather considerable information that implies movement. By *expanding the context* (Minuchin & Fishman, 1981) and *using the client's language* (Watzlawick, 1978) the therapist can broaden her/his natural inclination to speak from a cognitive level to include vocabulary from an affective level. When the above client accepts that the therapist is *confirming the reality presented*, he is ready for a suggestion at a behavioral level.

Example (2)

Therapist: Not being able to concentrate sounds *frustrating*, particularly when working on a Ph.D.
Client: It *is* frustrating. I don't know how she could do this to me. She knows how important the next few weeks are.
Therapist: Did you drive yourself over today?
Client: Yes, I did.

Therapist: So, you are able to concentrate *some*, but not to the degree to which you would *like*.
Client: Right.

The therapist has altered the original phrase, "I can't seem to concentrate," to the suggestion, "So, you are able to concentrate *some*." This is a gentle *reframing* (Watzlawick, Weakland, & Fisch, 1974) and a vote of confidence that he has resources to help himself. Not everything is happening *to* him. If the verbal and nonverbal language of the client is receptive, the therapist may proceed. The client has been offered no reason to be guarded in-session, his language has been utilized, and his reality has been understood. When under threat the conscious mind will draw upon the analytic logic and language of the left brain hemisphere (Watzlawick, 1978). Since no threat is perceived, the right brain hemisphere, housing mood and a holistic world-view, is more accessible. Its natural proclivity for attuning itself to homonyms and other plays on words makes the last phrase of the preceding example either an opportunity for some humor at the conscious level or a word puzzle to be solved at the unconscious level. The degree of concentration and the Ph.D. *degree* are not proceeding at the *degree* he would like. This is a message to the unconscious mind to rally in favor of the self. Such fortuitous therapeutic responses may abound in sessions where neither therapist nor client are guarded. *Spontaneity* (Minuchin & Fishman, 1981) on the part of the therapist sometimes ministers to a key issue more efficiently than a deductively derived series of questions.

Had the client reacted against the compliment that he could concentrate *some*, the therapist would have been cued that the rules of the client's usual system were being violated (Minuchin & Fishman, 1981). This would have to be explored.

Example (3)

Client: I never said I couldn't concentrate at all. I just said I couldn't concentrate when I read.
Therapist: You are quite right. Did I give you the impression I misheard you?

The therapist is signaled that she/he has just touched a nerve. The idea of *wrongness is quickly righted*. Then *the question is answered with a question*, a well-known method of getting out of hot water by getting out from under the microscope. The client is then subtly directed to engage in his own inner search (Rosen, 1982) which helps the clinician buy time to develop strategy for the next interchange. The question is a yes/no variety. If the respondent says, "Yes," the therapist can apologize and straighten out the matter. If he says, "No," the therapist is out of a bind and can still straighten out the matter.

Example (4)

Client: No, it wasn't that.
Therapist: Well, I could understand if you thought I was jumping to conclusions about your concentration. The news from your wife sounded like it hit you as a terrible shock. That would be enough to muddle anyone's thinking.
Client: The biggest shock is how quickly she moved her things out. We had been arguing a lot about the last year or so but just two weeks ago we had talked about going into marriage counseling, getting things ironed out, and raising our children together. She said I only talked about things instead of doing them. But she wasn't straight with me.

The above example depicts the clinician's option to return to confirmation of the client's reality under the condition of client resistance. This *backpedaling* pays off and relaxes the client out of his one-upmanship. Minuchin and Fishman (1981) point out that a therapist does not always have to be correct with interventions; if she/he "goes beyond the threshold of what is acceptable, the system will correct itself."

Hypotheses may be formulated about the client's system based on his behavior with the therapist. The interviewer gets a chance to see what the client is like when he is under stress, something his partner may have found intolerable. In this case the client tends to feel criticized and view circumstances as happening *to* him. When the therapist mirrors his reality by conveying understanding and by suggesting, "That is enough to muddle anyone's thinking," the client becomes freer to go on with his story. Defensiveness decreases to the point that he mentions his wife's criticism of *him* though he appears not to be able to stick with this thought and switches to his wife's foibles instead.

Recognizing the Rules Which Maintain the Problem

Conjecture regarding the possible dynamics of the marital system suggests rules by which the client approaches relationships, rules the therapist will have to respect in the development of strategy. Perhaps this student was preoccupied with his studies and paid only lip service to his wife's requests for counseling and her wishes for shared parenting. Perhaps she expected him to read her mind. Perhaps neither of them could tolerate criticism and both were inept at resolving conflict. Without the benefit of the other party's presence, the divorce therapist is choosy about what realities to confirm, bolstering those that are protective of self-esteem and avoiding comment on either the relationship or the absent party. The persistence of attachment (Weiss, 1975) is reason enough to presume that the client will fluctuate back and forth about his marital choice. He is in pain because of his investment in the marriage. An attack on the marriage or a negative remark about his wife may be taken as self-injury. What the therapist searches for and eventually finds is the client's *pattern* of relating under stress which is the rule, "Criticism invites closedness." Avoidance of criticism at this point encourages the client to be more open to what the therapist has to say down the road.

The client summarizes the problem as, "She wasn't straight with me." He seems to be trying to sell the idea that he has been victimized. This may give him cause to see a lawyer but it does not give a therapist much with which to work because it places the problem outside himself. The therapist in the next example must get the client's attention back to his own dilemma and his own resources in meeting it. The technique utilized is that of a combination "*kick and a stroke*" (Minuchin & Fishman, 1981).

Example (5)

Therapist: Your fist gathers strength as you speak of her while the rest of you goes *helpless*.
Client: I wasn't aware of that.
Therapist: If your fist could do the talking for you, what would it say?
Client: That I better get my act together or in two weeks I'm a dead duck.

The divorce therapist appeals to whatever survival instinct is available and can get away with addressing the client's helplessness and passivity by suggesting that there is unutilized strength that is begging for expression. Since this "fist" idea has attention-getting value it can be used again by *expanding the theme*.

Example (6)

Therapist: What is the worst thing that could happen in the next two weeks?
Client: If I just sit and mope and don't get my proposal done, I won't get the go-ahead to do my research in time. It could delay my whole program by a year.
Therapist: Where can your *fist* go for help if it gets tired of prodding you all by itself?
Client: I don't think my major professor will be very understanding but I do have a friend in the same program who knows that Cindy and I were having problems. He's divorced himself.

In assisting the client to walk through his worst fears it is discovered that he is not dwelling on his loss of the relationship. His focus is on the immediacy of his problem of concentration and it is this for which he is asking for help. If he finds success with what he has presented as a problem, he is more likely to make his other needs known. Erickson in Rosen (1982) recommends offering no more for the client than he is willing to do for himself. In order to make it more likely that he will do for himself, potential support systems are explored.

Example (7)

Therapist: Would this friend think you capable of finishing the proposal given your circumstances?
Client: Probably not.
Therapist: And what do you believe your chances are?
Client: If I can concentrate, I can finish. If I can't, I won't.

The client's reaction to the word "helpless," the fact that he is a Ph.D. student, and the fact that he predicts an outcome opposite from his more pessimistic friend helps formulate another hypothesis about a rule by which he lives: "Competition is worthwhile." Information is not gathered in a vacuum but tests the client's readiness for a task relevant to the presenting problem. The very pride which keeps him from discussing the emotional aspects of an imminent divorce is also the pride that makes him competent in his work. It may not be adaptive later on to hold feelings inside but it may be highly adaptive in the next two weeks. A strategic therapist follows the client's lead in identifying the problem. The client is expected to follow the therapist's lead in carrying out its solution.

Developing a Task Which Makes the Original Rules Obsolete

Example (8)

Therapist: There is a way around your problem but you won't like it.
Client: Try me.
Therapist: I really don't think you will like it.
Client: Just tell me what it is.
Therapist: So be it. This week you will know that you are no good at studying. You can study all you like the second week but this first week you must revel in your helplessness for all it is worth. Think of anything to avoid studying. You have told me that you can only finish if you can concentrate and this week you will not be able to. At the end of the second week you will treat your friend to dinner if you have not finished the proposal and ask him to tell you, "I told you so," because he figured you probably wouldn't finish anyway. *When* you do finish by the second week you can present a copy of the proposal to me and announce, "I told you so,"—and I will remember, *yes* you did.

The use of the *paradoxical injunction* in this sequence, "You can only study if you don't study" is only a variation of *symptom prescription* (Haley, 1976a). What has been changed is the *pattern* of not studying (Rosen, 1982). Instead of trying to study and not studying for two weeks, the therapist alters the *opportunity* to study and stipulates that this is out of the question for the first week. The way the therapist sets bait tantalizes the client into being hungry for hearing the task and ravenous for studying—the very thing he is not allowed to have. This may be analogically perceived as a *metaphor* for the relationship he cannot have. At present it is easier for the client to talk about the concentration he does not have with the implication that he is in a helpless, involuntary state. To make concentration competitive with "I told you so" from either the friend to the client or from the client to the therapist makes the involuntary a voluntary proposition (Watzlawick, 1978, 1983).

The task makes it impossible for things to just happen *to* the client. He can either lose out to his friend or be triumphant with his therapist, but his response now becomes one of choice. The first part of the message is another play on words, a juxtaposition of "know" and "no," but the last part of the message is an upbeat "yes" (Rosen, 1982). To further the probability of success, the word "*when*" is used, engendering hope (Erickson, Rossi, & Rossi, 1976), rather than "*if*," associated with failure; and it is paired with a positive, present-oriented verb, "*do finish*," as opposed to its negative counterpart phrased in the past tense, "*have not finished*." Even if the client begins studying ahead of time he still must associate this success with the therapy. The divorce therapist attempts to create situations that make it very difficult for the clinician to lose and very likely that the client will win. This obviates a situation where one has to win at the expense of the other.

Divorcing individuals who come to therapy prepared to engage in heavy catharsis and exploration of where they went wrong in marriage are often startled by an approach which dwells on immediate concerns. Such a startle response disrupts rigid mental sets and foggy emotional states during a crisis period and can be a more empathic intervention than allowing a self-destructive course to continue. This is especially true when the divorcing client questions her/his own capacity to salvage a constructive lifestyle apart from marriage.

In early therapy, there is a big difference between reassuring a client with words and providing an experience where, much to the client's surprise, she/he finds reassurance in the resources she/he brings to the situation. The former minimizes the seriousness of the situation; the latter capitalizes upon it. There is nothing magical or mysterious about how the divorce therapist figures out what sort of experience will have the potential of being not only supportive but corrective. This is accomplished by asking factual questions about the client's life circumstances, measuring these facts against the client's perceived reality, identifying the client's language, noting patterns of behaving that make an already difficult situation even more difficult, and disrupting those typical patterns of response. When the client's pain is acute enough to seek therapy, even small gains can be quite relieving.

Considering that the divorcing client is often overwhelmed at the outset of therapy, the divorce therapist can best help by adopting a "first-things-first'' approach. Discovering what will make things a little bit better in the most profound way sometimes takes a lengthy interview, something the examples presented do not readily expose. It is at times necessary to investigate whether the marriage is really over, whether there are stressors the client has neglected to mention, whether there are other people besides self to whom the client is responsible such as children, and whether the client's social network is a bane or a blessing. These are all factors which, if not checked out sufficiently, can confound proper assignment and completion of tasks.

Use of paradoxical injunction is not akin to ''shooting from the hip'' (Weakland, 1982). However, when the therapist uncovers the client's own rules which are interfering with productive functioning, she/he can assist in efficiently bringing about a new set of rules via paradox, a second-order change (Watzlawick et al., 1974), ''the difference that makes a difference'' (Bateson, 1972). When the client goes from ''I can't seem to help myself'' (an involuntary state) to ''I *can* help myself'' (a voluntary action), she/he discovers serendipitously that she/he can get along in life without the former spouse. One interview or task may not bring about this realization fully but little ''aha's'' of success along the way counter self-doubts and build self-confidence.

Developing Underutilized Capacities

In the foregoing examples the therapist structures a task based on the assessment that the client handles stress by ''closedness,'' by preoccupying himself with his wife's put-downs, and by criticism of those who are perceived as criticizing him. There is a competitive thread to these tendencies that the therapist weaves into the fabric of the task.

The task for the therapist is to incorporate what a client already does well in the directive in order to develop an underutilized capacity. The client in the examples becomes open to studying and to therapy by being required to be closed. He cannot be closed to studying the first week without being open to therapy and following the directive. If he becomes open to studying he is already benefiting from the therapy and gets caught up in the momentum of being open to it. The only thing he can be closed to is his former perspective.

Concluding Early Therapy

During early therapy the most ''*noble ascriptions*'' (Todd & Stanton, 1981) are applied to anything the client does to help her/himself through the divorce. A big deal is made out of the completion of tasks. The divorce therapist acts as a positive though not pushy advocate, encouraging the client to ''go slow'' and not make changes too fast. She/He sets therapeutic goals to reveal to clients a present, a future, and a different way of looking at the past. She/He helps hook people up with appropriate resources whether they be hard-to-find babysitters or free financial counselors. At the very least, she/he helps keep uprooted lives interesting until divorcing clients can set goals all their own. When they've reached that point, they are well into mid-therapy.

MID-THERAPY

Once the reality that life will never be the same again hits home, the client is faced with another reality—that what is not the same will inevitably have to be different. When the client is no longer just reacting to change but wants some say about how change will occur, the divorce therapist can assume that early has given way to mid-therapy. Perhaps the client used to present herself as a doormat when he showed up out of the blue to see the kids, but she now lays down the law of the land. Maybe he used to think that the single life would be utopia, but now he likens it to running away from home—a poor substitute for running toward something better. The distinction between these two phases is, of course, not always clear since divorce adjustment is cyclic rather than linear (Crosby, Gage, & Raymond, 1983). All reactivity does not cease. But once a divorcing individual has tasted the freedom of calling the shots alone and seen this method work, the dependency inherent in just reacting to the former spouse becomes less dominant.

The challenge to the therapist in early therapy is to help the client discover that life not only goes on but that one's own resourcefulness can successfully, if not surprisingly, rise to the occasion. In mid-therapy the therapist must assist the client in setting reachable goals with tasks that reflect less *obvious* direction from the therapist and more self-imposed direction from the client. Success becomes less associated with therapy and more associated with the client's own sound judgment.

The guideposts for what *is* sound judgment may be assessed by keeping abreast of the client's legal advice and its implications for ongoing relationships. Behavior that aggravates the situation may be stymied by either *blocking* or *reframing*.

Example (1)

Client: My lawyer told me to avoid any altercations with Cindy before the hearing, but I just know I'm going to see her with her boyfriend at our friend's wedding. She'll make some crack about my not having a date and that'll be all it takes for me to lose my cool.

Therapist: Would Cindy lay odds on you losing your cool or finding it?

Client: She's counting on me blowing up for sure. She wouldn't know how to handle it if I stayed cool.
Therapist: Disappointing her like that could just ruin her whole day.

Here, the rules of conduct are, "She/He who frustrates first, wins" and "Better you be frustrated than me." Disappointing her is devilishly more fun that letting her get away with a crass wisecrack. The therapist simply associates disappointing the former wife with the client finding his cool. He can concentrate on disappointing her easier than he can concentrate on not losing his temper. Trying not to do something makes doing it too attractive. Blocking the effort at avoiding altercations and reframing the situation as an opportunity to frustrate her helps the client look out for himself in spite of himself.

Tasks may be left more open-ended, leaving the client to fill in the blanks. Plotting the course becomes more clearly one's own success that way.

Example (2)

Client: I know that getting together for lunch with this woman I met is only a phone call away and I know she's the kind of person I could really talk to. Somehow I keep talking myself out of it.
Therapist: This matter needs to be studied more carefully. Keep track of all your arguments to yourself and *write them down.* Be as creative as you like but *write them down.* Even if it takes every scrap of paper you can lay your hands on *write them down.* Hand me your list next time and we'll discuss it further.

The client's directive is phrased as a command in such a way that the client cannot miss the opportunity to get out from under it in the name of adult independence. Not following the task at all would make the client's request for help look like a red herring, like companionship is not desired yet. Following the task will be so repulsive that making the phone call will appear easier. The client can meet the goal by doing more than the therapist apparently dreamed was possible. Stumping the commanding therapist, meeting a goal, and exercising "independent" judgment become irresistible.

Sometimes the smallest tasks seem insurmountable to a client. Whatever the size of the task it can be divided into smaller tasks (Rosen, 1982). The principle is the same whether a displaced homemaker is looking for a job, an ambitious undertaking, or a spurned husband just doesn't feel like doing his usual chores.

Example (3)

Client: I have mail sitting on my desk from the last two weeks that I haven't even opened.
Therapist: Is opening the mail the problem or had you intended to read it?

Client:	Well, I really ought to get around to both.
Therapist:	Reading it is too much for this week. This week it is enough that you open it—unless you think this is beyond your capabilities. Are you physically able?
Client:	Yeah.
Therapist:	Do you think that you could physically open the mail this week—or is that too much?
Client:	No, I could open it.
Therapist:	All right. Be careful that you don't look outside the envelope to see who it's from or peer inside to the contents. No need to get ahead of yourself.
Client:	But my bills . . .
Therapist:	They'll just have to wait till you're up to it.

The therapist frames the impossible task as a little less impossible. She/He creates an "*illusion of alternatives*" (Haley, 1967; 1976a) and the client can choose between opening the mail and reading it. This suggestion is more readily accepted because the therapist takes the client's comment very literally about the mail not being opened. The right brain hemisphere cannot resist the appeal of puns (Watzlawick, 1978). The therapist's presumption about the client's limitations is incentive enough to outdo the expectations in therapy. She/He frames an emotional issue as a question of physical competence. *Adding curiosity to incentive*, she/he adds the caveat against reading. When the therapist is foiled, she/he can be pleasantly surprised.

Example (4)

Client:	I went ahead and paid my bills.
Therapist:	Well, I'll be jiggered.
Client:	I know you told me to wait but . . .
Therapist:	You knock my socks off. You're just going to have to tell me when I should step aside.

There's that word "*when*" again, this time associating the client's speaking up for self with budding signs that therapy is no longer needed. The client works best when given some permission to fail.

Example (5)

Client:	I was doing really well until Timmy started acting up. I really yelled at him and scared him half to death. I held him and told him I was sorry, but it was a long time before he stopped crying.
Therapist:	Some days are just going to be "one-step-forward-two-steps-back days." Sometimes there's too many "all-of-a-suddens" all of a sudden.

A positive frame cannot be put on every situation, especially for single parents. To do that would be communicating that divorce is unimportant, that the marriage was unimportant, and that the effect of divorce on the children is unimportant. Parents need to know that their concerns about their children are real and that their desire to be better parents, especially after the marriage ends, is appropriate. Therapists who pontificate about the kids' resiliency in a crisis run the risk of sounding like they are disqualifying the love and protectiveness parents want to offer.

Example (6)

Client: I don't seem to be able to be both father *and* mother to him.
Therapist: There are certain limits to being one human being.
Client: I'll probably never be in a position to be with him all the time like his mother can.
Therapist: You may be right. From you he'll get conversations with a wise, older sage, a model for manhood, and a host of other quiet gifts that can only be unwrapped over time.

Metaphorically, the therapist communicates that the father's concern about his limitations makes perfect sense and that there will be less intimacy for him until he sees what kind of young man he has raised. Creating new realities does not always mean negating the client's. Embellishment of an *understandable reality* gives it a slight twist and makes it at least bearable.

During mid-therapy, the therapist fosters the client's impulse to get on with life and does not block grief over loss as much as rechannel it. Legitimate anger is reframed as energy, strength, and self-protection; sadness as the depth of one's ability to care; a sense of failure as the realization that one can learn. Erickson often used *anecdotes* (Haley, 1967; Rosen, 1982) to make a point about the vicissitudes of life without sounding preachy in the process. "I can't" was not a popular phrase as far as he was concerned.

Example (7)

Client: Now that I'm getting a divorce my father says I'll never amount to anything.
Therapist: And do you remember at 10 months how your father said, "That boy will never learn to walk"?
Client: I don't remember.
Therapist: Just as well.
Client: I was too young, I guess.
Therapist: And when you put out one leg in front the other would collapse and then you landed on your rumpus and started all over again. This time you took two steps but you fell forward and landed on your hands and you got up and fell backwards and went off, crawling for a change of pace till you were up for more adventure. You really were your own man then, you know?
Client: But I'm not a baby anymore. People expect babies to fall.
Therapist: And in looking right past what people expect you will find you're your own man after all.

It is particularly important during mid-therapy to normalize cyclic returns to fundamental issues of grief resolution (Crosby et al., 1983) and persistence of attachment (Weiss, 1975). In the foregoing example the therapist gives the client permission to go beyond even what she/he as the "expert" expects. Just as parents, when raising a child, assume less and less responsibility, the therapist likewise seeds *responsibility messages* that spell out that she/he is needed less and less. When the client has gone from associating self with failure, to therapy with success, to self with success, only finishing touches are required for the final stage of recovery in late therapy.

LATE THERAPY

The last sessions of therapy are designed to consolidate ongoing messages that the client can be successful in reorganizing life under changing circumstances. While sometimes the chemistry between therapist and client is such that both arrive at the decision to terminate simultaneously, quite often one has reached the decision before the other. Both situations are opportunities to reinforce gains.

When the client's bid to terminate comes as a surprise to the therapist, progress must be weighed in terms of the original goals of therapy. If these have been met the decision can hardly be considered premature. If these have *not* been met and the client is eager to be let go gracefully, the therapist can still seed some thoughts which help maintain the client's dignity even if she/he has not been particularly cooperative: "You know, I often got the impression that I wasn't getting to the heart of things. Perhaps you'll let someone else know how to do that better." This ends therapy on a positive note in case the person wants to return to it at another time or in case she/he has plans to see another therapist. Notice that the therapist does not let the client fully off the hook and plants a *responsibility message* to let the new therapist know the situation. The ambiguity in the way the message is phrased helps the client save face.

If the client's original goals have been met and she/he has simply run out of goals, this very realization can be applauded and slight transgressions can be normalized.

Example (1)

Client: I realize I should've called earlier to cancel the last appointment.
Therapist: Do you have anything you want to work on now that you're here?
Client: Not really.
Therapist: When you start cancelling appointments and running out of things to talk about I start figuring you're handling your life on your own. Maybe therapy has become just so much extra baggage.
Client: I was wondering if we would get to that.

When the therapist suggests termination prematurely, the client may have good reasons for hanging on that are worth exploring. A vote of confidence may be offered without threatening the client that the rug will be pulled out too soon.

Example (2)

Client: Don't let me go yet. I'm not quite ready.
Therapist: Oh?
Client: No.
Therapist: What will have to happen before you're ready?
Client: I need to know I can get through our wedding anniversary date.
Therapist: That *would* be a victory, wouldn't it?

As therapy comes to a close it is an excellent time to once again review the client's progress and *underscore productive themes*. The client has a right to know what she/he is doing differently that works.

Example (3)

Therapist: Remember when you used to dread going home alone?
Client: Yeah, now I can't wait to get home to "hear the quiet" after sitting in traffic for a half hour.
Therapist: When you began to associate quiet with comfort, you found that you could relish your "alone time."

Catch phrases act as markers (Davis & Davis, 1983) for past sessions and help anchor the future with the same productive realities. By the time therapy ends, the divorcing client has laid a former life to rest.

Example (4)

Client: I know that I'm still going to have my ups and downs but I feel like I'm more ready to meet them.
Therapist: I couldn't put it better myself.

When the therapist hands over the gauntlet to the client, as in the last example, the divorcing individual is signaled that she/he is quite recovered from a need for therapy. Another bridge has been crossed, an analogic message that the client has journeyed from old realities to new ones.

A CASE STUDY

A 44-year-old woman referred by her physician requested service from a large university's Marriage and Family Therapy Center. The presenting problem was that her "husband kissed and left" her and her feelings of "rejection" were leading to uncontrollable crying and fears that she was going "crazy." She explained her husband had a drinking problem and had left her many times before but this time it was for good. She reported feeling "like a yoyo" with his repeated separations and reconciliations. The woman, who will be referred to here under the pseudonym of "Dottie," intimated that she did not feel in control of her own decisions. She was adamant that even though she was distraught she was not a danger to herself or others, which was *reframed* as an indication that she *could* make decisions.

The couple reportedly had a marital union of 22 years, resulting in two sons and two daughters. The sons were living apart from each other but on their own, and at the time of therapy Dottie's husband was living with one of them. The two daughters were still living in the family home at the ages of 18 and 22. By all reports the daughters appeared to be making a favorable adjustment to the parents' final separation. They were given the option of joining the sessions but declined.

At first Dottie appeared highly agitated in addition to her reactive despair. Her responses were highly tangential and she wanted to tell her story from childhood on. Being redirected to her immediate problem, she focused on her crying which she feared would interfere with her thinking while working as a part-time veterinarian's assistant. It was clarified that this was Dottie's second marriage, the first occurring at the age of seventeen and ending in divorce. Dottie shared that she had pleaded with her husband to come with her for therapy only to be told that *she* was "the one with the problem." His attitude apparently persisted throughout her therapy.

The first session ended with the self-drawn conclusion that Dottie was tired of being a "yoyo" to her husband and that she would have to learn to treat herself well rather than wait for her husband to show caring. Since she tended to speak in *metaphor*, the therapist mirrored this type of communication. When she said she wished she could just decide to never cry again, the therapist likened this to a wish to never go to the bathroom again. This broke her tension and jarred her to attentiveness. She discovered that she could stop crying in-session. The crying itself was redefined as "not the problem." Rather, *reframing* the problematic situation as "worrying about crying" set the stage for the first task.

Dottie was directed to practice getting more comfortable with crying by arranging private time a half-hour a day to really get into her crying. Talking herself through the crying was framed as "self-caretaking." If she found that she had trouble "getting into crying" she was to go ahead and pretend (Madanes, 1981) that she was already "into" it. The therapeutic rationale was that the uncontrollable would be brought under specific parameters of control and therefore crying would no longer be an uncontrollable, scary activity. The paradoxical injunction "Cry in order to not cry'' was designed to effectively jumble up the client's own rule of ''I shouldn't do what my body is going to spontaneously do on its own.'' A change in rules was prescribed to bring about change in the system (Watzlawick et al., 1974).

Dottie's sense of uprootedness was unusually short-lived. She came to the second session announcing that she had not liked the task because ''crying is not the problem.'' Recognizing that Dottie had remembered this suggestion but was not attributing it to therapy, the therapist accepted her criticism and asked for clarification of her *real* problem. She said she needed to learn how to ''take charge'' of her own life. She was already socializing with friends and feeling guilty because she was having fun without her husband. *Using the client's language*, she was encouraged to ''go slow'' with ''taking charge.'' Her next task was to write a letter to her husband, explaining to him her ''take charge'' change in attitude. The letter was to be written to him in such a way that she could feel good about it. Consistent with the ''go slow'' theme, she was not to send the letter. Since she was already identifying her own goals, she was given an open-ended task which would give her considerable success in discovering her own decision-making capacity.

Structurally, the therapist assessed that the client had perceived her marriage as a one-up/one-down arrangement. Simply reversing the tables would be no second-order change in rules (Watzlawick et al., 1974). Going from ''My husband runs my life'' to ''I run my husband's life'' would be inadequate and would invite even more chaos. Dottie was shooting for a lifestyle of ''I run my *own* life.''

Dottie ''forgot'' her next appointment and did not write the ''go slow'' letter. Instead, she spoke directly with her husband and explained to him her decision to divorce. This she accomplished with the assuredness of knowing she was making her ''own decision'' and she phrased things in such a way that she ''could feel good about it.''

During her fourth contact Dottie noted that she wanted to rid herself from bitterness as she had from her guilt, indicating that she did not want to feel emotionally tied up with her former partner. She was encourged to ''go slow.'' Perhaps she was not ready to give up bitterness. Since marriage had been typified as self-constraining, her next problem of loneliness was redefined via *reframing* as her first opportunity to ''run free.'' This was an appealing thought to her. Dottie appeared to be toying with the idea of getting involved in another relationship which would have the potential of confounding her grief process over her marriage (Weiss, 1975; Fisher, 1981). Also, she was devoutly religious and was worried that she would feel guilty over another relationship while still married. The rule she was trying to get out from under was ''I follow the man's lead.'' It occurred to her female therapist that the best way to support her quest for male companionship and to caution her at the same time was to split the messages from the therapist by incorporating comments from an unseen male supervisor. In this way, Dottie would have the opportunity to work out issues with men and with authoritative men all at the same time. The male supervisor was quoted as saying she would never be able to say "No" to a man who wasn't good for her.

A series of tasks gave her the chance to find success in her relationships with men. It had been predicted in-session that she would find "feeling free" tiresome sometimes and loneliness an easier feeling to have. She metaphorically described her ups and downs as "mountains and valleys." She had come up with a game-plan for her "valleys" so as not to say "Yes" to the first man who came along as predicted by the male "expert." With the directive to write a conversation depicting a "come-on" that would be hard to say "No" to but one she could handle, Dottie returned with reams of potential scenarios she felt she was ready to handle.

In preparation for the holiday season both client and therapist predicted a downward swing. This was normalized as "inevitable"—*not* a crisis. Dottie built upon the success of getting through Thanksgiving without her husband but she then focused on her feelings of being "victimized" by her son who apparently was siding with his father. Her forgetfulness for a related task was positively connoted via *reframing* as indicating that, with the stress of the holidays, she was not yet ready to work on her relationship with her son. Once she got through Christmas without a therapist being around, she was told this was evidence she was "needing therapy a lot less."

In order to reinforce the client's continued success arrangements were made to have a treatment team act as "Greek chorus" (Papp, 1980) behind a one-way mirror. Her last task had been to go to a singles club and spend the first 15 minutes by herself, worrying about "what people might think," since this had been a stumbling block to getting on with her life. When she announced that she had tried to worry but was not able to and would just have to worry about what *she* thought instead, the team applauded. She reported that she had met a new man at the club and felt conflicted about involvement with him. Her next task was to carry the "congratulations" of the male supervisor with her on her second trip to the singles club, a vote of male support that she would be able to handle this man. She returned glowing in that she had recognized her skill in "laying down ground rules in the relationship." This confidence carried over into her relationship with the son as well.

Termination had been suggested earlier but had been rightfully delayed by the client until she got through the holidays and the divorce became final. She was "almost" ready but followed suit with the format of *symptom prescription* and predicted her own relapse.

Dottie's fourteenth session was her last. Her relapse was just one more "valley" that she found she could handle. Her recovery was reviewed in sequence from her first crying spells to her victories handling men. Themes of "running free" and being "in charge" were underscored. She accepted the gauntlet by acknowledging that the therapist had gone from "therapist" to "friend."

On last report Dottie came up and hugged a *different* male supervisor from the Center who happened to have been giving a talk on divorce to the singles club. She was just sure he had been the one she had received congratulations from after proving him "wrong."

CONCLUSION

Divorce is a singularly singular activity. Efforts to bring dividing couples together for conjoint sessions or mediation (Haynes, 1981) are not always successful or necessarily even advisable. Without the option of doing therapy with a whole system in-session, systems analysis may still be inferred from work with a divorcing individual. Structural-strategic techniques may be implemented to lend support until new realities of success are discovered. It is possible to create the reality that the therapist or the therapy are wrong and still provide the experience that the client is a very right and worthwhile human being. When the divorcing client experiences success with a new present and future, the past appears less wrong, and the therapy has been right enough indeed.

REFERENCES

Bateson, G. (1972). *Steps to an ecology of mind.* New York: Random House.

Crosby, J. F., Gage, B. A., and Raymond, M. C. (1983). The grief resolution process in divorce. *Journal of Divorce*, 7, 3-18.

Davis, S. L. R. and Davis, D. I. (1983). Neuro-linguistic programming and family therapy. *Journal of Marital and Family Therapy*, 9, 283-291.

Erickson, M. H. (1962). The identification of a secure reality. *Family Process*, 1, 294-303.

Erickson, M. H., Rossi, E. L., and Rossi, S. I. (1976). *Hypnotic realities*. New York: Irvington Publishers.

Fisher, B. (1981). *Rebuilding: When your relationship ends.* San Luis Obispo, California: Impact Publishers.

Haley, J. (Ed.). (1967). *Advanced techniques of hypnosis and therapy: The selected papers of Milton H. Erickson.* New York: Grune & Stratton.

Haley, J. (1976a). Development of a theory: A history of a research project. In C. E. Sluzki and D. C. Ransom (Eds.), *Double bind: The foundation of the communicational approach to the family.* New York: Grune & Stratton.

Haley, J. (1976b). *Problem-solving therapy*. San Francisco: Jossey-Bass.

Haynes, J. M. (1981). *Divorce mediation*. New York: Springer Publishing Company.

Minuchin, S. and Fishman, H. C. (1981). *Family therapy techniques*. Cambridge, Massachusetts: Harvard University Press.

Papp, P. (1980). The Greek chorus and other techniques of paradoxical therapy. *Family Process*, 19, 45-57.

Rosen, S. (1982). *My voice will go with you: The teaching tales of Milton H. Erickson.* New York: W. W. Norton & Company.
Sprenkle, D. H. and Storm, C. L. (1983). Divorce therapy outcome research: A substantive and methodological review. *Journal of Marital and Family Therapy*, 9, 239-258.
Stanton, M. D. and Todd, T. C. (1981). Engaging "resistant" families in treatment, III: Factors in success and cost-efficiency. *Family Process*, 20, 261-293.
Watzlawick, P. (1978). *The language of change.* New York: Basic Books.
Watzlawick, P. (1983). *The situation is hopeless, but not serious.* New York: W. W. Norton & Company.
Watzlawick, P., Weakland, J., and Fisch, R. (1974). *Change: Principles of problem formation and problem resolution.* New York: W. W. Norton & Company.
Weakland, J. (1982). Workshop on "Applied Therapeutic Communication" at George Warren Brown School of Social Work, Washington University, St. Louis, Missouri.
Weiss, R. (1975). *Marital separation.* New York: Basic Books.

From Divorce to Remarriage: Implications for Therapy with Families in Transition

Margaret Crosbie-Burnett
Constance R. Ahrons

ABSTRACT. This article identifies for therapists potential problem areas in binuclear families, particularly around the time of a remarriage. Based on published literature and the authors' observations, the issues described focus on the courtship period, common expectations of family members, ambiguity and transition of roles, and permeability of boundaries. The development of the stepfamily is delineated. Examples from cases and guidelines for therapeutic intervention are included.

At an ever-increasing rate, therapists in the 1980's are encountering a new population of clients—members of binuclear families. The binuclear family represents new nomenclature and is a way of conceptualizing, as one family system, the two interrelated households that result when spouses divorce (Ahrons, 1979). Although divorce does create new households with single parents, it results in a single-parent family only when one of the parents, usually the father, has no contact with the family and no longer performs a parental function. However, for many divorced families in which father has continued his parenting relationship after divorce, the "single parent family" is a misnomer. More appropriate and functional terminology is generated by conceptualizing divorced families as binuclear families, which consist of two one-parent households, thus reserving the term single-parent family for those families which truly consist solely of one parent.

The terminology we use in our thinking about divorced families is linked closely with our therapeutic guidelines and intervention strategies. The equating of the single-parent family with the universe of divorced families arises from our notion of divorce as a pathological event which inevitably results in the demise of the family system. This has resulted in

Margaret Crosbie-Burnett, Ph.D., is Assistant Professor, Department of Counseling, School of Education, The University of Wisconsin, Madison, WI 53706.

Constance R. Ahrons, Ph.D., is Associate Professor, The School of Social Work, The University of Southern California, Los Angeles, CA 90089.

© 1985 by The Haworth Press, Inc. All rights reserved.

both research designs and models of clinical practice which have ignored the noncustodial parent as a member of the family. But as we change our formulation to include a systems perspective, we can then view divorce as a process of family transitions which result in changes in both the equilibrium and the structure of the original family system. Although the family reorganization that results from marital disruption frequently reaches crisis proportions and alters the life course of the family system itself, it does not necessarily result in family disintegration or dissolution (Ahrons, 1980). However, when there are children and both parents desire to continue their parenting roles and responsibilities, new rules need to be established which will guide postdivorce interactions and relationships among family members.

Given the current rates of divorce and remarriage we can anticipate that approximately 40% of the children born in the 1970's will spend some portion of their growing-up years in a binuclear family, living in both one-parent households and in stepfamily households. Too often we do an injustice to divorced families by labeling the remarried custodial household as *the stepfamily*, relegating the noncustodial remarried household to a position outside the family. Indeed, members of the latter household, a part-time stepfamily for at least one set of children, have the challenging task of acquiring the flexibility to cope with a family identity which can vary from a child-free couple to a family with many children, some unrelated to others. When we broaden our focus to include the two remarried households, we have a complex binuclear system of two stepfamilies and their respective extended families. The importance for the child of the two stepfamily households may vary according to how the family redefines itself postdivorce, but their interrelationships are critical to the functioning of the linked family system (Jacobson, 1984) and, therefore, to clinical practice (Sager, Brown, Crohn, Engel, Rodstein, and Walker, 1983).

The focus of this article is to identify for therapists some of the unique issues and potential problem areas for binuclear families when one of the divorced parents remarries, and to suggest guidelines for therapeutic interventions directed toward these issues. Since binuclear families are complex, both structurally and dynamically, the models established for working with nuclear families are inadequate to meeting their needs.

COURTSHIP PERIOD AND EXPLORATION OF EXPECTATIONS

The intensity of romance during the courtship period will bias a couple's expectations about their family life; in a remarriage this gulf between fantasy and reality is more problematic. First, most binuclear family members believe that a remarriage will "reconstitute" a nuclear family in the remarrying household. Noncustodial parents may fear being shut out; the fear of losing their biological children may be coupled with jealousy and/or relief that the ex-spouse has a new partner. The remarrying couple and the residential children often expect that everyday living will resemble the family life of the previous, intact family (Fishman and Hamel, 1981). If one of the partners has not been previously married, he or she is particularly vulnerable to the dream of the ideal traditional family.

Second, an individual who marries a parent must understand that she or he is marrying a parent-child family group, whether or not the parent has custody. Children will be an integral part of their married life and the stepparent will share the parent's time, space, emotional energy, and perhaps, finances with the children. If the stepparent resists this, resentment will abound.

Third, couples often enter remarriage with the expectation that everyone in the new stepfamily will instantly love everyone else. Stepparents may go to great lengths to overcome the "evil stepparent" image and win a child's love; at the very least, they expect to be appreciated for what they bring to the family. Because children frequently do not comply, the biological parent needs to be especially supportive of the stepparent's efforts to give to the family.

Conversely, many stepparents expect themselves to love their stepchildren and feel guilty when they do not. When the stepparent is a noncustodial biological parent, this is complicated by their ambivalence about parenting their new partner's children. It is indeed a sensitive communication issue to ask for support from your new spouse for not loving his or her children!

Fourth, stepparents need to accept the reality that they cannot replace the biological parent of the same sex in the children's family schema, unless the children are very young and do not have contact with their noncustodial parent. Stepparents who are physically unable to have their own biological children, or who have lost contact with their biological children, are particularly vulnerable to wanting stepchildren to accept them as "the mom" or "the dad." Naturally, the children's response is frequently to keep the stepparent at arm's length emotionally, causing frustration and resentment. This is compounded when the custodial biological parent adds her or his emotional clout to the pressure on the child to shift allegiance from a noncustodial mother or father to a stepmother or stepfather. Demanding that a child reject one of his or her parents in order to be loved often causes psychological distress for the child (Wallerstein and Kelly, 1980). Children adjust to divorce and remarriage much better when *all* of their parents give them permission to enjoy themselves in both households (Visher, 1984). Stepparents need not feel threatened by a child's attachment to her or his noncustodial parent. In a study of stepfamilies Crosbie-Burnett (1983) found that stepfather-stepchild relationships were better when the child had regular contact with the noncustodial parent. It appears that children are capable of loving multiple parents; it is the adults who have been socialized to think in terms of only one "real" mother and one "real" father.

Fifth, custodial parents often have expectations that their new partners will behave according to traditional American family sex roles. Mothers may look forward to having a man to "get these kids back in line." Fathers often expect their new wives to take over the nurturing, entertaining, carpooling, cooking and washing duties for his children when they come to visit him. Even when new stepparents accept that they are marrying more than an individual, they may be quite resistant to being a second parent, especially according to traditional American sex roles.

Sixth, while courtship and remarriage may be a time of romance and excitement for the adults, it is often a time of crisis for the children. The more the couple is caught up in their dreams, the less they can see and hear any signs of distress in the children. Like the noncustodial parent, children's anxiety stems from the loss of predictability. The cause of this loss has two levels—societal and individual. Unlike nuclear families, there is no social prescription for the behavior of members of stepfamilies; worse, there are negative images of stepparents in our cultural mythology. Therefore, children often experience the normal fear accompanied with approaching the unknown. As the number of stepfamilies increases, this problem should decrease. On the individual level, a new person or persons have entered the binuclear family; how this will affect the stepfamily household and the many interpersonal relationships within the entire binuclear family has received little attention in the literature. Some of the possibilities are reflected in children's common concerns: "Will my new stepparent be nice to me? Will I be able to go to Dad's as much now that he has a family of his own? Will I have to move away from my friends? Will Mom still love me if she has another baby? Will I have to share my room with stepsiblings?"

Because remarrying adults do not want their hopes and dreams blemished, they often do not hear their children's concerns. When this happens, the therapist usually needs to facilitate productive communication between the children and the adults. This includes supporting the children in expressing their fears and expectations, which vary tremendously depending upon the age of the children, whether or not they are involved with their noncustodial parent, whether or not they like the new stepparent, etc.

Seventh, unresolved feelings about events in the family's history and the subsequent changes in relationships and living arrangements can play havoc in the new stepfamily. Naturally, if the remarriage occurred soon after divorce, there is a higher probability of unresolved feelings between various family members. The following are common examples: Children often hope that their biological parents will reunite, in which case they may be resentful of the remarrying couple for dashing those hopes. Ex-spouses who quickly remarry after seeking a divorce because their partners were "the whole problem" may not have learned to take responsibility for their part in a couple relationship and are likely to continue to blame ex-spouses for all problems that may arise in the continuing co-parenting relationship, and new spouses for problems in the stepfamily. Ex-spouses who were rejected by their previous partners may still be in love with, or very dependent upon, these persons; they may feel intense hostility. Unless these kinds of feelings are resolved, they will become components of the remarried family's dynamics.

A major problem with the courtship period is that the exploration of expectations does not usually occur. Consequently, remarrying couples overwhelmingly report that they were unprepared for the complications of stepfamily living (Schlesinger, 1978). If a therapist is fortunate enough to see the couple and their children before the remarriage, discussion of everyone's expectations is crucial. More frequently a stepfamily will seek counseling after the remarriage has taken place. When the courtship is brief and the couple did not cohabit, many of the potential problems are upstaged by the new romance. Not unlike first marriages it is not until after the honeymoon period that the issues surface. But whether the couple does seek premarital counseling or arrives after the honeymoon period, a discussion of their expectations is necessary. This discussion should include behaviors that individuals are both willing and unwilling to do. Remarrying adults often find it difficult to say what they are not willing to do, because they have very high performance expectations for themselves and a need to please their partners. The therapist may need to help clients to be realistic about their feelings and their future performance. Expressing limitations is a sensitive subject and clients often need permission and support from the therapist for doing this.

BOUNDARIES WITHIN THE BINUCLEAR FAMILY

It is useful to conceptualize the issues that binuclear family members bring to therapists around the time of a remarriage under two major constructs: boundaries and roles. Boundaries in a binuclear family exist between households and between individuals within households in a manner that is much more complex than boundaries within and around nuclear families. Similarly, many of the roles and interpersonal relationships in a binuclear family are not only ambiguous, but they are also in transition when a remarriage occurs.

The conceptualization of the binuclear family assumes two households or subsystems of the family with persons having dual membership across the two (Ahrons and Perlmutter, 1982). Unlike the relatively impermeable boundary that surrounds a nuclear family, households within the binuclear family system need to have permeable boundaries which facilitate the exchange of children, money, and decision-making power (Walker and Messinger, 1979). This is quite different from the cohesion and sense of unity and autonomy of the nuclear family.

Change of Custody and Split Custody

It is not uncommon for a change in custody, with the possible result of split custody, to occur around the time of remarriage. The reasons vary. Any of the adults or children involved may be the instigators. Sometimes remarrying noncustodial parents return to court in an effort to gain custody. Sometimes the custodial parent perceives children to be threatening her new marriage and wants them out of the house. Many times it is the child who wants the change, either because she does not want to live with the new stepparent, because she wants to care for or become emotionally closer to the noncustodial parent, or because she is a maturing adolescent searching for new experiences. Often a change in custody is a combination of these factors, for example, in the case of an adolescent who had been wanting to live with the noncustodial parent for some time, but was with a custodial parent who was not ready to release her only companion until she had a new partner.

Whatever the specific situation may be, the therapist needs to be mindful of the following guidelines while addressing the change of custody issue: The therapist and family members alike may be attributing the desired change solely to the remarriage, while the change may be mostly a function of the developmental level of the child. Many adolescents desire to live with the noncustodial parent, and many custodial parents want that change also, whether or not there is a remarriage in the family network. The therapist needs to help the family explore the reasons for the desired change. This exploration could, of course, reveal reasons related to the remarriage; for example, a child's desire to change households may be masking resistance to developing intimacy with a new stepparent or to the changing roles in the remarrying household.

The therapist should also help the family explore negative *and* positive consequences of the change. This requires letting go of the traditional belief that it is unfortunate to split up siblings or that children should have to learn to get along with someone the parent has brought into the household. A change in custody may be a viable option for everyone concerned. However, the therapist would do well to encourage the family members to allow time for readjustment after remarriage and not to make any rash decisions, including a change in custody.

When a change in custody does occur, there are emotions to resolve. The rejected parties may feel devalued and unloved; there may also be a sense of relief at the termination of a difficult situation. If a child has left a custodial parent and new stepparent, the custodial parent may experience a loyalty crisis and may believe that the price for having a new partner was losing a child. While there is no research data on this topic, clinical experience suggests that the concept of control and feelings of loss of control pervade this issue. Family members who are left behind may need support in grieving the loss of the child who changed households; children who are forced to change certainly need assistance in coping with the many different feelings they may have. In addition, helping binuclear family members to reconceptualize their family network as an extended family with many households may ease the pain of rejection and loss—the child is not leaving the family; he is only changing households.

Movement of Children Between Households

The movement of children back and forth from their primary residence to the residence that they visit can present problems for all involved. The custodial biological parent and stepparent feel the lack of autonomy and control over their family life; plans must always include consideration of whether or not the residential children and/or any visiting children will be included in household activities. This means coordinating with the needs and plans of binuclear family members in one or more other households. Cooperative scheduling of children's movement between households is difficult at best, but when the divorced parents have a hostile relationship, breaking agreements about picking up or delivering children can be used as a weapon in a battle between ex-spouses (Ahrons, 1981). Children who live in these situations often report feeling like pawns caught in a war that they wish were not even being fought (Wallerstein and Kelly, 1980).

These hostile situations exacerbate the loyalty problems children commonly have (Lutz, 1983). Children who spend time in two households have many potential sources of guilt: guilt about favoring one of their biological parents, guilt about liking a stepparent more than the biological parent of the same sex, guilt about preferring the remarried household to the single parent household because it may appear more "normal" to peers. In addition, children frequently find it stressful being "the kids" for two families; many children also report worrying about and feeling parental toward the noncustodial parent who has not remarried. For example, a daughter may become "Daddy's little homemaker" when she visits him. Consequently, children may have mixed feelings of relief and rejection when a noncustodial parent remarries.

Another problem frequently underlying the relationship between children and the noncustodial parent is the fear of losing each other. One manifestation of this is the reluctance to express anger with each other for fear that the visitation time will end before resolution is reached. Another manifestation is the choice to emotionally separate from one another before there is a chance of rejection. The themes in these dilemmas are trust and control between parents and children across two households. Can a noncustodial parent trust that his or her child will want to continue a relationship when the parent has little control over the child because he or she lives in another household? A remarriage in either household can magnify this fear. Children fear that they may be replaced by new stepsiblings or half siblings in the noncustodial parent's household; the noncustodial parent fears being replaced by a stepparent. The therapist can help clients to accept their underlying feelings, which are quite normal reactions to the situation, and to empower the individuals by bringing to their awareness the many ways that they do have control in a relationship, even when it bridges the boundary of two households.

When we take the perspective of a remarriage family who plays host to visiting children, other issues emerge. In the typical situation, it is the husband's children who visit the household. The wife and her custodial children often feel invaded by the interlopers. The wife/stepmother frequently loses her husband's attention and gains more housework and child care. The children who live in the home may have to share bedrooms, bathrooms, time with friends, and their mother's and stepfather's attention with the stepsiblings. The children who visit can feel unwanted and out of control.

In addition to this disruption of the usual routine, a visit by noncustodial children can be particularly unpleasant if the custodial parent of the visitors feels threatened and not given the visiting children permission to enjoy themselves, but instead has given them orders to "not let that other woman touch you" or "not let her kids boss you around." This is another example of the permeability of a household boundary to the intrusive influence of a member of another household in the binuclear family. Needless to say, resentment of visiting children can occur. In that case the husband/father can feel torn between loyalty to his visiting children and loyalty to the individuals in his household. The therapist can help this part-time stepfamily through the processes of a needs assessment for all individuals, problem-solving, and negotiation of a compromise. Coping with visitations is an example of the conundrum with which many men struggle—having remarried because they lost their families in a divorce, and then finding themselves in the position of having more family than their time, energy and money can support.

Exchange of Money Between Households

The flow of alimony and child support monies between households further blurs the boundaries and exemplifies the interdependence of families within the binuclear family system; the finances of one household may be interwoven with the finances of one or more other households. This exchange of money per se might not be of interest to a therapist, were it not for money being a metaphor for emotional issues. For example, withholding or delaying payment of monies to one's ex-spouse may be an effective way to disrupt normal functioning in his household. Furthermore, children often perceive the amount of money that a noncustodial parent spends on them as symbolic of her love for them. If a noncustodial parent's standard of living is higher than the children's, they are likely to feel resentful. When differences in standard of living exist within one household, due to different sources of support for different children, jealousies abound. In some states, the income of a divorced parent's new spouse is taken into consideration when the court sets the amount of child support that the noncustodial parent is required to pay. While this may be good for children financially, it promotes resentment of one's stepchildren. A therapist would be wise to inquire about the financial situation in the binuclear family; it will serve as another clue to understanding observable behaviors and underlying feelings.

Sharing Decision-Making Power in the Coparenting Relationship

The agreement between divorced parents to share decision-making power concerning the lives of their common children creates another means by which two households are linked together by permeable boundaries. The increase in the incidence of joint legal custody arrangements formalizes this agreement for more and more divorcing parents, even though there is a dearth of evidence that joint custody actually promotes cooperation between ex-spouses (Derdeyn and Scott, 1984). The interdependent cooperation required to successfully share this decision-making power necessitates continued contact between ex-spouses at a level that is more than cursory. This continuation of one function of the previous marriage can be threatening to the new marriage. There are some preliminary findings that suggest that too much contact with ex-spouses may not be conducive to a happy remarriage (Clingempeel, 1981). Although we do not have sufficient data yet to know how much contact works for which types of former spouses relationships, it appears that a moderate amount of contact is necessary for functional coparenting. Furthermore, current research indicates that fathers who continue to share decision-making with their former wives continue to be more involved with their children postdivorce (Ahrons, 1983; Bowman and Ahrons, 1984).

Obviously, unresolved emotions about one's ex-spouse can play a part here. When divorced parents are spending excessive amounts of time on coparenting issues, it may mean that one or both of them have not psychologically divorced. When this is the case, a remarriage is particularly threatening to the ex-spousal relationship, and it is not unusual for the non-remarrying ex-spouse to respond to the threat of loss by intensifying contact in the coparenting relationship. The contact can be hostile or friendly. Fighting over decisions about their children can be an acceptable avenue by which they continue their own hostilities. Conversely, the process of successfully working together "for the sake of the children" can make them feel emotionally close and even affectional toward each other. It can be nostalgic of good times during their marriage. Naturally, a new spouse might also feel threatened and, in turn, might resent stepchildren for being the reason why the coparental relationship exists. The decision-making issue is further complicated by the question of inclusion of the stepparent into the process. How much decision-making power should stepparents have? This has implications for the well-being of the stepfamily. There is some evidence that shared decision-making between the new couple about children's behavior is associated with subjective feelings of closeness (Ihinger-Tallman and Pasley, 1982).

Maintaining a functional coparental relationship that does not detract from the remarriage is a balancing act for the remarried parent. It requires establishing definitive boundaries in the ex-spousal relationship while keeping flexible boundaries in the parental relationship. This separation of spousal and parental roles is the basic task in the coparental relationship. The difficulty for the family and for the therapist is that there is no one correct set of behaviors that define these abstract notions. Each individual family member has her own connotation of definitive boundaries and flexible boundaries. The task of the therapist is to help family members share their ideas and wishes about behaviors that will promote boundaries that are appropriate for their own unique family situation. Negotiation and compromise are likely to be part of the process.

Because the research on binuclear family functioning is still in the embryo stage, families are not aware of most of the new findings and theory development about remarriage families. Hence, therapists need to assume responsibility for educating their clients and helping them translate the new knowledge into functional behavior and realistic expectations. For example, recent research suggests that excluding the noncustodial father from the family system results in more emotional distress for fathers (Ahrons, 1979; Grief, 1979; Keshet and Rosenthal, 1978; Mendes, 1976), mothers (Brandwein, Brown, and Fox, 1974; Hetherington, Cox, and Cox, 1976; Weiss, 1979) and children (Hetherington, 1979; Jacobson, 1984; Wallerstein and Kelly, 1980). Ahrons and Perlmutter (1982) note the importance of providing the family with a new way of thinking about themselves. By labeling the family as a binuclear family and acknowledging, when appropriate, the existence of two households of family, the stepfamily itself forms a different, more expansive definition of their family.

BOUNDARIES AND RELATIONSHIPS WITHIN THE STEPFAMILY

Inclusion of the Stepparent Into the One-Parent Household

Narrowing the focus from the binuclear family system to the remarrying household reveals similar, but more subtle, issues about boundaries between members of the new stepfamily. It is helpful to remember that the one-parent household was an ongoing group prior to the remarriage; the new stepparent is trying to penetrate the boundary of that group and be accepted as a legitimate member. If the remarriage occurs soon after a divorce, children often resent a stepparent's "trying to take Daddy's place" in the group, whether or not this is the case. The noncustodial parent may still be psychologically present while being physically absent. As noted by Boss (1977), it is frequently this type of boundary ambiguity which creates distress in the family. Furthermore, children sometimes irrationally blame a stepparent for their parents' divorce even when they know that their parent had not met the stepparent until after the divorce.

If the remarriage occurs long after a divorce, the one-parent household has had time to adjust to the loss of an adult member of the group, has redefined roles and relationships and, usually, has become a functional group. In this case inclusion of the stepparent into the group is a different problem. Because members of one-parent households have shared difficult times, they can be intensely cohesive. New stepparents sometimes report that breaking into the one-parent household group is like breaking into a fortress. The previously single-parent may continue to feel protective loyalty toward her children; the children can be defensive about losing their prior parent to a new spouse. In addition, the new stepparent is entering a well-established family culture with its own set of norms, habits, traditions, communication patterns, and "in" jokes. If the stepparent moves into the house or apartment of the one-parent household, he is even more of an outsider.

Many stepparents in this situation report feeling out of control, a normal response. Bids for control and power within the family group are camouflaged in arguments about trivial issues. For example, a heated debate about whether the potatoes should be mashed or baked on Thanksgiving has little to do with potatoes; it is a covert negotiation for power in the family. While it is quite normal for the stepparent to feel the frustration and powerlessness of an outsider, it is his behavioral response to these feelings that may be problematic. If the stepparent responds hostilely or withdraws, assimilation into the group is even less likely. Explaining one's feelings and asking for support from the biological parent and, perhaps, from the stepchildren is a more difficult but more adaptive response.

The biological parent in the household holds the key to the stepparent's psychological acceptance into the group. The biological parent's responses to the stepparent's attempts to participate in the group communicate to the children whether or not they must treat him as part of the "in-group." She or he models consideration or unconcern for the stepparent's needs and feelings and supports or sabotages the assertions of the stepparent. A toss of the hand or lift of an eyebrow communicates to a child that his or her behavior toward the newcomer is acceptable or unacceptable. The therapist must pay close attention to the subtle communication related to this issue of inclusion of the stepparent.

Why would a biological parent not promote complete inclusion of the new stepparent into the family group? First, giving another adult equal status in the family means sharing leadership power. Although the biological parent may welcome sharing family responsibilities, giving up the accompanying leadership rights is more difficult. Second, a biological parent can feel jealous of a growing friendship between stepparent and stepchild; this is more likely if the parent-child relationship has been stormy.

From the children's perspective inclusion of the stepparent has another twist. First, if the biological parent marries someone suddenly or without the children's "approval," the children are also likely to feel out of control. Like adults, the children may react with hostility toward or withdrawal from the stepparent or the family. Manifestations range from acting out in school to alcohol or other drug abuse to staying secluded in one's room and being hyper-alert in the presence of the stepparent. Second, children often fear that they will lose the attention and loyalty of the biological parent—that the stepparent will come between them and their parent. For only children, this fear is more acute and may have some basis in reality. Crosbie-Burnett (1983b) found that stepfamilies with one custodial child from a prior marriage and one or more children born into the remarriage reported being significantly less happy than stepfamilies with one custodial child and no additional children, and than stepfamilies with two custodial children from a prior marriage with and without additional children.

Third, eldest children have an additional issue. During the readjustment of roles in the one-parent stage of the household, the eldest child (sometimes the second eldest) often assumes some of the responsibilities that were shared by two parents. The eldest child may care for younger children, shop, cook, clean, and do laundry. Along with gaining responsibilities is a rise in status and power within the family. The eldest child often becomes the single parent's partner in making decisions about the household and younger children, and confidant with respect to personal issues. If this eldest child is the opposite sex of the biological parent, he or she is often encouraged to be "the man" or "the woman" of the house. This child straddles the intra-familial boundary that separates children from adults. When the single parent remarries, the eldest child becomes displaced in the adult role he or she has assumed, and stands to lose the concomitant status and power. Consequently, this child may spend a great deal of energy sabotaging the inclusion of the new stepparent into the family group. It is one thing for the previously single parent to say to this child, "Thank you for helping me; now you can go back to being a kid." It is another thing for the child to be able to relinquish the adult role and return to being one of the children. It should be noted that, occasionally, this eldest child is happily relieved of the responsibilities and welcomes displacement by a stepparent.

What can the therapist do to ease this inclusion process? Most importantly, she or he can help people to have realistic expectations—readjustment after remarriage takes about two years (Visher and Visher, 1979). The therapist can also explain the principles of group dynamics that concern the entry of new group members. Further, he or she might help the children discover what they could gain by accepting the new stepparent. If the children have nothing to gain and stand only to lose by the remarriage, the chances for family happiness are slim.

The Stepparent Role

A key aspect in the process of inclusion of the stepparent into the family is the formulation of his or her role. Because there is no social prescription for the role of stepmother or stepfather in modern stepfamilies, confusion and misunderstandings about what the stepparent "is supposed to be doing" in the family abound. As noted above, family members often have contradictory expectations. The positive side of the ambiguity is the flexibility to tailor the stepparent role to fit the unique needs of each stepfamily. These needs vary widely depending upon the age of the children, the amount of contact with the noncustodial parent, the type of relationship the stepparent would like to have with the children, the type of relationship the biological parent would like the stepparent to have with the children, etc.

The creation of a role definition for the stepparent is rarely done in an explicit, organized manner. Instead, the role is covertly negotiated by all family members through arguments about specific behaviors, stand-offs, attempts at discipline, playing one parent against the other, sabotaging, manipulating, and the like. These are the symptoms that the therapist sees.

The therapist can be very helpful by giving structure to the negotiation process. Each of the stepparent's interpersonal relationships needs to be negotiated. Usually, the most delicate relationship is between stepparent and stepchild. Satisfaction with this relationship appears to be more central to family happiness than is satisfaction with the marital relationship (Crosbie-Burnett, 1984). We suggest that negotiation begin with the stepparent and the eldest child, and should be as behaviorally specific as possible. This means answering questions like: What am I willing to do? What would I like to do? What am I unwilling to do? What would I like you to do? What would I like you not to do? Sometimes children will refuse to negotiate any relationship with a stepparent, out of loyalty to the noncustodial parent, especially if there is competition between the two. An uncooperative child may become amenable to the process if the therapist explains that the child is being asked to negotiate a working relationship, not necessarily a loving relationship.

It is important to remember that the goal of this process is to create a relationship that maximizes answering the needs of the two individuals, not to subtly manipulate these two into a relationship that fulfills someone else's fantasy (including the therapist's) about how the family *should* function. After this dyad has tentatively agreed upon their relationship, the support of the other family members, especially the biological parent, is crucial. If they are uncomfortable with the relationship, for whatever reason, they will sabotage it. Family members' concerns and feelings about the tentative agreement can be addressed by having the family fantasize positive and negative repercussions of the negotiated relationship. Other relationships can then be negotiated in similar fashion. Overt negotiation of relationships can help family members feel more in control; hopefully, they will have less need to act out or withdraw.

Stepparents and stepchildren need to establish a friendship before the children will accept discipline from the stepparent (Stern, 1978). Younger children, of course, accept the discipline sooner than older children. This means that the biological parent should continue to do the disciplining after the remarriage, until the stepchildren have a trusting, friendly relationship with the stepparent. He or she should begin disciplining slowly, first supporting the biological parent's rules, and later, disciplining more independently. This prescription assumes that discipline is part of the negotiated role for the stepparent. This is not true in all stepfamilies, especially when the children are older adolescents.

The Biological Parent

The biological parent is the pivotal person in the stepfamily. She or he is a member of both the previously one-parent household and the conjugal couple, two subgroups within the stepfamily. As such, she or he is likely to feel caught in the middle when her spouse's needs conflict with her children's needs. In the initial adjustment after remarriage, the spouse and/or the children may set up conflicting demands to see where loyalties lie. In the process of trying to meet everyone's needs (sometimes this includes the ex-spouse's), the biological parent may experience role overload. This is similar to the role overload that a remarried noncustodial parent feels when the children visit, but the custodial parent has more control over the situation.

This phenomenon of conflicting loyalties is a major difference between intact families and stepfamilies. In intact families, the children often hold the marriage together; in stepfamilies, the children pull the marriage apart. If the couple has both "hers" and "his" children, it is even more imperative that the couple squeeze into their already overstressed schedule some time for themselves. Clinicians report that many remarriages are distressed because the pivotal biological parent has not changed primary allegiance from the children to the new spouse.

Integration of the Stepfamily

Although the stepfamily has permeable boundaries and may change its composition frequently as children move from household to household, it can still build some identity and cohesion of its own. First, we recommend that each dyad regularly spend one-to-one time together away from other family members in an activity that is pleasurable for both parties (e.g., movies, restaurants, athletic events, museums, shops). Second, the stepfamily can enjoy planning and implementing new family traditions (Visher and Visher, 1979). The brainstorming should include all stepfamily members and the decision-making process should be consensual in order to maximize the chances for success. If the new tradition is forced on anyone by a subgroup within the stepfamily, the activity wil not build family cohesion.

As with any group, having fun together and working through difficulties together builds group identity and cohesion. Stepfamilies are no exception.

CONCLUSIONS

Binuclear families are a new family form; the collective wisdom regarding solutions to problems is still small. In addition, there are so many variants of binuclear families that solutions need to be individualized to each family configuration. What are the implications of this situation for the therapist? First, since there are so few cardinal rules to teach the family, therapists must take a facilitative role, and help the family reach their own unique solutions. They can teach the family members communication skills, values clarification, problem-solving, negotiation, etc. Second, when working with binuclear families, therapists must constantly be alert to their own culturally conditioned and academically trained normative biases about how *healthy* families function. These norms tend to be based on intact families and their generalization to binuclear families and stepfamilies is inappropriate.

Third, when an individual or family presents itself, therapists must remember to perceive the group of individuals in his or her office as part of a larger family system. By asking the clients about other people in the system (ex-spouses and their new partners, noncustodial biological children, stepchildren, half siblings, stepsiblings, grandparents), the therapist begins to discover the quality of each of the many relationships between the members of the entire binuclear family. Unlike nuclear families, primary parent-child relationships and coparental relationships bridge two households. Due to the potential emotional intensity of these relationships, the behavior of individuals in the binuclear family system has an impact on others that can extend far beyond one's own household. Therapists must always be mindful of this cross-household influence when they are seeking explanations for individuals' behavior.

Perhaps the most important thing that a therapist can do for binuclear family members is help them to feel normal. They are living in a stressed system; most of the feelings of being burdened, jealous, threatened, out of control, and the like, are quite normal responses to the situation. At the societal level, the cultural ideology regarding families and the economic and legal institutions have not yet responded to this emergent family form. There is little validation or support when families turn outward for help. Simply sharing this information with clients can relieve much of their guilt and self-doubt. The next step is to build their sense of self-efficacy about coping with the chronic stresses inherent in the binuclear family. If family members can achieve this and, better yet, maintain a sense of humor about their difficulties, they can enjoy the intrigue of living in this most modern of family structures.

REFERENCES

Ahrons, C. R. (1979). The binuclear family: Two households, one family. *Alternative Lifestyles*, *2*, 499-515.

Ahrons, C. R. (1980). Divorce: A crisis of family transition and change. *Family Relations*, *29*, 533-540.

Ahrons, C. R. (1981). The continuing coparental relationship between divorced spouses. *American Journal of Orthopsychiatry, 51*, 415-428.

Ahrons, C.R. (1983). Predictors of paternal involvement postdivorce: Mothers' and fathers' perceptions. *Journal of Divorce, 6*, 55-59.

Ahrons, C. R., & Perlmutter, M.S. (1982). The relationship between former spouses: A fundamental subsystem in the remarriage family. In L. Messinger (Ed.), *Therapy with remarried families*. Rockville, MD: Aspen Systems Corporation.

Boss, P. (1977). A clarification of the concept of psychological father presence in families experiencing ambiguity of boundary. *Journal of Marriage and the Family, 39*, 141-151.

Bowman, M., & Ahrons, C. R. (1984). *Impact of legal custody status on fathers' parenting postdivorce.* Unpublished manuscript, University of Wisconsin-Madison.

Brandwein, R. A., Brown, C. A., & Fox, E. M. (1974). Women and children last: The social situation of divorced mothers and their families. *Journal of Marriage and the Family, 36*, 498-514.

Clingempeel, W. G. (1981). Quasi-kin relationships and marital quality. *Journal of Personality and Social Psychology, 41*, 890-901.

Crosbie-Burnett, M. (1983, October). *Impact of remarriage on labor force participation, divorce decree modification, ex-spousal relationship, and extended family reorganization.* Paper presented at the annual meeting of the National Council on Family Relations, St. Paul, MN. (a)

Crosbie-Burnett, M. (1983, August). *Models of well-adjusted stepfamilies.* Paper presented at the annual meeting of the American Psychological Association, Anaheim, CA. (b)

Crosbie-Burnett, M. (1984). The centrality of the step relationship: A challenge to theory and practice. *Family Relations, 33*, 459-463.

Derdeyn, A. P., & Scott, E. (1984). Joint custody: A critical analysis and appraisal. *American Journal of Orthopsychiatry, 54*, 199-209.

Fishman, B., & Hamel, B. (1981). From nuclear to stepfamily ideology: A stressful change. *Alternative Lifestyles, 4*, 181-204.

Grief, J. B. (1979). Fathers, children and joint custody. *American Journal of Orthopsychiatry, 49*, 311-319.

Hetherington, E. M. (1979). Divorce: A child's perspective. *American Psychologist, 34*, 851-858.

Hetherington, E. M., Cox, M., & Cox, R. (1976). Divorced fathers. *The Family Coordinator, 25*, 417-428.

Ihinger-Tallman, M., & Pasley, K. (1982). *Parental coalition in remarriage.* Unpublished manuscript, Washington State University, Pullman, WA.

Jacobson, D. S. (1984, April). *Family type, visiting and children's behavior in the stepfamily: A linked family system.* Paper presented at the annual meeting of American Orthopsychiatric Association, Toronto.

Keshet, H. F., & Rosenthal, K. M. (1978). Fathering after marital separation. *Social Work, 23*, 11-18.

Lutz, P. (1983). The stepfamily: An adolescent perspective. *Family Relations, 32*, 367-375.

Mendes, H. (1976). Single fatherhood. *Social Work, 21*, 308-312.

Sager, C. J., Brown, H. S., Crohn, H., Engel, T., Rodstein, E., & Walker, L. (1983). *Treating the remarried family.* New York: Brunner/Mazel.

Schlesinger, B. (1978). *Remarriage in Canada.* Toronto: Guidance Centre, Faculty of Education, University of Toronto.

Stern, P. N. (1978). Stepfather families: Integration around child discipline. *Issues of Mental Health Nursing, 1*, 50-56.

Visher, E. B. (1984). Personal Communication.

Visher, E. B., & Visher, J. S. (1979). *Stepfamilies: A guide to working with stepparents and stepchildren.* New York: Brunner/Mazel.

Walker, K. N., & Messinger, L. (1979). Remarriage after divorce: Dissolution and reconstruction of family boundaries. *Family Process, 18*, 185-192.

Wallerstein, J. S., & Kelly, J. B. (1980). *Surviving the breakup: How children and parents cope with divorce.* New York: Basic Books.

Weiss, R. S. (1979). *Going it alone.* New York: Basic Books.

Sibling Relationships in Families of Divorce

Mary M. Eno

ABSTRACT. This paper considers the role of sibling relationships in families of divorce. The nature and functions of sibling relationships are first discussed in light of current research and family theory. This theoretical background is used to support the notion that sibling relationships are not only affected by divorce, but can also be an important resource in helping children through post-divorce adjustment. Several case studies are presented which provide support for this perspective. Finally, suggestions are made for the clinician interested in applying knowledge about siblings in the family therapy setting.

INTRODUCTION

The separation of a couple or family is an occurrence which has, in some way or another, closely touched the lives of most American adults. This new reality is captured in a recent cartoon in which a smiling little girl addresses her doll by saying, "I just want you to grow up and have a normal happy live . . . love, marriage, children, separation, divorce, then love, marriage, children, separation, divorce, then love . . ." It is the kind of cartoon which may sometimes draw tears rather than laughter. A child of divorce who recently happened to see the cartoon did not find it funny.

Divorce is hard on people, perhaps especially children. In the last few decades, social scientists and clinicians—stirred, in part, by the strong reactions children have to hearing their mother say, "Daddy and I have decided to separate"—have directed their attention to learning more about the special significance divorce has for children (Wallerstein & Kelly, 1980), its effects on their development (Hetherington, Cox & Cox,

---

Mary M. Eno, Ph.D., is Director of the Post-Masters Certificate Program in Family Therapy at the Philadelphia Child Guidance Clinic, 34th and Civic Center Boulevard, Philadelphia, PA 19104.

Work for the case studies was supported by a grant to the Families of Divorce Project of the Philadelphia Child Guidance Clinic by the Pew Memorial Trust.

I wish to thank Betsy Wood, Douglas Sprenkle and Dan Wagner for their helpful suggestions on earlier versions of this chapter.

Very special thanks to Marla Isaacs, Director of the Families of Divorce Project, for her friendship and support in making this research possible.

© 1985 by The Hawrth Press, Inc. All rights reserved.

1977, 1979; Hetherington, 1979), and how clinicians might aid them and their families to steer through the divorce aftermath as successfully as possible (Abelsohn, 1983; Isaacs, 1981). Studies and reports of clinical work have, of course, varied in their approaches and conclusions, but one striking fact that emerges from the review of the literature is that sibling relationships in families of divorce have been almost altogether overlooked. There are no studies which attempt to document the effects of divorce on the sibling relationship or vice versa.

Sibling relationships are clearly important and variable. Broadly speaking, recent clinical and experimental studies of siblings have established that the sibling relationship is unique in a child's plurality of relationships and contributes to many aspects of child development and family functioning. Within the last few years, several substantial works have been published which give new prominence to siblings (Lamb & Sutton-Smith, 1982; Bank & Kahn, 1982; Dunn & Kendrick, 1982).

Despite recent attention given to the topic, sibling relationships are still the least studied of all family relationships.[1] Still, previous sibling research has contributed to our understanding of siblings in a number of areas. For example, through his research, Cicirelli (1972, 1982) has demonstrated that siblings affect cognitive development and can enhance learning. Previous research has also demonstrated that siblings influence affective development (Bowerman & Dobash, 1974) and development of personal identity (Bank & Kahn, 1982). Dunn and Kendrick (1982) have documented the impact of the second born child on family relationships. They and others (Bryant & Crockenberg, 1980) have concluded that age and sex of children and family composition are key variables influencing family dynamics. For example, the intensity of sibling bonds relates to the age and sex of the children—siblings close in age and of the same sex are usually closer to each other emotionally (Cicirelli, 1972, 1982). Bank and Kahn (1982) maintain that strong sibling bonds occur when there is "high access between siblings; the need for personal identity; and insufficient parental influence."

While some researchers (e.g., Bank & Kahn, 1982; Abelsohn, 1983; Coleman, 1978; Rosenberg, 1980) have focussed on the sibling relationship as a unit of therapeutic intervention, the corpus of such research remains limited. Perhaps this shortcoming is due to the fact that there is, as yet, no theory of healthy sibling relationships over the lifespan. Therefore, to establish specific intervention strategies aimed at the sibling relationship may seem premature. It is the opinion of this author that there is sufficient clinical data on siblings to justify developing clinical interventions for families of divorce whose children are having difficulty adjusting.

Even in the absence of a theory of healthy sibling relationships, it is clear that, for better or for worse, siblings of divorce are bound together by their common family background and their shared experience of the separation. Yet, how siblings may act as friends or enemies to each other in the post-divorce adjustment period and to what extent sibling interactions contribute to or hinder post-divorce adjustment, remain largely unexplored. The poignancy of this oversight was made apparent recently when, after a two-hour clinical session with a woman who had just decided to leave her husband of twelve years, I reentered the reception room where the woman's two children were waiting. There, her youngest child was curled up on his older sister's lap. By listening attentively to her stories, the children "allowed" their mother to talk with me without interruption. This peaceful scene brought to mind a sharply contrasting moment in which I had been told that, following their parents' decision to separate, the two school-age sons had engaged in a vicious fight in which they literally tore the shirts off each other's back.

This chapter is based on my own clinical work as a family therapist, as a clinical associate of the Philadelphia Child Guidance Clinic's Families of Divorce Project, and on case studies of four families of divorce (Eno, 1983). The latter study focussed on the lives of eight children between the ages of 6 and 11 who had made significant adjustments both inside and outside the family as a consequence of their parents' marital separation which occurred between 8 months to 2 years prior to the onset of the study. It is important to keep in mind, therefore, that the material presented is oriented toward the post-divorce period and not the period of immediate separation. Data were collected through structured interviews with parents, teachers, and children, as well as from observations made of children's daily activities at home and at school.

Sibling relationships vary greatly in relation to the ages and number of the children in the family, so a relatively narrow focus has been chosen to prevent overgeneralization, a problem which already characterizes much of the work on siblings.

THE PRIMACY OF THE SIBLING RELATIONSHIP IN POSTSEPARATION FAMILIES

Whatever their particular circumstances, separated parents are faced with a new constellation of needs and demands with regard to their own adult lives and the lives of their children. It is not uncommon, in clinical practice, to observe separated parents worry over decisions which seem and at times do require choosing between their children's needs and their own. Such choices have special significance in families of divorce since they are often characterized by a marked decrease in the availability of one or both parents. A single parent may have to find employment and may be emotionally preoccupied with his or her own very adult activities, friends, or romances. Or, a parent may be absent altogether. Unfortunately, it is often precisely when a parent is least available that the children most need parental attention to help them deal with their confusion, anger, and sorrow.

With family size contracted and parents less available, the sibling relationship stands out in relief—siblings count more for each other, for better or for worse. Although the sibling relationship does not exist independently of other family relationships, it is, to some extent, a separate world. The sibling relationship is distinct from any other family relationship and, during the process of marital separation, maybe a place away from entanglement in spousal affairs. Alone in a bedroom, children can entertain, teach, challenge and wound each other. In short, through their relationship they can distract themselves from a home life which may seem horribly disrupted, and thereby buffer at least some of the distress emanating from the marital subsystem.

In order to assess whether and how siblings might be helping or hurting each other in adjusting to changes at home, the therapist must consider two key dimensions of post-divorce family life: (1) siblings solidarity, and (2) parent-child coalitions.

SIBLING SOLIDARITY: INTRAGENERATIONAL DIALOGUE

Siblings create a world for themselves which is separate from, and sometimes unknown to, other family relationships. Theirs is an intragenerational dialogue[2] active throughout the lifespan. The separate world of siblings, not unlike children's relationships with their peers, operates on many levels and takes diverse forms. Three dimensions of sibling relationships which are especially relevant to families of divorce will be briefly discussed.

Sibling Rituals

During many kinds of life transitions, including divorce, it is not uncommon for families to forego family rituals in an effort to cope with new, very pressing daily demands. Many family therapists and researchers have claimed that the existence of family rituals is central to their well functioning and, conversely, that their absence undermines successful adjustment. For example, Isaacs (1983), in her study of divorce, found that when bedtime rituals were disrupted in the first year of the separation, the children had more behavior problems. Given the importance of rituals in family life and the possible deleterious effects of their disruption in the post-separation period, it is remarkable that so little attention has been directed to sibling rituals in families generally, and in families of divorce more specifically.

Though generally tacit, siblings often have their own rituals which are fundamental to the continuity and stability of their relationship. In the case of marital separation and the adjustment following, sibling rituals may be inadvertantly dropped which can disrupt the children's sense of security. For example, in one case, described in detail later, the Davis siblings joined each other on the TV room couch every Saturday morning where they would huddle together under a blanket and enjoy the pleasure of early morning cartoons before their parents awakened. When their parents separated, the ritual continued uninterrupted. Similarly, new rituals may emerge as a result of the separation. In the case of another sibling pair—the Belfields—immediately following their parents separation the two children began to sleep in the same bedroom, where their mother reports that she could hear them laugh and talk long after their bedtime. In both cases, sibling bonds were maintained or strengthened through rituals unique to that relationship.

Sibling Play

Researchers and clinicians alike have noted that much of sibling interaction takes the form of playful activity. In fact, in three of the four families of my study, play was the dominant mode of interaction between siblings: it was play that most often brought the children together and was the principle means by which they belonged to each other. In the one family where neither child was doing well with their peers—the Roslycks—the siblings had no history of playing together. Whether or not siblings are able to play together and, whether sibling play is carried over contagiously into family life, is important for the therapist to consider. In clinical practice it is not unusual to hear parents report that their children's play diminished or increased following their separation. Just what causes these changes is not known, but it is safe to say that a lengthy discontinuation of sibling play cannot bode well for child adjustment. Regardless, sibling play is central to family life and can be an important dimension in helping families of divorce.

Sibling Conflict

Equally compelling, is the issue of sibling conflict. There is probably no other childhood relationship in which children express as much continuous hostility toward each other as the relationship between siblings. Again, to the dismay of parents and clinicians alike, there are no norms for what constitutes healthy sibling conflict, although a number of researchers state that aggressive interaction is a primary mode of sibling interaction and is an important means by which children learn how to effectively handle their hostile feelings (Abramovitch, 1979). A common complaint of parents who are in the process of marital separation is that the fighting between their children increases. Since there are so many reasons why children fight—to make contact, to play, to increase or decrease proximity, to seek revenge—it is important for therapists to carefully examine this dimension of the sibling world. The limits to what is healthy are not known, except in extreme cases when physical and mental injuries are common or severe. In one family discussed later—the Roslycks—the mother described fights which occurred regularly among *her* adult siblings some of which still result in trips to the hospital for fractured ribs and broken noses. More difficult to assess are sibling fights similar to the one described earlier where the two boys—ages 10 and 8—tore the shirts off each other's back. At the same time, many siblings will boast of how they fight "just for fun." Taking diverse forms, assessing the nature and extent of sibling conflict in families of divorce can prove helpful in treatment.

PARENT-CHILD COALITIONS FOLLOWING MARITAL SEPARATION

Parent-child coalitions can strongly influence sibling relationships, particularly in families of divorce where their impact can be very destructive. To understand how parent-child coalitions affect siblings, it is helpful to review the theoretical basis underlying the concept of coalitions.

The idea that families have structures is a central feature of family therapy theory. Family structure is conceived as a consequence of repeated transactions within the family. Through repetition of such transactions, an organized pattern is formed. This pattern is based on overt and covert rules regarding how, when, and to whom family members relate. While certain dimensions of family structure are idiosyncratic, others are fairly universal. For example, all families have some sort of hierarchy with regard to the power and authority of individual family members. Characteristic of family hierarchies is the power differential between parents and their children and that between older and younger siblings. Minuchin's (1974) structural family therapy, through which these ideas have become familiar, assumes that an intergenerational hierarchy—between parents and children—is essential for healthy family functioning. Conversely, a skewed hierarchy which is sustained over a period of time—such as occurs when, for example, younger children have more rights and responsibilities than their older siblings—becomes the source of problems.

Another hallmark of family structure is the differentiation of family members into subsystems which are determined by age, gender, or interests (i.e., parental subsystem, sibling subsystem, mother-infant subsystem). Subsystems are delimited by boundaries, a term which is used to denote the regulating distance between individuals or subsystems which protects the functioning of the system.

Subsystems sometimes take the form of a coalition—that is, a situation in which two family members join together against a third person (Minuchin, 1974; Caplow, 1968). While such coalitions may be unintentional, they are active and can be observed through patterns of family interaction. Parents often coalesce to carry out a task in relation to their children; siblings may do the same in relation to their parents. Such intragenerational family coalitions are integral to family functioning. Coalitions can also be cross-generational. A father and his daughter, for example, may gang up on the mother whenever she expresses an opinion. Whether a cross-generational coalition is harmful depends on its degree and duration. Ongoing stable parent-child coalitions threaten the integrity of family functioning in intact as well as separated families.

Parent-child coalitions create special difficulties in separated families where one parent is absent from the home. In two-child families, a parent-child coalition—e.g., between the mother and one of her children—leaves the other child alone inside the family. The child is excluded and has no allies. Disagreements between him and his mother cannot remain dyadic, for his sibling will somehow be brought into the conflict in his mother's camp. Likewise, a sibling argument will signal the mother (either directly or indirectly) to side with one of her children against the other. The repeated failures of the one child to successfully engage either family member in a dyadic interaction leaves him at risk because a whole range of interpersonal skills are developed in dyadic interaction. A broken generational boundary not only jeopardizes the developing competence of the alienated child by actively favoring one child over the other, but also harms the functioning of the sibling subsystem. And, although the coalesced parent and child may temporarily have feelings of increased self-worth, such gains are illusory and do not increase the ability to function well in other relationships.

Part of the therapist's task is to determine whether or not a stable parent-child coalition exists in a given family. Importantly, patterns of identification in families are not necessarily synonymous with patterns of parent-child coalitions. In two-child families, there tends to be a common pattern of identification among family members—each child identifies with a different parent, a pattern termed "split-parent identification" (Schachter, 1982). (Ordinarily, children's identification with their respective parents is consistent with the parents' identification with their children.) Patterns of identification can be found by direct questioning—"Who are you most like, your mom or your dad?" However hesitant, most children will have a respone to that question. Yet, patterns of identification do not necessarily reflect parent-child coalitions, and the therapist who is seeking to assess family structure should be careful not to confuse these dimensions of family life.

The following cases illustrate the difficulties that parent-child coalitions can create in families of divorce, some circumstances which mitigate their adverse effects, differences between patterns of coalition and identification, the mutual support that siblings can provide in the presence and absence of parent-child coalitions, and the damaging effects of the absence of solidarity between siblings.

The Roslycks: Parent-Child Coalitions and Sibling Enmity

Both Mr. and Mrs. Roslyck[3] agree that long before their separation their two children were each parked squarely in different parent camps—the older child, Kristie (age 11), with her father, the younger child, Nicholas (age 10), with his mother. The children had been pulled into their parents' marital struggles for so many years that by the time the separation occurred, each child identified with and "belonged to" one parent. As siblings, when they were not fighting bitterly, they avoided each other. When they *were* fighting, the parents were in the middle supporting one child against the other. Mrs. Roslyck cannot remember a time when Kristie and Nicholas played together.

When the family was intact—however disquieting the home life had been—at least each child had an ally. But, once Mr. Roslyck moved out, Kristie was left unprotected inside the family. For example, Kristie would lose most arguments with her brother because Nicholas would quickly call in his mother and she would take Nicholas's side. Similarly, Nicholas would jump into conflicts between Kristie and her mother, using this occasion to lodge yet another complaint against his sister.

In this family, underlying the mother's overt behavior is a set of attitudes that subtly influence the texture of family life. Mrs. Roslyck had split her children into the "good child" and the "bad child." When she was asked to describe her daughter, she chose the words "forward," "guarded," and "strange." In contrast, she said that she herself was like her son—Nicholas was a "nice, cooperative kind of kid" who "never gives me any grief." Kristie and Nicholas also agreed that Nicholas is "like his mom" and Kristie is "like her dad", a pattern of identification which parallels the coalitionary structure. Mr. Roslyck's post-separation involvement with the children was limited to one afternoon every two weeks which, until recently, had only included Kristie. Therefore, he was not present to offer support to "his child," and she was not able to solicit it from other family members. As a result, Kristie launched heavily into relationships with peers with which she had little success.

A strong parent-child coalition, particularly when the other parent is absent, can have a whole panoply of deleterious effects on the excluded child, such as causing him or her to become deferential, angry, or depressed in other social situations. The child who cannot win at home may lose hope of winning elsewhere. This can be directly seen in Kristie's behavior when she is with Nicholas.

Within months after the separation, Kristie was showing signs of stress at home and at school. Typical evidence of the lack of connection between her and her brother was revealed in the children's behavior a few minutes before an interview with the therapist. Kristie was observed trying to engage Nicholas in some kind of interchange. She spoke to him, copied his movements in an exaggerated way, and smiled at him. Once or twice Nicholas glanced her way, but otherwise ignored her completely. Later, Kristie was consistently deferential to Nicholas. Her deference was especially visible when they constructed a building together using colored blocks, an assessment tool which was used as part of the sibling interview. Often, Kristie made a suggestion or placed a block on the toy construction. Nicholas ignored the suggestions and he usually removed whatever building-block additions his sister had made. Kristie never actively protested over this, although she showed signs of frustration by becoming whiny and tense, and she virtually relinquished her responsibility for the overall task. What is particularly striking about this imbalance is that it is the younger and not the older child who carried the weight. Ordinarily, hierarchical imbalances between siblings favor the older child, a phenomenon which has inherent logic and which is generally not the source of serious problems unless the older child's role is overplayed.

In Kristie's case, it can be surmised that her relationships with people outside the family were affected by her failures at home. While the exact nature of the connection between family and peer relationships is not known, there are data which suggest that when children's post-divorce problems persist beyond the initial transition period, they are likely to take the form of difficulties in establishing and maintaining peer relationships (Hetherington, Cox & Cox, 1977, 1979; McDermott, 1968). Kristie's difficulties at school were apparent in a brief interaction during a lunch period. After finishing her meal, Kristie sat at a table where a group of lively young girls were talking and laughing. Kristie initiated a conversation with one of the girls and the latter did not respond. Again, Kristie tried to get her attention; the girl then changed her position, presenting Kristie with her back. Kristie slumped down into the bench, and then sidled up to the girl yet another time. Again the girl did not respond. After a momentary pause, Kristie turned and went off by herself.

Kristie's classroom teacher noted that this sort of behavior was common. Kristie was not like the other children. He said, apologetically, that she was "a blah child" and that this "carries over socially because the children don't find her interesting." Thus, Kristie's behavior with her only "peer" at home could be seen in her relationships with peers at school, with the same disastrous consequence. Although research has just begun on the topic, current work suggests that sibling relationships in the family may be a bridge to understanding peer relationships outside the family (Furman & Buhrmester, 1980).

Inside the family, a two against one phenomenon is a harsh reality with potentially enduring deleterious consequences for all family members. Currently, Kristie is having a particularly hard time holding up under the forces against her. Kristie's struggle to deal with the separation—synonymous with the loss of her only ally in the family—is exacerbated by a brother who is planted firmly alongside his mother, and the father is, for the most part, unavailable. Before the separation, the sibling conflict paralleled that of their parents' not because the children were modeling themselves in their parents' likeness, but because the sibling conflict could not be resolved within that generation. In the Roslyck family, sibling conflict was waged across generations, and thus the children never learned the skills required to resolve problems by themselves. Fighting sometimes reached serious proportions. They seldom enjoyed each other's company, since neither parent supported an affectionate bond between them. Affectionate bonds were established in this family, but only between parent and child in two, separate, adversarial camps. Once the parent of one camp left, one child was left alone, neither competent to defend herself nor to elicit positive regard from others.

In the Roslyck family, the sibling relationship was a source of pain for both children—by omission or commission. Sturdy parent-child coalitions prevented the development of a sibling bond, and elevated the younger child to a position of authority over his older sister, further distorting the natural hierarchy in the family. Parental hostility which continued beyond the separation kept the children actively divided. There was no reason to believe that the children had been supported in whatever tenuous connections they may have made with each other over the years.

The Belfields: Sibling Coalition as a Factor Counteracting a Parent-Child Coalition

In families of divorce, the harmful effects of a stable parent-child coalition on the sibling relationship are sometimes mitigated by other aspects of family life. The Belfield family is a case in point. Mrs. Belfield has custody of her two children, Alison (age 11) and Charles (age 10), after separating from her husband eight months previously. She claims that her children "are extremely close" to each other, neither more nor less than before the separation. Part of the reason for this is propinquity—while Mrs. Belfield is away at work every day, the children manage for themselves both mornings and afternoons. This they did long before the separation occurred and, according to their mother, it has worked well for the children. An opportunity to alter the arrangement has been present throughout, since Mrs. Belfield's mother has offered to keep the children with her, either full-time or during the after-school hours. But Charles and Alison prefer to be home alone.

Since their parents' separation, they also prefer to sleep in the same room at night even though they each have their own bedrooms. Usually Alison travels to Charles's room, where he relinquishes his own bed to her and sleeps on the floor. During the night, their mother reports, they talk, whisper, and giggle for hours at a stretch. Household chores, which Mrs. Belfield assigns to each child individually, are nearly always divided up in a different manner by the children. For example, Alison might be asked to wash the dishes while Charles is expected to clean the dining and living rooms. Instead of carrying on as planned, one or the other of the children will initiate a switch. Other times, one child will just do the other's chores and the favor will be returned later. When I questioned the logic behind this chore switching, Charles strongly claimed that his and Alison's system was "better," even better than if their mother entered in and assigned the chores to meet each child's wishes. In summary, Charles and Alison make decisions and take actions which keep them constantly interacting with each other. This is not to say that they always get along well. Although they tell each other secrets, have special rituals which only they share, and engage in much mutual activity, they often argue with each other and boast of their disagreements.

Significantly, many of these disagreements end with Mrs. Belfield's supporting her daughter. Both children admit that their mother "sides most" with Alison, a fact which coincided with my observations of the family's interactions. On a number of occasions during the interview, Charles and his mother were in active disagreement with each other. Each time this happened, Alison entered into what had been a dyadic interchange and sided with her mother against Charles. Mrs. Belfield always permitted this alliance to occur, making no attempt to keep Alison out and continue the dyadic interchange with Charles. However, at other times the children acted with solidarity, laughing and teasing each other as their mother tried to engage them in a more serious conversation and calling themselves "the wicked kids" because their mother sometimes thought they were "bad." Thus, despite the mother-daughter coalition, the children managed to draw strength from their own coalition, finding in each other comrades who would help weather the difficult post-separation period.

Although Mrs. Belfield has sole custody and the major financial responsibility for the children, Mr. Belfield makes regular visits and daily phone calls with Alison and Charles. While everyone agrees that Mr. Belfield does not "take sides" with one child against the other, he is slightly more involved with Charles than with Alison. This involvement provides Charles with another important base of support in the family.

As this family structure illustrates, sibling solidarity and cross-generational coalitions in families of divorce are not always mutually exclusive. At times, Alison is in coalition with her mother, at times with her brother. In contrast, Charles's position as youngest child remains stable. The question here is what keeps the intragenerational dialogue between siblings alive in the face of a parent-child coalition which often excludes one child.

There are a number of factors that mitigate the effects of parent-child coalitions in the Belfield family. For one, Mrs. Belfield has consistently worked full-time. Thus, long before the separation, her children were accustomed to being on their own and having to resolve difficulties without the aid of an available parent. Secondly, Mrs. Belfield encouraged closeness between her children, even took pride in how much they seemed to enjoy each other's company. Thirdly, Mr. Belfield is not engaged in an active coalition with one child, though he provides some additional support for Charles. Furthermore, the marital separation was relatively calm and Mrs. Belfield kept a close check on the way her unfriendly feelings for her former husband might translate into actions which would hurt the children, especially Charles. Finally, while a stable parent-child coalition exists, it does not dislodge the natural hierarchy established by birth order since Alison, by virtue of her age, has a legitimate edge over Charles in terms of rights and responsibilities.

Thus, in contrast to the situation in the Roslyck family, the sibling relationship in the Belfield family is a strengthening influence during the post-separation period and helps counteract the effects of the mother-daughter coalition and the instability caused by the parents' marital separation.

The Davises: Siblings Who Sustain a Separate World

Separating after 10 years of marriage, Mr. and Mrs. Davis decided that Mrs. Davis would take custody of their two children, Stephen (age 10) and Paul (age 8). Mrs. Davis went back to work full-time; Mr. Davis agreed to spend three evenings a week and one weekend day with the boys. While not entirely amicable, the separation occurred without the children becoming entangled in marital conflicts.

What is striking about the Davis family is that only one coalition exists, the boys' intragenerational coalition as siblings. When either boy attempts to get their mother to join with them against their brother, she declines. Illustrating this is a conversation in which Mrs. Davis countered Stephen's grumpy claims that he was a bad football player. I interrupted to ask Mrs. Davis whether Stephen often put himself down, to which she replied, "Oh, definitely. All the time . . . He doesn't think he's good at anything." She then turned to Stephen and asked, "Am I correct?" At this point, Paul eagerly entered into the conversation and claimed, "Yes!" Rather than disregarding Paul's comment or incorporating his position to strengthen hers, Mrs. Davis swiftly turned to Paul and said, "Who asked you?" Paul laughed and returned to the blocks he was playing with, and Mrs. Davis carried on the conversation with me. But even though Mrs. Davis does not join forces with either of her children, the boys freely defend and join forces with each other. Once Mrs. Davis teased Paul about his schoolwork, and Stephen entered the conversation to strengthen Paul's position. On another occasion, I made a joke to Paul about something he was doing, and Stephen came over and defended his brother. Along with an earlier claim the boys made that neither of their parents had "favorites" between them, interactions between Mrs. Davis and her children support the evidence that mother-son coalitions are not permitted to form.

When the boys were with their father, the same pattern was evident. Neither boy coalesces with their father against the other, nor does the father join together with one boy against the other. Even though Mr. Davis identifies more with Stephen, it does not translate into coalitionary interactions.

Stephen and Paul are very attached to and integrally involved with each other. They are together mornings, after school, evenings, and weekends, often without their mother or father present. Frequently, when they are given a choice to do otherwise, they choose to be together. They share certain rituals—watching Saturday morning cartoons, chore-switching, riding the bus to school together every day, playing certain games at certain times—and consider themselves both alike and different from each other. Theirs is a relationship characterized by a lot of play and a considerable amount of conflict. All family members agree that the boys generally resolve their own difficulties. To confirm these observations of their behavior, I asked the boys whether one of them ever called, "Mom!" in the middle of one of their fights. They both said no, and when I asked, "How come?" this dialogue ensued:

P: Too busy fighting.
S: Well, you figure you're gonna feel bad 'cause your mom's gonna come and yell and scream and . . .
P: . . . then you get in trouble.
S: . . . and in one way you get punished and it might be the other one, the other brother's fault.

And later, when Stephen was asked whether his mother might not be a better judge of "who was right or wrong," he replied, "Well, if she didn't *see* it, she wouldn't know." Clearly, the Davis brothers have developed skills which give them confidence that their clashes can be resolved through their own tacit rules and expectations.

In the Davis family, separate worlds exist between parents and children. Stephen and Paul share thoughts, feelings, and experiences which are not part of their combined or independent relationships with their mother or father. In addition, most of their arguments occur when their parents are not even present. On the other side of the generation gap stands both parents, who likewise sustain a life of their own independent of their children. Certainly, the fact that Mrs. Davis works full-time creates a structural boundary. Further, she does not discuss "adult" concerns with her sons, neither job-related problems nor her continued feelings of anger toward their father.

The Davis brothers have managed to sustain a relationship which has been a stabilizing influence for each of them throughout a difficult time. The development of this solidarity seems to be integrally related to the absence of parent-child coalitions both before and after the parent's separation, and parental encouragement of their children's sibling relationship.

CLINICAL IMPLICATIONS

Given the limited amount of research on sibling relationships, it would be premature to design a set of reliable clinical interventions that would be successful in different family contexts. What has been presented is a sense of the importance of sibling relationships, rather than a prescription for therapy. Nevertheless, it is possible to give some preliminary indications of how we might go about assessing the role of siblings in families of divorce, and some examples of appropriate interventions.

While the adjustment of separated parents is integrally related to the adjustment of their children, the therapist's first obligation is to assess how the children are surviving the separation. Naturally, children have the most to lose and the least control over their environment. Yet, intervening at the level of the child necessitates the involvement of other family members.

It is important to keep in mind that the goal of therapy with families of divorce is to assess how children and parents are functioning and to help facilitate changes which are needed for healthy adjustment. Here, the paradigm for change is change, and not insight: it is assumed that it is better for children to find ways to play together than to understand why they don't.

Sibling Sessions

One important way of assessing how well children are adjusting individually and as siblings is to arrange for a session or part of a session where siblings are seen without their parents present. In this session, the therapist can explore different dimensions of their relationship and their perceptions of the way that their parents are involved in that relationship. Areas to be explored may include conflict, ritual, play and the children's verbally expressed reactions to the separation. Techniques for gathering information must be created on the basis of the therapist's clinical judgement of the parents' and children's comfort with the situation. For example, in his sessions with adolescent siblings of divorce, Abelsohn (1983) directly questioned the siblings about how they and their parents were adjusting to the separation. In my study of younger school-age children, the siblings were also questioned directly about family matters, but in order to understand the situation further, they were asked to engage in a videotaped building block task so that they might be observed as they interact in less verbal ways.

Techniques must correspond with desired goals. For instance, in the building block task, children were asked to make something "tall, strong and beautiful"[4] in a limited amount of time. The contradictory descriptions of "tall" and "strong" created a slightly tense situation, resulting in mild disagreements between the children. The form these disagreements took and the ways the children resolved them were useful in the process of assessing how the children handled conflict between them. Later, the children were told my perceptions of how they handled the situation and asked whether it was "typical of how things went at home?" Each sibling pair confirmed my observations of their interactions.

In addition to assessing sibling conflict, it is important to explore the ritual world of siblings. For young children this presents certain difficulties, since direct questioning often does not elicit the relevant information. One can approach the issue indirectly, however, by asking the children to describe a typical Saturday, or after-school period. In other words, the therapist can discover along with the children whether they engage in some activities regularly. Parents can also be helpful in this area since they often have opportunities to observe and support their children's ritualized activities.

Siblings, young and old, can usually express what they enjoy doing together. In addition, their forms of play can be observed in the session: the therapist might use games or humor, or leave the session and video-tape the children's spontaneous interactions. In such circumstances, the absence of any form of play, as with the Roslyck siblings, is immediately noticeable. Observations of their interactions can be discussed later with the siblings and their parents.

Family Sessions

Families of divorce become two families and therapy sessions should, for the most part, reflect this reality. Therefore, assessing structural characteristics may occur by meeting with the mother and the children separately from the father and the children. In each case, the therapist can explore whether parent-child coalitions exist and, if so, how stable they are. In addition, the therapist can also observe how the parents' presence affects siblings interaction.

In cases where stable parent-child coalitions exist, the therapist can intervene through "unbalancing," a structural family therapy technique with demonstrated usefulness (Minuchin & Fishman, 1981). Briefly, unbalancing refers to a process of undermining a pattern of interaction which is considered to be dysfunctional for the family. Two obvious means of achieving this goal are by strengthening the relationship between the parent and the non-coalitionary child and actively blocking coalitionary interactions in session. For example, in the Roslyck family, the therapist might help find ways for Mrs. Roslyck to do a joint project with her daughter, and for Mr. Roslyck to do the same with his son. Or, the therapist might actively block parent-child coalitions in sessions.

Therapists can also assist parents in supporting their children's sibling world. In the Davis family, for example, it would be important to reinforce the ways that Mrs. Davis manages to provide her children certain distance from her own adult world. Or, Mrs. Roslyck could be encouraged to facilitate family activities, which might begin the long process of closing the gap between her children. It would be equally important to assist the Belfield and Roslyck siblings in finding ways to resolve conflict between them, while encouraging their parents to avoid becoming involved themselves. For the Roslycks, such an intervention would first require that Mrs. Roslyck ensure the children's protection, since the sibling conflict has reached dangerous proportions. Therapists can also help facilitate recognition of the natural sibling hierarchy created by birth order (except in the case of twins) and, similarly, support age-appropriate care-giving between the children.

CONCLUSION

The period following the separation of a couple is a time of crises and transition. As a result, adults and children have needs which are different than at other times in the family's development. How well families are able to meet these special needs determines, at least in part, later ability to adjust well. Sibling relationships—an important dimension of family life in intact families and perhaps even more important in families of divorce—have been generally overlooked. While siblings cannot substitute for parents, they can provide for each other at least one safe and predictable world inside a family with notably altered features.

As a clinician working with families of divorce, it is important to consider the sibling relationship and how it might be helping or hurting the children as they try to adjust to their parent's separation. One key aspect is sibling solidarity—the nature and significance of the life that siblings share away from direct parental influence. Another key aspect of this relationship is family structure: do stable parent-child coalitions exist and, if so, in what ways are they affecting the ability of siblings to be a resource to each other during post-divorce adjustment? As a therapist, it is important to explore whether pre-divorce rituals between siblings have been sustained, whether children are able to play with each other, and if sibling conflict reaches dangerous proportions. Therapeutic interventions which directly attend to the sibling relationship are just beginning to be explored, and thus there is room for creative and thoughtful invention for family-oriented therapists. In light of the above cases and others like them, it is clear that the sibling relationship can threaten a child's recovery or temporarily sustain a stable and lively micro-culture during an unstable time.

NOTES

1. The majority of sibling studies have been concerned with birth order, where the underlying assumption is that birth order in and of itself has a significant effect on the individual. This body of research has been criticized for serious methodological and theoretical problems (Sutton-Smith & Rosenberg, 1970; Altus, 1966; Schooler, 1972; and Schvaneveldt & Ihinger, 1979).
2. The idea of "intragenerational dialogues" between siblings is attributed to David Abelsohn of the Families of Divorce Project.
3. All names have been changed to protect family member's anonymity.
4. The building block task was suggested to me by Steve Bank.

REFERENCES

Abramovitch, R., Carter, C., & Lando, B. Sibling interaction in the home. *Child Development*, 1979, *50*, 997-1003.

Abelsohn, D. Dealing with the abdication dynamic in the postdivorce family: A context for adolescent crisis. *Family Process*, 1983, *22*, 359-384.

Adams, V. The sibling bond: A lifelong love/hate dialectic. *Psychology Today*, June, 1981, 32-47.

Altus, W. Birth order and its sequelae. *Science*, 1966, *151*, 44-49.

Bank, S. Hansels and Gretels: A study of extremely loyal sibling groups. Presented at American Psychological Association, APA Symposium: *Life span perspectives on sibling socialization*, New York, Sept. 1, 1979, Chaired by Brian Sutton-Smith.

Bank, S., & Kahn, M. *The sibling bond.* New York: Basic Books, 1982.

Bell, R., & Harper, L. *Child effects on adults.* Lincoln, Nebraska: Univ. of Nebraska Press, 1980.

Bowerman, C. & Dobash, R. Structural variations in inter-sibling affect. *Journal of Marriage and the Family*, 1974, *36*, 48-54.

Bryant, B. & Crockenberg, S. Correlates and dimensions of prosocial behavior: A study of female siblings with their mothers. *Child Development*, 1980, *51*, 529-544.

Bryant, B. Sibling relationships in middle childhood. In M. Lamb and B. Sutton-Smith (Eds.) *Sibling relationships: Their nature and significance across the life span.* (Chapter 5), Hillsdale, N.J.: Erlbaum, 1982.

Caplow, T. *Two against one: Coalitions in triads.* N.J.: Prentice-Hall, 1968.

Cicirelli, V. The effect of sibling relationships on concept learning of young children taught by child teachers. *Child Development*, 1972, *43*, 282-287.

Cicirelli, V. Sibling influence across the lifespan. In M. Lamb and B. Sutton-Smith (Eds.) *Sibling relationships: Their nature and significance across the lifespan.* N.J.: Erlbaum, 1982.

Coleman, S. Siblings in session. In E. Kaufman & P. Kaufman (Eds.) *The family therapy of drug and alcohol abusers.* N.Y.: Gardner Press, 1978.

Coleman, S. Sib group therapy: A prevention program for siblings from drug-addicted families. *The International Journal of Addictions,* 1978, *13,* (1), 115-127.

Dunn, J., & Kendrick, C. *Siblings.* Cambridge, Mass.: Harvard Univ. Press, 1982.

Eno, M. Four families of divorce: Case studies of sibling and peer relationships. Doctoral dissertation, Univ. of Pennsylvania, 1983.

Furman, W., & Buhrmester, D. The contribution of siblings and peers to the parenting process. In M. Kostelink (Ed.), *Patterns of supplementary parenting, 2,* N.Y.: Plenum Press, 1980.

Hartup, W. The social worlds of childhood. *American Psychologist,* 1979, *34,* (10), 944-950.

Hetherington, M., Cox, M. & Cox, R. The aftermath of divorce. In J. Stevens & M. Matthews (Eds.), *Mother-child, father-child relations,* Washington, D.C., NAEYC, 1977.

Hetherington, M., Cox, M. & Cox, R. Play and social interaction in children following divorce. *Journal of Social Issues, 35*(4), 1979.

Hetherington, M. Divorce: A child's perspective. *American Psychologist,* 1979, *35*(10), 851-858.

Isaacs, M. Treatment for families of divorce: A systems model of prevention. In I. Stuart and L. Abt. (Eds.) *Children of separation and divorce: Management and treatment,* N.Y.: Van Nostrand Reinhold, 1981.

Isaacs, M. Children's long term adjustment to divorce. Paper presented at the American Orthopsychiatric Association Annual Meeting, Toronto, April, 1984.

Lamb, M. & Sutton-Smith, B. *Sibling relationships: Their nature and significance across the lifespan,* N.J.: Erlbaum, 1982.

McDermott, J. Parental Divorce in early childhood. *American Journal of Psychiatry,* 1968, *124,* 1424-1432.

Minuchin, S. *Families and family therapy.* Cambridge, Mass.: Harvard Univ. Press, 1974.

Minuchin, S., & Fishman, C. *Family therapy techniques,* Cambridge, Mass: Harvard Uni. Press, 1981.

Rosenberg, E. Therapy with siblings in reorganizing families. *International Journal of Family Therapy,* 1980, *3,* (2), 155-158.

Schachter, F. Sibling deidentification and split-parent identification: A family tetrad. In M. Lamb & B. Sutton-Smith (Eds.), *Sibling relationships: Their nature and significance across the lifespan,* N.J.: Erlbaum, 1982.

Schooler, C. Birth order effects: Not here, not now! *Psychological Bulletin,* 1972, *78,* (3), 161-175.

Schvaneveldt, J. & Ihinger, M. Sibling relationships in the family. In W. Burr, R. Hill, F. Nye & I. Reiss (Eds.), *Contemporary theories about the family,* N.Y.: Free Press, 1979.

Sells, S., & Roff, M. Peer acceptance-rejection and birth order. *Psychology and the schools,* 1964, *1,* 156-162.

Sutton-Smith, B., & Rosenberg, B. *The sibling.* N.Y.: Holt, Rinehart & Winston, 1979.

Wallerstein, J., & Kelly, J. *Surviving the breakup,* N.Y.: Basic Books, 1980.

Weisner, T., & Gallimore, R. My brother's keeper: Child and sibling caretaking. *Current Anthropology,* 1977, *18,* (2), 169-189.

Wood, B. & Talmon, M. Family boundaries in transition: A search for alternatives. *Family Process,* 1983, *22,* 347-357.

Youniss, J. *Parents and peers in social development.* Chicago: Univ. of Chicago Press, 1980.

COMPREHENSIVE VIEWS OF THE FIELD

The Comprehensive Divorce Treatment Center: The Divorce and Marital Stress Clinic Model

Emily M. Brown

ABSTRACT. The comprehensive divorce treatment center provides a constellation of services to people who are encountering problems in maintaining and/or ending their marriage. Clients are at different points along the marriage-divorce-remarriage continuum when they first come to the center, but typically are highly dissatisfied with their present situation, whether that be their marriage or the aftermath of their separation or divorce. The center's goal is to help clients resolve the immediate crisis, and to assist them in recognizing and changing problematic behavior patterns. Services offered include short and long term counseling and therapy, educational programs, and divorce mediation.

The case has been made for services for the divorcing, and numerous mental health and family agencies have incorporated such services into their offerings. A somewhat unique approach is the center providing comprehensive services for the divorcing family.

It might be asked why there is a need for a divorce center, given all the marriage counseling centers throughout the United States. Historically, the marriage centers wanted no part of divorce. Success meant keeping couples together, not helping them end their marriage. Those who saw a need for divorce counseling and tried to interest the established marriage and family agencies received a chilly response until very recently. Therefore, as with many new ideas, the innovative work in developing divorce services was done outside the mainstream, usually in small private organizations which focused on one or more aspects of divorce. Some retain a narrow focus, for example providing services only to children of divorce. Others address issues all along the continuum of marriage/divorce/remarriage. Many of the traditional agencies have modeled their services for the divorcing after these programs.

This article will describe a comprehensive divorce treatment center,

---

Emily M. Brown, A.C.S.W., L.C.S.W., is Director of the Divorce and Marital Stress Clinic, 1925 N. Lynn, Suite 900, Arlington, VA 22209.

© 1985 by The Haworth Press, Inc. All rights reserved.

and discuss its philosophy, its clientele, and its services. It is based on many years of experience in developing programs and offering services to divorcing families at the Divorce and Marital Stress Clinic in the Washington, D.C., area, and providing consultation to and networking with other divorce centers.

GOALS AND PHILOSOPHY

The concept of a comprehensive divorce treatment center is based on several principles:

1. Divorce is a complex process which affects all family members, and thus a variety of services are needed.
2. Mental health, family systems, and conflict resolution techniques are the tools of choice.
3. A comprehensive approach facilitates resolution of emotional issues and minimizes dysfunctional behavior and the use of adversarial tactics.
4. Marriage and divorce are points on a continuum (not discrete entities) and any divorce-related program needs to allow for movement in any direction along the continuum.
5. Coordination with the legal system and with other professionals is an essential element.
6. Marital problems are often the "tip of the iceberg" and issues such as depression, phobic behavior, and addictions must be addressed.

The process of divorce is lengthy and complex. The spouse initiating the split usually takes from one to two years to arrive at the decision to separate. After separation it takes about a year for either spouse to gain any sort of stability, and a minimum of another year to resolve the attendant long-term issues. If the marriage has been a lengthy one it takes longer, as it does for those whose resources, skills, or coping abilities are lesser. Children meanwhile are affected by the stresses between their parents and by the changes in the family and they in turn react to the situation. For many children it takes about a year to get back on track after parents separate (Wallerstein and Kelly, 1980, p. 308). Some adults and some children never recover from the trauma of divorce. It should be noted here that this is not attributable to divorce alone, but divorce is merely one in a series of negative events from which the individual has insufficient resources (personal and otherwise) to recover.

CLIENTELE AND PRESENTING PROBLEMS

The comprehensive divorce center serves people who are encountering problems in maintaining and/or ending their marriage (or primary) relationship. They can be viewed as ranging along a broad continuum, from those who want help in resolving the problems in a first marriage to those who are experiencing problems years after a divorce or in a subsequent marriage or divorce. The common issues are intimacy, power, and loss. The continuum is shown in Figure 1. Not everyone who divorces is distressed enough to seek help. Many do however—one study found that almost three-fourths of the women and more than a third of the men in the sample were in therapy at some point during the divorce process (Luepnitz 1982, p. 128, 142).

The divorce treatment center must be a marriage center as well. Couples considering divorce or even already separated need the option of working on the marriage if they so choose. Marriage and divorce are not opposites, but are points along the same continuum. Remarriage is another point along the continuum, and clients who have divorced often return for help in preparing for and handling the problems that come with blending families. To adequately serve families who are considering or in the process of divorce the center's services must address all points along the continuum. Clients can and do move in either direction along the continuum as well as repeat the cycle. Clients present themselves in various ways: individually, as couples, in regard to a child, or sometimes as a family. The initial visit may be at any point along the continuum. The services needed vary depending on the presenting problem, and on which family members have come for help.

Couples who choose to come to a divorce center to work on marital problems generally have fairly serious issues and at least one spouse has considered the possibility of divorce. Resolution of the marital issues however, still appears to the couple to be a possibility. Individuals who request help in resolving marital problems at this point are giving a slightly different message: there are secrets (usually an affair) the person wants to talk about before engaging in marital work, or the individual wants seriously to consider divorce and wants to do so alone.

When the first contact with the couple comes about as a result of a decision to separate, the request is likely to be for practical help (information, mediation), or the partner who is leaving is covertly saying to the clinician "I'm leaving, here's my spouse, you take care of her (or him)". Individuals presenting at this point are either the initiator who wants help

Figure 1: MARRIAGE-DIVORCE-REMARRIAGE CONTINUUM

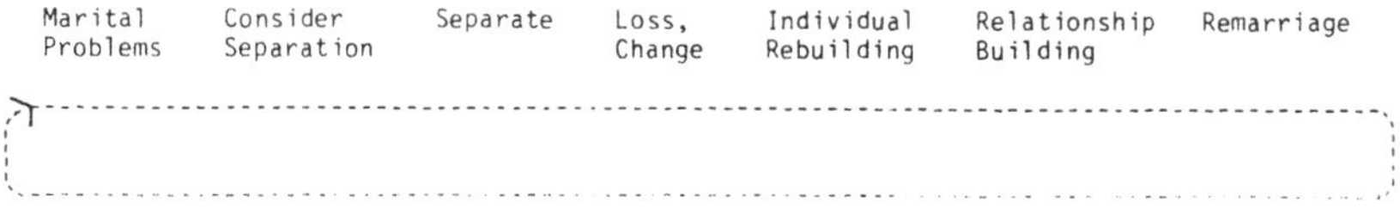

with guilt, with practicalities, or with "making sure my head is on straight", or the non-initiator who wants to prevent the separation or who is emotionally distraught.

In the first few months after separation, it is the non-initiator who is likely to seek help. The issues revolve around loss of grief, and depression is a common and serious problem. During the same period, couples who have separated and want to consider reconciliation may initiate marital therapy. Later in the process, initiators again seek help after having managed very nicely for awhile. The catalyst is an inability to function as desired, particularly with regard to relationships, which the individual attributes to unfinished elements of the divorce. Figure 2 shows the steps in the emotional process of divorce for the initiator and the non-initiator.

Children are always distressed when parents separate, but often go to great lengths to protect their parents from awareness of their feelings. Parents, who may be preoccupied with their own issues, are only too glad to see the children behaving well. In other cases acting out behavior is obvious but viewed as temporary. Thus children's issues tend not to be the presenting problem until months or even years after the separation. Luepnitz' study (1982) provides further evidence of this pattern. Even though a majority of parents (probably middle class) used therapy at some time during the divorce process, only a fraction brought their children in for therapy (p. 128-129, 142).

Divorced people who are beyond the rebound period (the first two to three years after the separation) tend to be somewhat cautious about remarriage. Former clients often come back when planning to remarry, and others seek help for the first time to prepare for remarriage. Remarrieds also come for help when they run into difficulties in the new marriage, usually in regard to children, or when problem patterns from the first marriage crop up in the new marriage.

For many people, the issues of divorce are the tip of the iceberg. Behavior patterns developed in response to events of the distant past contribute to the demise of the marriage. Although withdrawing from intimacy, or inhibiting one's anger may be intended to lessen or prevent future losses, these strategies serve as a self-fulfilling prophecy. To resolve the issues of marriage and/or divorce, the meaning of these behaviors must be understood and the patterns changed.

SERVICES

Three types of services are needed by those struggling with relationship problems and with loss: information, practical guidance, and therapeutic help. Comprehensive divorce treatment centers usually provide all three, typically offering educational programs, divorce mediation, and counseling and therapy. Clients can choose to use a single service or any combination of services in any order.

While counseling and therapy are the heart of the program, information and assistance with the immediate situation often come first. Educational programs are used to provide clients with data about legal and economic aspects of divorce, a description of the emotional process, information about various relationship issues, and referrals to appropriate resources.

Figure 2: Steps in the Emotional Process of Divorce

Initiator		Non-Initiator
Deny problems/possibility of split Consider possibility of separation Anger and blame Loss, grief, helplessness Guilt failure Detachment Decision	Decision-Making Phase	Deny problems/possibility of split
Separation	End of Marriage	Separation
Cope with massive change in living patterns Develop new social relationships Explore new opportunities and challenges Understand marital breakdown, including own contribution Accept responsibility for own actions Reassess values and needs Set long-term goals Develop autonomy	Marriage Still Primary Referenece Point Marriage Not Primary Reference Point Restructuring Phase	Acknowledge fact of separation Anger and Blame Loss, grief and helplessness Guilt and failure Manage day-to-day activities Implement small decisions Develop new social relationships Accept separation/divorce Explore new opportunities and challenges Understand marital breakdown including own contribution Accept responsibility for own actions Reassess values and needs Set long-term goals Develop autonomy

Copyright © 1976 Emily M. Brown

Generally these are evening seminars with a limited attendance. The "Legal and Economic. . ." seminar is the most popular one at the Divorce and Marital Stress Clinic and is attended by those on the brink of separation. It is unique in that the participants do not want to share their personal situation. The next most popular seminar is "Meeting People", where the participants have been separated for some time and are eager to share. In addition to providing valuable information, seminars can also be used by the staff to test out ideas about client needs, and to develop visibility in the community.

Divorce mediation is a relatively new service, first pioneered in the early 70s (Coogler, 1978; Haynes, 1981). It is a process for making decisions about the "business of marriage", and uses techniques drawn from the field of conflict resolution, law, and therapy. Some mediation models deal only with parenting arrangements, but others address all the issues which must be resolved when couples separate. Mediation is a short process, taking from eight to fifteen hours over the course of a few days or a few months. With the development of mediation training programs, mediation has spread rapidly throughout the country. Existing divorce centers have been eager to add mediation to their program, and mediation has been the catalyst for the development of new divorce centers. The mediators in a mental health setting are often therapists, but mediation and therapy are typically set up as separate processes. At our Center neither the mediator nor the therapist functions in the other role with the same couple.

It is only with great effort that individuals and couples extricate themselves from unsatisfying or destructive behavior patterns. To do so usually requires therapy, which is the primary service of many divorce treatment centers. The basic modalities are: (1) crisis intervention and long term treatment for both individuals and couples, (2) group therapy which is often the treatment of choice for separated and divorced individuals who are struggling with grief or examining their own difficulties with relationships, (3) individual and group treatment for children, and (4) family therapy for married, remarried, and single parent families.

Divorcing clients tend to be of two types: those who want help with the crisis and those who also want to resolve the underlying issues. Crisis oriented services may last a few weeks to a few months. Those who choose to take an in-depth look at what has happened continue in treatment for one or more years, the length depending on factors such as age, length of the marriage, degree of dysfunction, motivation, and the rate of movement. Some individuals deal only with the crisis initially, and come back later to resolve other issues. Almost twice as many women as men seek therapy to deal with the issues of divorce. However men who do come in are more likely than women to continue past the crisis to examine the underlying issues. Whether this is because women have less money, or because it takes longer for men to overcome their early socialization, or for other reasons is not known.

Typical divorce center cases include the following:

> A 35 year old mother of 3 who had left her abusive husband. The initial focus of individual sessions was on protecting herself, obtaining legal help, dealing with guilt, and parenting. As she began to face her depression, group therapy was added. Next, the 10 year old daughter, a parental child, was seen by another therapist on the staff for a short period. Therapy terminated when the mother was functioning appropriately with her children, at work, and socially, and when she was no longer depressed. A year later her ex-husband committed suicide and she returned briefly for guidance in regard to her children. Several years later she came back again for counseling prior to remarriage.
>
> A 31 year old father who had become phobic after his wife had left him. He was seen with his wife, first to explore whether the marriage might be continued, and then to obtain closure. He was also seen individually. After it was clear the marriage was ending he began group therapy. Brief family therapy was used to interrupt family patterns that supported the phobic behavior.
>
> A 52 year old woman whose husband had left her for another woman shortly after the last child left home. Group therapy was used to help her develop self-esteem and assertive behavior.
>
> A 25 year old single parent whose depression was interfering with her limited parenting skills. She was seen individually at first, and then with her two year old daughter in sessions devoted to the development of parenting skills.
>
> A couple in their early 40s with two adolescent daughters, who were on the verge of separation. They were seen briefly as a couple to address emotional aspects of separation. They also used mediation to work out the terms of their separation agreement. After the separation the wife continued to come in to explore parenting issues and to change her pattern of impulsive behavior.
>
> A 37 year old father with custody who was in the midst of his second contested divorce, and was depressed. Individual therapy and later, group therapy were used to help him learn to get in touch with his feelings and to express them appropriately. Guidance on working within the legal system was also provided.

Short term divorce groups (six to eight sessions) have been popular in recent years. They appeal to a population which is largely committed to a "do-it-yourself" approach, but which is often "brittle" and more in need of help than those voluntarily choosing therapy. While these groups are useful in providing information and support, and in encouraging participants to consider using help in the future, by themselves they do not address the underlying issues in any meaningful way. A more useful approach is to offer ongoing therapy groups and a series of educational seminars for the separated and divorced.

Divorce groups which are limited to women only or to men only miss the mark. It becomes too easy to blame the opposite sex and avoid the painful work of self examination. Both marriage and divorce have to do with male and female issues, and it helps in the sorting out to be able to talk honestly to people of both sexes.

It is important that the divorce treatment center not become a social center. One of the tasks facing the divorced is to reestablish themselves in the world as individuals. The role of the divorce center is to help clients move in that direction, not to become a substitute for the real world.

A few centers have chosen to focus exclusively on children of divorce and their needs. These centers provide individual and group counseling for children, and often family therapy. Adult services are limited to those who will enhance parental functioning. Depending on how this is interpreted, mediation services and therapy for the parents may or may not be offered. The Children's Divorce Center in Woodbridge, Conn. makes a broad interpretation and is in fact a comprehensive divorce treatment center, though with a clear emphasis on children.

STAFFING

The staff of divorce treatment centers are mental health professionals from the fields of social work, marriage and family therapy, and psychology, with an occasional psychiatrist. Staff must have the ability to work with and weave together the individual and the relationship aspects of the issues presented. In addition to being competent clinicians they need to be knowledgeable about the emotional and the legal aspects of separation and divorce. They must be empathetic and respectful of people who are divorcing. They must be clear that their role is not to save marriages but to help all family members resolve their situation in as optimal a manner as possible. On occasion this means saving marriages, but often it does not, and whether or not the marriage is saved is not the therapist's decision.

Whether the therapist has been married or divorced is relatively unimportant. It is important that the therapist have some life experience. Individuals who have gone from high school to college to grad school need some seasoning before they work in this type of setting. If the therapist is divorced it is important that his or her own unfinished issues be kept separate from the client's issues. Those professionals who have an attitude of "Oh, you poor dears," toward children of divorce and a condescending attitude toward the parents do not belong on the staff of a divorce center.

When there are questions about medication or hospitalization, consultation with a psychiatrist is indicated. Most divorce centers have an arrangement with a psychiatrist to provide these services and to consult on cases, particularly the more difficult ones involving matters such as severe depression, suicide threats, addiction, and out of control behavior. Consultation may also be appropriate with the physicians of clients who have chronic physical problems such as epilepsy.

Since most divorce treatment centers are small organizations, staff members often perform more than one function. Therapy is the primary function but the clinician may also give educational seminars, or provide mediation. Special training is required for those doing mediation (Academy of Family Mediations). The small size of divorce centers facilitates both flexibility and innovation. Creative ideas for seminars, for professional training, and for clinical services for a particular population can be tested with a minimum of bureaucratic detail.

Full-time staff is often augmented by part-timers who work in the evening. This arrangement maximizes the clinical hours available in the evening, a desirable situation since after-work appointments are preferred by most clients. Single parents especially find it difficult, if not impossible, to schedule appointments during the work day.

FUNDING

Divorce treatment centers are located in the private sector and may be either profit or non-profit. If non-profit, a significant amount of time has to be devoted to raising funds, and the program has to be research oriented or flashy (new and different, and preferably for children) to attract funds. In addition to funding from grants, fees are charged for services.

The funding of for-profit divorce centers comes entirely from fees for services. Even so many of these centers use a sliding fee or some form of discount for clients who are financially strapped. In terms of fees charged to the public, there seems to be little difference between the for-profit and non-profit organizations.

Some divorce center clients have health or other third party insurance which partially covers the cost of therapy. Fees for educational seminars and mediation services, however, are not reimbursable.

During economic hard times, many families put off non-essential purchases. This includes counseling and therapy. Thus at the time economic pressures are added to other family problems, help is least available. Female-headed families, who comprise a significant part of a divorce center's clientele, are particularly vulnerable to economic pressures (Weitzman, 1975). When the economy improves, counseling is again considered for family problems, but the delay is likely to have caused further deterioration in the situation. The effects of recession are passed on to divorce centers in the form of declining income from fees, and slower payments. In addition, grant funds dry up. Divorce centers need to be prepared to trim their costs during periods of recession in order to survive.

RELATIONSHIP WITH THE COMMUNITY

As with all organizations, divorce centers must network with a variety of community members and organizations. These contacts enable the center to obtain or make referrals, and to gain or give access to information. The kinds of contacts important in obtaining referrals include churches, schools, hotlines, employee assistance programs, physicians, and other mental health practitioners. The most commonly made referrals are to lawyers, alcohol programs including Alcoholics Anonymous, career counseling, and singles organizations. Case consultations between professionals are common. Speaking engagements in the community provide an opportunity to gain visibility as well as offer expertise.

The relationship with the legal system is somewhat unique within the mental health profession. Divorce center staff must be knowledgeable about the legal aspects of separation and divorce. To this end staff tend to have frequent contact with domestic relations attorneys, consulting with them about clients, or about developments and issues in either field. Knowledge about the legal aspects of separation and divorce enables the clinician to help clients use the legal process appropriately, and to avoid negative legal consequences. For example, it may be therapeutically advisable for a woman to leave her husband, but she may in some states lose her right to alimony if she does. The therapist can alert the woman so that she gets the information she needs to make an informed decision before she acts. Divorce center staff are also knowledgeable about who the good attorneys are, and make referrals to those who promote conflict resolution, not conflict.

Interdisciplinary efforts in continuing education between lawyers and therapists have been initiated by several of the divorce centers. This has become more frequent with the advent of mediation. It's still true, however, that divorce centers refer more often to lawyers than vice versa, as lawyers tend to view psychiatrists as the preferred mental health practitioners. Divorce centers have a lot of education yet to do in this area.

ISSUES AND PROBLEMS

Finding an appropriate name presents a problem for divorce centers. The word divorce needs to be included to give an accurate picture, but has negative connotations for some people who, hoping to prevent divorce, shy away from such an organization. Others think that a divorce center provides only crisis intervention or mediation services. Organizations whose names reflect their focus on children fare a bit better.

Divorce centers are frequently confronted with questions about their effectiveness: i.e., how many marriages are saved. This is an inappropriate measure for many clients. More appropriate measures might be whether the behavior that was problematic has changed for the better, whether the children resume appropriate functioning, whether the depression ends, and whether the parents work out a cooperative relationship. Using these criteria, divorce centers are effective in helping many of their clients. In addition, they do help some couples save their marriage. Not all clients, however, want help in making changes. Some just want to feel better for the moment and they have the right to make that choice. The clinician, however, can help them be clear about the choice they're making.

SUMMARY

The concept of the divorce treatment center has to do with meeting the particular needs of the separating and divorcing, while at the same time facilitating movement along the marriage-divorce continuum—either toward a viable reconciliation or toward completion of the process of divorce (Brown, 1976). A variety of services and the opportunity to be flexible in combining them are hallmarks of the divorce treatment center.

Luepnitz points out that while divorce is painful and can be debilitating, "It can also be corrective, leading to higher levels of functioning" (1982, p. 154). This is the challenge for the divorce treatment center.

REFERENCES

Academy of Family Mediators Newsletter.

Brown, E.M. A Model of the Divorce Process, in Conciliation Courts Review. 1976, 14(2), p. 1-11.

Coogler, O.J. 1978. Structured Mediation in Divorce Settlement: A Handbook for Marital Mediators. Lexington, Mass.: D.C. Heath and Co.

Haynes, J. 1981. Divorce Mediation: A Practical Guide for Therapists and Counselors. New York: Springer.

Luepnitz, D. 1982. Child Custody: A Study of Families after Divorce. Lexington, Mass.: D.C. Heath and Co.

Wallerstein, J., and Kelly, J. 1980. Surviving the Breakup. New York: Basic Books.

Weitzman, Lenore J. The Marriage Contract: Spouses, Lovers and the Law. 1975. New York: Basic Books.

Divorce and Divorce Therapy: An Annotated Bibliography

Roslyn Garden Cantrell

Divorce became a national concern in the 1970s. Reasons for this concern are due to the divorce rate and the personal difficulties encountered by those going through the divorce process. Because of this, it is the rare therapist who does not come into contact with clients who are or will be affected by the divorce process in some way or form.

In this bibliography you will find what I consider to be the key works on the topic of divorce and divorce therapy. It is by no means an exhaustive list. However, included here are those works which have made their contribution to the divorce literature by adding to what already is known. Each adds in its own unique way.

The bibliography is written for any professional who is interested in learning about the more up-to-date information on divorce and divorce therapy. The materials have been divided into 11 categories to help interested readers find those works which will be most helpful to them. The sections are: Adjustment for the Divorcee; Children's Books; Custody; Extended Family; Mediation; Parenting and Children; Postdivorce Families; Schools; Theory, Therapy, and Research; Women's Issues; and Workshops.

ADJUSTMENT FOR THE DIVORCEE

Adam, John, & Adam, Nancy. (1979). *Divorce: How and when to let go.* Englewood Cliffs, NJ: Prentice-Hall, 227 pp.

Here is a behaviorally-oriented book which goes through the steps of divorce. The book is divided into three sections: Making the Decision, Carrying Through, and Afterward. In the first part, the authors give a good cognitive argument for not equating divorce to failure. They go through questions to ask oneself and activities to do in order to find out if an individual should divorce. Part II includes telling friends and relatives, helping your children, and legal and financial problems one will need to deal with. The last section discusses handling feelings; dealing with new roles, such as social life and single parenting; and working on personal growth.

Fisher, B. (1981). *Rebuilding: When your relationship ends.* San Luis Obispo, CA: Impact Publishers, 204 pp.

This is an excellent handbook for those going through the divorce process. Using the metaphor of climbing a mountain, Fisher divides the process into 16 rebuilding blocks. This most readable book normalizes what divorcees go through and gives suggestions of how to deal with each rebuilding block. Examples from those who have gone through his seminars are scattered throughout the book. At the end of each chapter is a list of statements for the reader to help see where along the journey one is.

Roslyn Garden Cantrell, M.S., is a family therapist at Parental Stress, Lafayette, IN, and a doctoral candidate in Marriage and Family Therapy in the Department of Child Development and Family Studies, Purdue University, W. Lafayette, IN 47907.

© 1985 by The Haworth Press, Inc. All rights reserved.

Gettleman, S., & Markowitz, J. (1974). *The courage to divorce*. New York: Ballantine Books, 267 pp.

The authors offer divorce as an alternative to a bad marriage. They profess that marriage is only one of many satisfying and normal options available in life. The main contribution of this book lies in its intent to view divorce in a positive way. They believe that society and our perceptions have caused all the anti-divorce literature. An excellent job has been done to show that divorce can be a healthy, constructive, fulfilling beginning for both parents and children.

Johnson, S. M. (1977). *First person singular.* New York: J. B. Lippincott, 367 pp.

This is an excellent book for the divorced individual. Using a rational-emotive approach, the book is divided into three parts. The first part deals with the difficulties of separating from a relationship. Part II is about living as a single person. This section includes an excellent chapter differentiating between being alone and being lonely. The author gives clear descriptions of how to deal with loneliness. The last section deals with different stages involved in developing meaningful relationships with the opposite sex in primary relationships. The author is not against marriage, but does a good job of giving credence to the single life as an acceptable life-style.

Krantzler, M. (1974). *Creative divorce*. New York: Signet, 240 pp.

Using his own experience and those of divorcees going through his seminars, Krantzler describes the steps one goes through when divorced. He defines divorce as a new beginning in which one can learn to use his/her untapped resources. Krantzler includes in the book nine emotional traps faced by divorcees and how to deal with each one. This is a good book for people right after the physical separation.

Smoke, J. (1976). *Growing through divorce*. Irving, CA: Harvest House, 143 pp.

For those wanting a Christian perspective, *Growing through Divorce* answers the bill. This is a helpful book for those adjusting to divorce. The main focus is whether an individual wants to just go through a divorce or is willing to grow through one. Each chapter ends with personal growth and discussion questions. Areas covered include letting go, assuming responsibility, finding a "family," new relationships, and remarriage. Personal growth experiences from members of a Christian singles group make up two of the chapters. A list of resources is at the end of the book.

Weiss, R. S. (1975). *Marital separation.* New York: Basic Books, 334 pp.

Here is a book for both one going through a divorce and the professional. Weiss describes the process of divorce and separation. He includes many accounts of those who are in the process to give the flavor of what it is like. Areas covered in the book are: why separation takes place, the emotional impact of separation, various aspects of relationships between the separating spouses and with friends and relatives of each, difficulties that are likely to come up with children, and establishing a new life. Weiss does a good job of explaining and demonstrating the attachment felt between separating spouses.

CHILDREN'S BOOKS

Gardner, R. A. (1971). *The boys and girls book about divorce*. New York: Bantam Books, 159 pp.
Gardner, R. A. (1978). *The boys and girls book about one-parent families*. New York: Bantam Books, 122 pp.

Gardner, R. A. (1982). *The boys and girls book about stepfamilies*. New York: Bantam Books, 180 pp.

Each book is written for both children and parents to read. They are written at the 3rd- to 4th-grade reading level, although younger children can understand as parents read. Each book includes an introduction for parents and one for children. An excellent description of each situation is told, including feelings that a child may expect and suggestions of how to deal with individual situations. It is highly recommended for parents and children to discuss issues covered in the books.

Rofes, E. (Ed.). (1982). *The kids' book of divorce: By, for & about kids*. New York: Vintage Books, 122 pp.

Addressing the subject of divorce from the child's point of view, here is a book written by twenty 11- to 14-year-olds who have either experienced divorce personally or through a friend or relative. They interviewed professionals and, also, used personal experience in writing the book. They explain what happens during the divorce process and give many suggestions on how to deal with divorce. Some topics included are: how parents should tell kids, legal issues, counseling, weekend Santa, stepparents, and gay parents. This book is appropriate for both parents and children.

CUSTODY

Committee on the Family Group for the Advancement of Psychiatry. (1980). *Divorce, child custody and the family* (Volume X, Publication No. 106). New York: Mental Health Materials Center.

This publication takes a family approach to child custody. A historical and legal background for custody decisions is first given. The chapter on the family approach to child custody determinations is excellent. Five, broad guidelines for custody decisions are given and examined. Different forms of divorce therapy are explored. They also discuss the role of the mental health professional in the litigation process. Finally, recommendations to the courts are given.

Folberg, J. (Ed.). (1984). *Joint custody and shared parenting*. Portland, OR: The Association of Family and Conciliations Courts, 350 pp.

Included in this book is a comprehensive, well-organized collection of articles dealing with joint custody. Although both views for and against shared parenting are presented, the editor's bias in favor of encouraging joint custody comes across clearly. The first section provides a historical perspective, definitions, different living arrangements, and a review of the literature. Chapters in the second part examine factors which may influence: (a) the decision to implement joint custody and (b) the success of shared parenting. Research findings are discussed in Part III, including what we know and what we have yet to learn. The last section deals with issues and trends in the law. Appendices include: (a) an excellent chart of state by state custody statutes and judicial interpretations and (b) a sample joint custody agreement with alternative provisions.

Galper, M. (1978). *Co-parenting: Sharing your child equally*. Philadelphia: Running Press, 158 pp.

Here is a source book for the separated and divorced family. To gather her material, Galper drew from her own experience and corresponded with and interviewed professionals and others who are successfully co-parenting. Topics coverd in the book include: a definition of co-parenting, how to actually do it, your relationship with your ex-spouse, and what the professionals say. Variations of handling different situations according to what is best for the individual family are stressed.

Howell, R. J., & Toepke, K. E. (1984). Summary of the child custody laws for the fifty states. *The American Journal of Family Therapy, 12*, 56-60.

The contribution of this article lies in its chart which summarizes the child custody laws for each state. The chart tells whether the following situations occur in each state: psychological investigation may be ordered by the court, neither parent preferred due to parent's sex, joint custody specifically allowed, non-custodial parent has access to child's records, similar relevant factors are used to determine custody, child's wishes considered by the court, parental conduct not affecting relationship with the child not considered, and grandparent visitation rights allowed.

Musetto, A. P. (1981). The role of the mental health professional in contested custody: Evaluation of competence or facilitator of change. *Journal of Divorce, 4*(4), 69-79.

Musetto presents two different roles for a therapist in contested custody cases. He examines the role of the evaluator of competence, which is based on individually-oriented concepts. After his critique of this role, he offers what he feels is a better one. The facilitator of change role, which comes from family therapy theory, is one in which the focus is on helping the family to change and resolve their issues in order for custody to be decided fairly. A case example is included.

Roman, M., & Haddad, W. (1978). *The disposable parent: The case for joint custody.* New York: Holt, Rinehart & Winston, 215 pp.

Written from the male point of view, Roman and Haddad argue their case for joint custody. They begin with a historical view of custody and continue in looking at the impact of divorce on the whole family. Backed up by research, they show how contact with the father, usually the non-custodial parent, is most important. To help their argument, they show how the role of the mother as a single parent is difficult. They demonstrate how parenting is a human, not a gender, trait. Roman and Haddad give excellent arguments for those objecting to joint custody. Examples of case studies are included. They realize that culturally induced attitudes are most difficult to change and give ideas on what can be done.

EXTENDED FAMILY

Fisher, E. O. (Ed.). (1982). *Impact of divorce on the extended family.* New York: The Haworth Press, 171 pp.

A forgotten area, the impact of divorce on the extended family, is explored in this collection of articles. Some of the topics examined include: the dynamics of relationships within the extended family after divorce and remarriage, the role of extended kin in the adjustment to divorce/separation, effects of those in the role of grandparents and parents of an adult son/daughter, visitation rights of grandparents, the beneficial impact of divorce on the extended family, and services and interventions for this population.

MEDIATION

The following books deal with divorce mediation. Each has a different way of dealing with the topic. All provide useful information.

Coogler, O. J. (1978). *Structured mediation in divorce settlement.* Lexington, MA: Lexington Books, 204 pp.

This is a handbook for marital mediators. Coogler provides definitions and clear directions for divorce mediation. Qualifications for mediators are also discussed. All forms used are included in the book.

Haynes, J. M. (1981). *Divorce mediation: A practical guide for therapists and counselors.* New York: Springer Publications, 193 pp.

Haynes combines some from the Coogler book and the Irving book. He believes that mediation involves both the role of therapist and that of mediator. Part I discusses the divorce process and how to deal with each stage as a mediator. The mediation process, itself, is covered in the second part. Analysis of nine mediation case studies is included in Part III. The last section looks at the implications for practice. Sample forms used are included at the end of the book.

Irving, H. H. (1980). *Divorce mediation: A rational alternative to the adversary system.* New York: Universe Books, 188 pp.

This book covers what divorce mediation is, how it came about, and uses case studies to show how it can be used. At the end of the book, Irving tells how a couple interested in mediation might proceed and where to go to find a mediator.

Saposnek, D. T. (1983). *Mediating child custody disputes*, San Francisco: Jossey-Bass, 326 pp.

Written from a systems perspective, this is a comprehensive guide for the professional who is wanting to mediate child custody disputes. Saposnek explains each step in the mediation process, with an excellent description of the beginning phase. Strategies used by children and parents that play into the custody dispute are discussed. The author describes interventions for eliciting cooperation and managing conflict. Both successful and unsuccessful case studies are given. Appendices include: California law on joint custody, mandatory mediation, and family conciliation courts; confidentiality forms; and sample mediation agreements.

Shapiro, J. J., & Caplan, M. S. (1983). *Parting sense: A couple's guide to divorce mediation.* Lutherville, MD: Greenspring Publications, 131 pp.

Shapiro and Caplan offer a book which fills the void for the layperson. Written by a lawyer and a psychotherapist, this book acquaints the reader with the concept and practice of divorce mediation, describes how joint custody works, and suggests that the family relationship is restructured, rather than terminated, with divorce. Areas covered are: (a) division of marital property, (b) spousal support, (c) child custody and parental access, (d) child support, and (e) tax considerations. Vignettes are used to help illustrate certain aspects of the mediation process. The authors include guidelines and forms used in mediation.

PARENTING AND CHILDREN

Cantor, D. W., & Drake, E. A. (1983). *Divorced parents and their children: A guide for mental health professionals.* New York: Springer Publishing Company, 182 pp.

Here is a book that familiarizes the reader with the current literature and research, while providing a sourcebook for mental health professionals who are working with divorcing families. At the same time, the authors present possible applications of this knowledge to the therapeutic process. Cantor and Drake give a wealth of information to help mental health professionals deal with the following areas: the effects of divorce on children, different approaches of working with both children and parents, ways to minimize the negative impact of divorce on children, custody arrangements, visitation, and parental dating and remarriage.

Francke, L. B. (1983). *Growing up divorced.* New York: Linden Press, 303 pp.

Through interviews with children and experts in the field, the author describes the effects of divorce on children according to their age level: babies and toddlers, preschoolers, 6- to 8-year-olds, 9- to 12-year-olds, and teenagers. At the end of each chapter is a section on what parents can do to help. The latter part of the book looks at the role that the institutions can and cannot fill. The schools, in many cases, become a second family to the children of divorce. The author describes how some schools are handling this situation. There is a good discussion of the role of the courts regarding mediation, custody, and childsnatching. Lastly, Francke discusses the role of government in relation to the family and divorce.

Gardner, R. A. (1976). *Psychotherapy with children of divorce.* New York: Jason Aronson, 534 pp.

Based on a psychodynamic orientation, this book focuses on the family elements that contribute to the psychopathological reactions of children to divorce. Gardner advocates having the parent who brings the child to therapy stay in the room during the session. He describes various reaction patterns of children and therapeutic approaches to dealing with these. An excellent chapter on special techniques that Gardner uses is included. Two chapters are devoted to advising parents. A lengthy chapter on litigation includes what to involve in a custody evaluation and recommendations for the therapist in court. There are many clinical examples throughout the book with a full-length case study at the end.

Hetherington, E. M., Cox, M., & Cox, R. (1981). The aftermath of divorce. In E. M. Hetherington & R. D. Parke (Eds.), *Contemporary readings in child psychology* (pp. 234-249). New York: McGraw-Hill.

This reading is a description of one of the best designed studies to date on the effects of divorce. The effects on mothers, fathers, and children are all included. Continued involvement of the non-custodial father proved to be most important. The study did demonstrate that a conflict-ridden intact home is more detrimental to all members of the family than a stable home where the parents are divorced.

Kurdek, L. A. (Ed.). (1983). *New directions for child development: Children and divorce.* San Francisco: Jossey-Bass, 93 pp.

The unifying theme of this collection of articles is the child's view of divorce. Each author has addressed some aspect of the question: What is the child's view of the divorce? Rather than relying on parent reports, these authors have gone directly to the children, themselves. Areas covered are: children's understanding of their parents divorces, young adolescents' responses, exploration of father-custody and mother-custody homes, correlates of children's adjustment, and a divorce adjustment project.

Newman, G. (1981). *101 ways to be a long distance super-dad.* Mountain View, CA: Blossom Valley Press, 107 pp.

This book is for the non-custodial parent who does not live close to his/her children. It is a series of ideas to make your relationship with your children special through ordinary means. This idea-book includes ways to liven up phone calls and ways to let your children know that their lives and what they do are important to you. Examples include using a different type of postage stamp on each letter for stamp collecting, playing long-distance chess, and sending clippings from the newspaper that will interest your children.

Nichols, W. C. (1984). Therapeutic needs of children in family system reorganization. *Journal of Divorce, 7*(4), 23-44.

In this article, Nichols believes that flexible treatment which is based on the needs determined during the ongoing assessment is the approach of choice. The major focus of intervention for children of separation/divorce is implied to be the reorganized family system, the continuing parental subsystem, and the reactions and adjustments of the child to this situation in relation to any changes that may affect the child's long-term development.

Oakland, T. (1984). *Divorced fathers: Reconstructing a quality life.* New York: Human Sciences Press, 201 pp.

Information on various problems and issues that fathers and children experience due to divorce is presented in this book. This book is written as a primer for a father to understand what he is going through, how his children are affected, and how to reconstruct his life. Topics covered include: psychological and social changes faced by fathers, understanding children and the effects of divorce, how to anticipate children's problems and how to deal with them, custody, legal issues, and managing a household. Some good lists are included in the book. These are: a checklist of signs of stress in children, what is included in child neglect, basic foods to buy, kitchen utensils and appliances needed, and how to be a sharp shopper.

Stuart, I. R., & Abt, L. E. (1981). *Children of separation and divorce: Management and treatment.* New York: Van Nostrand Reinhold, 365 pp.

This book, divided into four parts, is a collection of articles which deals with matters of child management and treatment in the divorce situation. The first section examines the legal rights and responsibilities regarding children of divorced parents and the attitude of courts and their staff. Part II explores the emotional and psychological factors involved in understanding and providing for these children. Topics covered here include developmental issues of children in divorcing families, the male single parent, and dealing with custody loss. The third part includes chapters on different child management problems growing out of divorce and separation. Areas covered include foster care, joint custody, the role of the school, gay parents, incarcerated parents, and adolescent pregnancy. The final section examines treatment within the family unit. The five chapters include the family system approach in various settings, failure to thrive, and the visiting relationships after divorce.

Wallerstein, J. S., & Kelly, J. B. (1980). *Surviving the breakup: How children and parents cope with divorce.* New York: Basic Books, 341 pp.

The California Children of Divorce Project is described in this book. Findings at the time of initial separation, one year later, and after five years are discussed in detail. The results are from parents, children, and the school. The authors look at the reactions of both parents and children at all three time periods. The chapter on how children responded to the divorce is an exceptionally good one. Using developmental theory, Wallerstein and Kelly describe the reactions of the children in their study according to their developmental stage. Another excellent chapter to help understand the process of divorce and its ramifications is the one on the implications of their findings.

POSTDIVORCE FAMILIES

Hansen, J. C. (Ed.). (1982). *Therapy with remarriage families.* Rockville, MD: Aspen Systems Corporation, 206 pp.

Here is a collection of articles, each authored by one or more practicing professionals. Knowledge and techniques are provided for the therapist who is working with family members going through the remarriage cycle. Articles have been arranged according to the temporal sequence of this process. Several articles look at the concerns and needs of children and adults in dealing with the losses they encounter in the separation process. Others explore concepts and techniques to assist the remarriage family with resolving their problems.

Sager, C. J., Brown, H. S., Crohn, H., Engel, T., Rodstein, E., & Walker, L. (1983). *Treating the remarried family.* New York: Brunner/Mazel, 388 pp.

This comprehensive book is a must for the mental health professional who is working with remarried families. The authors examine the remarried family on three levels: family systems, life cycle, and intrapsychic. This well-organized volume discusses in great detail the theory and structure, treatment, special issues, and prevention in dealing with this population. Case examples are well utilized by the authors to further elucidate remarried families. An Appendix of forms and checklists for the clinician to use is included.

Visher, E. B., & Visher, J. S. (1979). *Stepfamilies: A guide to working with stepparents and stepchildren.* New York: Brunner/Mazel, 280 pp.

Emotions felt by members of stepfamilies and intact families may be the same, but the structural differences of the two types of families produce differences in degree, complexity, and interactional elements. The Vishers help those in the mental health field realize this and give ways of dealing with stepfamilies. The first three chapters discuss the cultural characteristics, the structural characteristics, and research done on stepfamilies. The rest of the book looks at different constellations of family members in stepfamilies. They explore what difficulties to expect and how to deal with them as a therapist. The groups covered are: women as mother/stepmother, men as father/stepfather, the remarried couple, children, and the whole stepfamily.

Visher, E. B., & Visher, J. S. (1982). *How to win as a stepfamily.* New York: Dembner Books, 196 pp.

The Vishers cover mainly the same material as in *Stepfamilies: A Guide to Working with Stepparents and Stepchildren.* The difference lies in the audience to which the book has been written—stepfamilies, themselves. They do an excellent job of explaining stepfamilies and the difficulties they face. Included in these difficulties are: dealing with former spouses, grandparents of remarriage, legal issues, and helping children adjust. The Vishers have succeeded in normalizing stepfamily interactions. They realize that all families must deal with stress. At the same time, stepfamilies have some unique stresses not faced by an intact family. Information and suggestions are given on how to make a stepfamily work. References for stepparents and children are at the end of the book.

Weiss, R. S. (1979). *Going it alone: The family life and social situation of the single parent.* New York: Basic Books, 303 pp.

Through interviews of over 200 single parents and about 40 children of single parents, Weiss describes what it is like to be raising children alone. Much information is given; at the same time a real understanding of the single parent situation is shown. The following topics are covered: how one becomes a single parent, the way the household is structured and how it operates, relationships with children and ex-spouses, how they organize their social lives, the strengths and vulnerabilities in being a single parent, and ways that single parents manage. The book is filled with quotations and examples from Weiss' interviews. This is a good book for both the mental health professional and the single parent.

SCHOOLS

Allers, R. D. (1982). *Divorce, children, and the school.* Princeton, NJ: Princeton Book, 158 pp.

If the therapist plans on involving the school as part of the therapeutic program, this book will prove to be most helpful. The first half of the book describes both the child's and parents' experience of divorce. The role of the school is described in the last half. There is an excellent section on the symptoms of stress, the child's reaction to stress, and the causes of stress in relation to divorce. The role of the teacher is explored in relation to what would be helpful and what wouldn't. Allers also describes a program to be led by mental health professionals to help children of divorce in the school. A bibliography for children and adults is included.

THEORY, THERAPY, AND RESEARCH

Ahrons, C. (1983). Divorce: Before, during, and after. In H. I. McCubbin & C. R. Figley (Eds.), *Stress and the family: Coping with normative transitions.* New York: Brunner/Mazel, 102-115.

Divorce is conceptualized as a normative family transition in this chapter. Ahrons introduces the concept of the binuclear family as a useful family model. Using a case example, the author reviews the stressors involved with each phase in the divorce process and suggests functional and dysfunctional coping patterns at each stage. The five transitions are: (a) individual cognition, (b) family metacognition, (c) separation, (d) family reorganization, and (e) family redefinition. The chapter ends with implications for counselors and therapists.

Albrecht, S. L. (1980). Reactions and adjustments to divorce: Differences in the experiences of males and females. *Family Relations, 29*, 59-68.

Albrecht reviews the reactions of 500 male and female divorcees to the divorce experience and the adjustments made. It was found that there are differences due to gender, especially in the areas of stress, property settlement, changes in social participation, and effects on income.

Cherlin, A. J. (1981). *Marriage, divorce, remarriage*. Cambridge, MA: Harvard University Press, 142 pp.

Here is an examination of overall trends in the United States over the last several decades in relation to marriage, divorce, and remarriage. Cherlin believes that the 60s and 70s are more the norm of the century than the 50s, as many of us are lead to believe. He first looks at the demographic data and then the trends. Cherlin continues with explanations for these trends for each decace from the 1950s to the 1980s. Consequences of these trends for spouses, parents, and children are then explored. In his last chapter, Cherlin looks at differences in family patterns of black families and white families.

Espenshade, T. J. (1979). The economic consequences of divorce. *Journal of Marriage and the Family, 41*, 615-625.

Espenshade does an excellent job of summarizing the recent research on the economic consequences of divorce for husbands, wives, and children. One important finding is that the economic status of wives gets worse after divorce, while that of the husbands improves. The children's economic well-being is dependent upon which parent they live with. The author analyzes why this is so and discusses policy implications of the findings.

Frederico, J. (1979). The marital termination period in the divorce adjustment process. *Journal of Divorce, 3*(2), 93-106.

This article explores the dynamics of a couple during the period immediately prior to the decision to divorce. The author's contribution to the field lies in his concept of a marital Point of No-Return in relation to deciding to divorce. An excellent discussion of this concept follows.

Goetting, A. (1981). Divorce outcome research. Issues and perspectives. *Journal of Family Issues, 2*, 350-378.

Here is a review of the recent research findings on the effects of divorce on divorcing men and women and their children. The importance of this review lies in using only well-designed studies employing "normal," rather than clinical, subjects and appropriate control groups. One major observation from this article is that family discord may be a more important determinant rather than marital structure.

Goldsmith, J. (1982). The postdivorce family system. In F. Walsh (Ed.), *Normal Family Processes*. New York: Guilford Press, 297-330.

Using general systems theory, Goldsmith identifies the processes and patterns in post-divorce families. The main contribution of this chapter lies in viewing the postdivorce family as one that is normal, functional, and reorganizing. Looking at the structure, she breaks down the family into subsystems and discusses working with each one.

Isaacs, M. (1982). Helping mom fail: A case of a stalemated divorcing process. *Family Process, 21*, 225-234.

This article describes a systems approach to a problem of a symptomatic child due to her parents' separation. Background material is first given, with a case example elucidating how to put it into practice.

Kaslow, F. W. (1981). Divorce and divorce therapy. In A. S. Gurman & D. P. Kniskern (Eds.), *Handbook of family therapy*. New York: Brunner/Mazel, 662-696.

In this chapter, Kaslow gives an overview of divorce. Topics covered include: divorce statistics, factors which lead to divorce, various models of stages of the divorce process, the impact of divorce on children, intervention strategies, research on divorce therapy, and training of the divorce therapist.

Kaslow, F. W. (1984). Divorce: An evolutionary process of change in the family system. *Journal of Divorce, 7*(3), 21-39.

Kaslow explores divorce from a combination of family systems, individual life cycle and stage theory of development. The choice of treatment varies according to the following: where one is in the divorce process, one's ego strength, cognitive functioning, and social and resource networks. Kaslow includes an excellent chart which is made up of the stage, feelings, actions and tasks, and the most appropriate therapeutic interventions. Case vignettes are also presented to further elaborate Kaslow's thinking.

Kitson, G. C., & Raschke, H. J. (1981). Divorce research: What we know; what we need to know. *Journal of Divorce, 4*, 1-37.

Kitson and Raschke explore the divorce process through an extensive review of the literature. The main focus is on antecedents and consequences of divorce. They examine the sociological and psychological factors, the causes, and theoretical perspectives of divorce. The relationship of unmodifiable and modifiable factors in easing adjustment explored. Much information is shared in this clearly written review, with an excellent bibliography at the end.

Kitson, G. C., & Sussman, M. B. (1982). Marital complaints, demographic characteristics, and symptoms of mental distress in divorce. *Journal of Marriage and the Family, 44*, 87-101.

This article describes a study which examines divorcees' perceptions of their reasons for divorcing. Comparing these results to those of Goode's study in 1948, there are differences. Goode's study shows more reasons as instrumental, rather than expressive, as in the current study. Major differences between men and women are also reported.

Kraus, S. (1979). The crisis of divorce: Growth promoting or pathogenic? *Journal of Divorce, 3*(2), 107-119.

Using crisis theory, Kraus offers a positive theoretical model as an alternative to the pathogenic perspective on divorce. After critically examining divorce as pathogenic, Kraus offers her framework as a means for understanding both short-term and long-term reactions to divorce, as well as many variables that have an effect on these reactions.

Kressel, K., & Deutsch, M. (1977). Divorce therapy: An in-depth survey of therapists views. *Family Process, 16*, 413-443.

With the use of in-depth interviews, the authors discuss therapists' views on the criteria of a constructive divorce, obstacles that get in the way of this, and strategies used in divorce therapy. Techniques fall into one of three categories. Reflexive strategies are those used to help the therapist better understand the clients' situation and to join with them. Contextual interventions are those used to create the climate needed for decision-making. Substantive interventions include those that are intended to produce a resolution. Different strategies under each of the three areas are discussed.

Levinger, G., & Moles, O. C. (Eds.). (1979). *Divorce and separation: Context, causes, and consequences.* New York: Basic Books, 363 pp.

Included in this book is a comprehensive collection of articles to help one better understand divorce and its ramifications. The articles are often cited throughout the divorce literature. The wide range of topics in this volume include: perspectives on marital dissolution, social and psychological determinants of breakup, economic determinants, consequences and effects on the ex-spouses, and effects on families and children.

Raschke, H. J. (in press). Divorce and marital separation. In M. Sussman (Ed.), *Handbook of marriage and the family.*

Here is a review and analysis of the "state of the art" of the separation/divorce literature as of the early 1980s. Looking at contemporary theory and research, the thread of viewing divorce through the deviance perspective and its implications pervades throughout. This comprehensive chapter covers the contexts, correlates and causes, consequences and adjustment of both adults and children, legal aspects, and policy implications. This work is an excellent place to start in order to find where to read further in the key areas of divorce. The extensive bibliography, as well as the thorough literature review, makes this chapter a must to read.

Salts, C. (1979). Divorce process: Integration of theory. *Journal of Divorce, 2*(3), 233-240.

In this paper, Salts compares several models of the divorce process. Models compared are those of: Kessler, Bohannon, Wiseman, Froiland/Hozman, Levy/Joffe, Waller, and Weiss. It is concluded that the models are not in conflict with each other. Implications for counseling are discussed. A chart showing the comparisons is included.

Sprenkle, D. H., & Cyrus, C. L. (1983). Abandonment: The stress of sudden divorce. In C. R. Figley & M. I. McCubbin (Eds.), *Stress and the family: Coping with catastrophe.* New York: Brunner/Mazel, 53-75.

As illustrated in this chapter, the sudden divorce has its own unique circumstances with which one must deal. The authors examine both theoretically and practically one specific type of divorce—abandonment. Areas covered are: (a) the meaning of emotional abandonment in the family and its complexity, (b) why this stressor is so painful for all involved, (c) factors determining the level of stress experienced, (d) constructive and destructive coping methods, (e) useful interventions, (f) the constructive potential for the survivor, and (g) gaps in our knowledge and recommendations for future research.

Sprenkle, D. H., & Storm, C. L. (1983). Divorce therapy outcome research: A substantive and methodological review. *Journal of Marital and Family Therapy, 9*, 239-258.

Here is a substantive and methodological review of empirical studies related to divorce therapy. The six areas that the 22 studies are divided into are: (a) mediation, (b) conciliation courts counseling, (c) consumer evaluation, (d) divorce groups, (e) separation techniques, and (f) marriage counseling with divorce as an unintended outcome. An excellent chart comparing the studies is included. There is strong evidence for the superiority of mediation to traditional adversary methods for custody and visitation disputes. There appears to be an increase in the number of reconciliations in the short-term for those using conciliation counseling. Due to the weakness of the methodologies of many of the studies, other conclusions remain tentative. The authors critically answer what we know and what we still need to know about divorce therapy. Suggestions are made for further research and practice.

Storm, C. L., & Sprenkle, D. H. (1982). Individual treatment in divorce therapy: A critique of an assumption. *Journal of Divorce, 6*, 87-97.

The authors critically examine the commonly help maxim that the treatment of choice in divorce therapy is working with the individual. Conjoint and family treatment are explored as alternatives. A model of divorce therapy is offered using all 3 modes of therapy. Storm and Sprenkle propose conjoint and/or family treatment as most effective in the decision making and restructuring stages. Individual treatment is the most appropriate for the recovery phase.

Weltner, J. S. (1982). A structural approach to the single-parent family. *Family Process, 21*, 203-210.

This article focuses on the problems implicit in the structure of a family unit which includes one parent and at least one child. Specific therapeutic approaches are discussed. Two priorities examined are support of the executive system function and establishing generational boundaries.

WOMEN'S ISSUES

Colleta, S. D. (1983). Stressful lives: The situation of divorced mothers and their children. *Journal of Divorce, 6*(3), 19-31.

Interviewing 72 divorced and married mothers, the results of this study suggest that the negative situation of divorced mothers and children are largely due to the low income that so often is a reality for divorced mothers, rather than father absence.

Langelier, R., & Deckert, P. (1980). Divorce counseling guidelines for the late divorced female. *Journal of Divorce, 3*(4), 403-411.

Based on research, this article offers divorce counseling guidelines for females who divorce after being married a minimum of 20 years. Guidelines are given in the six following areas: emotions, divorce grounds, finances and budgeting, children, lifestyle changes, and independence.

Robertson, C. (1980). *Divorce and decision making: A woman's guide.* Chicago: Follett, 206 pp.

This is an excellent how-to book for women going through the divorce process. It is full of information, activities, and questions that one needs to ask as she goes through a divorce. If the information is not included in the book, the author tells where to look for it. Part I deals with emotional supports, values, plans for the future, and decision-making ability. Part II deals with specific decisions that need to be made in the following areas: legal help, the divorce settlement, children, money, careers, and social life. The last chapter discusses the use of assertiveness in implementing decisions. An excellent bibliography and list of resources is included at the end of the book.

Thomas, S. P. (1982). After divorce: Personality factors related to the process of adjustment. *Journal of Divorce, 5*(3), 19-35.

According to this study, those individuals who scored high on the following personality traits achieved the best adjustment to divorce: dominance/assertiveness, self-assurance, intelligence, creativity/imagination, social boldness, liberalism, self-sufficiency, ego strength and tranquility. Passivity, lack of self-assurance, dependency, shyness, and conformity all hinder adjustment to divorce. These traits are also sanctioned by society as ones acceptable for women. The implications of this are discussed.

Women in Transition. (1975). *Women in transition: A feminist handbook on separation and divorce.* New York: Charles Scribner's Sons, 538 pp.

Here is another how-to book for women in transition, including divorcees. It is geared to middle- and working-class women. Although in a few areas it is outdated, it is packed with down-to-earth information on the following areas: emotional support, children, the law, financial resources, living space, and taking care of oneself. The section on the law gives much needed information. The section on financial resources is another excellent one. It includes what to do if on welfare, how to get a job, sexism at work, educational resources, and financial resources such as savings, loans, and insurance. At the end of the book is a national list of centers where women can go for help.

WORKSHOPS

Callahan, B. N. (1979). *Separation and divorce.* New York: Family Service Association of America, 129 pp.

This is a manual for a 10-session workshop on separation and divorce. Format for the sessions include mini-lectures, role playing, exercises, and discussion. Topics covered through this educational model are: the emotional impact of divorce, ties to the past, children and divorce, legal aspects, anger, loneliness, sex and dating, remarriage, and looking ahead. Each session is structured with all needed information and handouts included.

Davidoff, I. F., & Schiller, M. S. (1983). The divorce workshops as crisis intervention: A practical model. *Journal of Divorce, 6*(4), 37-53.

The authors describe a series of six weekly workshops available to women. Topics that are included are as follows: the emotional impact of separation and divorce, grief and mourning, the death of the marriage, coping with new realities, single parenting, legal aspects, and crisis as growth.